Theodore O'Hara

Theodore O'Hara
Poet-Soldier of the Old South

Nathaniel Cheairs Hughes, Jr.,
and Thomas Clayton Ware

The University of Tennessee Press • Knoxville

Frontispiece: Theodore O'Hara, ca. 1850. From Edgar Erskine Hume, *Colonel Theodore O'Hara, Author of The Bivouac of the Dead* (1936).

Library of Congress Cataloging-in-Publication Data

Hughes, Nathaniel Cheairs.
  Theodore O'Hara : poet-soldier of the Old South / Nathaniel
Cheairs Hughes, Jr., and Thomas Clayton Ware. — 1st ed.
    p. cm.
  Includes bibliographical references and index.
  ISBN 1-57233-008-2 (cloth: alk. paper)
  1. O'Hara, Theodore, 1820–1867—Biography. 2. Poets,
American—19th century—Biography.
  I. Ware, Thomas Clayton, 1929– . II. Title.
  PS2488.H75 1998
  811'.3—dc21
  [B]   97-33770

In memory of my father, Lindsay Ware,
whose interest in Theodore O'Hara quickened my own.

And for my wife Judy, whose presence on this journey
made it possible.
        T. C. W.

To my three understanding daughters, Mitzi, Kathaleen,
and D'Arcy, of whom I am proud.
        N. C. H.

There is something beyond the grave;
   death does end all,
and the pale ghost escapes from the vanquished pyre.
    —Sextus Propertius, *Elegies,* bk. 4, viii.

On Fame's eternal camping ground
   Their silent tents are spread,
And Glory guards with solemn round
   The bivouac of the dead.
    —Theodore O'Hara, "The Bivouac of the Dead"

Contents

Illustrations

Figures

Maps

Preface

As Thomas Wolfe observed in *Look Homeward Angel,* a destiny that leads the people of one nation to another is strange enough, but a destiny that leads a talented individual—and thence his progeny—into foreign regions and to ambivalent fame becomes touched by "that dark miracle of chance which makes new magic in a dusty world." Thus it was with Kean O'Hara, one of the "wild geese" who fled Ireland in the late eighteenth century and found his destiny in Kentucky—and there begot his son, Theodore, fated to become one of America's most quoted authors, one whose work became formally used by the federal government and yet to contemporary audiences one of its least known.

Perhaps no artist in recent centuries, with the possible exception of English poet Thomas Gray—certainly no American, not even Edgar Allan Poe—became so closely identified with cemeteries or so widely cited in them as Theodore O'Hara, once regarded as "Uncle Sam's Official Poet." Lines from O'Hara's elegiac poem "The Bivouac of the Dead" have been immortalized in wood, marble, and granite, in steel, on slabs, on memorial tablets, and on the tombs of soldiers in state and national graveyards across the land—especially throughout the South, and most notably, perhaps, across the archway of both sides of the General George B. McClellan gate to Arlington National Cemetery, the original entrance to that site.

One account tells us that a stanza of O'Hara's elegy was inscribed on a rude memorial nailed to a tree on the battlefield at Chancellorsville, Virginia, shortly after the fighting in 1863. A passage of "Bivouac of the Dead" is engraved on a military monument in Boston, still another on an obelisk in a cemetery in Greenville, South Carolina. In the Confederate burial plot on the battlefield at Perryville, Kentucky, the central monument features a quatrain of O'Hara's work on three of its four sides. In Europe, lines from the poem were etched on a memorial column marking a major battle of the Crimean War. One American traveler reported encountering a passage in a cemetery in London. Reading the relatively little that has been written about this man and his major elegy, one gets the sense that during the height of the vogue which the poem apparently enjoyed during the later decades of the nineteenth century and the early twentieth, it was regarded as the ultimate expression on the subject of death—especially the death of military men. During that vogue, the poem became the official elegiac utterance in American Civil War cemeteries—Antietam, Gettysburg, Shiloh, Stone's River, Vicksburg, among others—and in the burial grounds at the Custer Memorial at Little Big Horn in Montana. But the poet's name never once appears with his lines in these public places. In our time the recognition the poem still receives certainly overshadows the fame of its author, though that author's life and career led him into some of the most exciting and important events of his time—and by extension, some of the most dramatic and consequential occasions of the history of the United States in the mid-nineteenth century.

Aspects of his background involve the remarkable courage of his Irish Catholic forebears in their departure from a country split by religious oppression and abuses of royal power, the conjoining of distinguished families in the haven which the provinces of Maryland offered, the emigration of his father to the wilderness of Kentucky, and the establishment of a proud tradition of private education in the bluegrass region of that state.

Theodore's own talents and restless nature led him into several careers—teaching, law, and journalism—as well as into a variety of military experiences, including skirmishes with Indians on the western frontier, front-line encounters in the war with Mexico, an ill-fated filibustering attempt to free Cuba from Spain, and wide-ranging service with the Confederacy in the Civil War. He was truly a man who participated in the rapidly changing pageant of his times; yet few of the millions of people who have read his eloquent lines in graveyards across the country or in their own high school and college American literature anthologies—or in newspapers across the country on Memorial Day—have had little conception of the poet, or of the adventurous man who wrote that moving elegiac poem. O'Hara himself would never have anticipated the official uses of his work or the anonymous universality of the poem's sentiments.

Except for some of his writings, few, in fact, of his principal endeavors seem to have yielded him complete success or satisfaction. With all of his natural gifts, plus his education, gregariousness, and breadth of experience, he remained a curiously isolated, even tragic figure, never quite fulfilling the promise of superior achievement conveyed so vividly during his childhood and adolescence. He appears to have had little of the proverbial luck of the Irish—indeed, quite the opposite. He never married, although he was strongly attracted to the company of young women; never lived for long in one place; never, or so it appears, found the appropriate sense of identity, direction, and purpose to bring into steady focus his impressive energies, his versatility, or his aspirations. F. Scott Fitzgerald once said, "There are no second acts in American life," an observation which could readily apply to Theodore O'Hara's career, although one soon comes to recognize that his repertoire certainly featured an impressive array of opening scenes, testifying to the brilliance of his potentialities, but also to a peculiar lack of what his fellow Southerners would term "staying power."

The idea for this study of Theodore O'Hara, ironic as it now seems, emerged from a casual conversation the two of us had in an office facing onto an ancient burial plot in Chattanooga, now a quasi-national cemetery in which a number of disintegrating Confederate grave markers may be found, a hallowed ground oddly marked by the stone towers of the U.S. Army Engineer Corps embracing a black iron gate, criss-crossed with the battle flag of the old Confederacy.

The conversation began with congenial questions about current academic activities and drifted to the subject of that cemetery across the street, with its ill-proportioned towers and lovely oak trees. We discovered that we were both Victorians at heart, at least in our fascination with grave markers and the marvelous stories they contain. We talked a while about the forlorn Confederates buried there, most of them lost to posterity without having been identified with proper markers, and then we began to discuss Civil War personages who interested us, including Theodore O'Hara.

Our chat ended with a mutual agreement to carry on the discussion at a later time. That later discussion resulted in a recognition of just how much we had in common in our curiosity about this enigmatic and elusive figure, an author whose relatively small literary achievement had received so much acclaim and so little public acknowledgment, a soldier whose endeavors in several military campaigns seemed to be but were not well documented, and in total a man whose life involved many dark passages, most of which led to misfortune.

We discovered not only that O'Hara intrigued us but also that we had both been collecting O'Hara material for years. As a youth, Tom Ware had known Marie O'Hara Branham (Theodore O'Hara's grandniece) and had learned about Theodore and the O'Haras, a branch of his family that had been systematically denied him because of lingering animosities. Nat Hughes had encountered Theodore O'Hara first when researching the life of William J. Hardee. O'Hara was a colorful subordinate of Hardee's in the Second Cavalry Regiment. Our second conversation quickened into an excitement about a possible project.

Our individual research efforts have carried us into a number of physical byways (libraries, archives, schools and churches) and to large cities (Boston, Washington, D.C., New Orleans, Louisville, Sligo, and Dublin among them), small towns in Georgia and Kentucky, and in rural Ireland, large cemeteries and small graveyards, the smallest of them all in the almost forgotten village of White Sulphur, Kentucky, where Theodore's father Kean O'Hara lies buried. We decided to divide the writing responsibilities: Tom Ware authored chapters 1, 2, 5, and 12, and Nat Hughes wrote chapters 3–4, 6–10, and 11. Every chapter, of course, has been reviewed by both of us, and we bear mutual responsibility for the merits and demerits of the entire work.

Researching and writing the biography of O'Hara has been a pleasure for us, made so in large measure by the people we have met, who in so many instances have assisted us most generously. One, Antonio R. de la Cova of Amelia Island, Florida, read the entire manuscript and offered a number of helpful suggestions. To all these we express our deepest gratitude:

The staff of the Lupton Library, University of Tennessee at Chattanooga: Dr. Joseph Jackson, Dean of Libraries, Bill Prince, Neal Coulter, Ray Hall, and Athena Hicks; Heather Grothe, Carlotta Cooper, Susan Smith, and Brad Shoop of the University of Tennessee—Chattanooga English Department; Michael P. Musick and Stuart L. Butler, Military Reference Section, National Archives; Charles J. Boyle, Spring Hill College, Mobile, Alabama; Barbara S. Edwards, *Danville Advocate-Messenger*; John White, Southern Historical Collection, University of North Carolina; Ralph Poore, *Mobile Press Register*; John J. Slonaker, Chief, Historical Branch, U.S. Army Military History Institute, Carlisle, Pennsylvania; Caldwell Delaney, Director, City of Mobile Museum Department; Jay Higginbotham, Mobile Municipal Archives; Claire McCann, Special Collections, University of Kentucky Libraries; Mary Margaret Bell, Manuscripts Curator, Kentucky Historical Society; John R. Lassiter, Chattahoochee Valley Regional Library; William C. Richardson, Kentucky Department of Libraries and Archives; Marion Pokriots, Scott's Valley, California; Ron Bryant, Kentucky Historical Society Library; Dorothy C. Rush, Library, Filson Club, Louisville, Kentucky; James J. Holmberg, Curator, Filson Club; Sarah Lambert, Girls Preparatory School; Robert E. May, Purdue University; Fred Bauman, Library of Congress; Dr. Richard Sommers, United States Military History Institute, Carlisle, Pennsylvania; Mrs. W. T. Hays, Jackson, Mississippi; Bob Wheeler, New Haven, Connecticut; Jim Ogden, historian, Chickamauga-Chattanooga National Military Park; William F. Sherman, National Archives; Virginia J. H. Cain, Archivist, Woodruff Library, Emory University; The Reverend Jim V. Bills, Christ Church, Chattanooga, Tennessee; Charlotte Kennedy, Chattahoochee Valley Regional Library; Phil Gillis, Chattanooga Bi-Centennial Library; E. Raymond Lewis, Librarian, United States House of Representatives; and the late Dr. Charles R. Lee, Centre College, Danville, Kentucky. And to the University of Chattanooga Foundation for making possible the research in County Sligo and Dublin, Ireland, Tom Ware wishes to acknowledge special gratitude.

Chapter 1

An Irish Odyssey

Theodore O'Hara was a native Kentuckian, born February 11, 1820, probably in Frankfort; but the odyssey which led to his birth in that green sector of this dusty world originated in the early 1790s in the west of Ireland, a time and place of remarkably widespread and inventive violence, reaching deeply into parts of the country not implicated in burgeoning insurrection. Almost no one, it appears, could remain neutral.

The success of the American Revolution had intensified the desire for freedom among Ireland's oppressed people, both Protestant and Roman Catholic. Coincidentally, revision of various penal codes against Catholics began in the mid-1770s, and dictates outlawing the Catholic Church itself were repealed by 1782. Ireland's own "Great Liberator," Daniel O'Connell, was but a child when colonial American warships cruised off the coast of his home county of Kerry, yet he would recall that exciting episode for years.[1] To him and doubtless to others of O'Connell's countrymen, the career of John Paul Jones remained a symbol of heroism. Indeed, the economic and military constraints which the war produced in England led to the easing of some restrictions which Irish merchants had experienced. Thus the American success became a beacon for Ireland's own aspirations.

The French Revolution, with its further emphasis on the Rights of Man, prompted Wolfe Tone in 1791 to form the Society of United Irishmen, an organization formally representing the passionate spirit that had pervaded the country since news of the Declaration of Independence. Within this charged political atmosphere, the odyssey of the O'Hara family—and for our purposes, specifically that of Kean O'Hara—began, from the area of Collooney in County Sligo. Attributions about the origin of this branch of the O'Hara family have been varied. One family document indicates that they were originally from a "baronny" of Layney in County Sligo. Another comment suggests that they were from Galway. But as with many Irish families, the belief that passed through the generations was that they were descended from royalty, thus: "The O'Hara's [sic] were descendent from the King of Munster in the third century of the race of Heben—O'Hara's [sic] occupied Mumes before the noblemen of other countries were in existence."[2]

In that west county of Sligo, in the parishes of Ballysdare and Kilvarnet, the family surname may be tracked back through some thirty generations, and the given names of the males have recurred with consistency, Kean and Charles among the more prominent. In Annaghmore, the "Big House" of the O'Hara estate is still intact, its current master Dermott O'Hara. The house is a repository of painting of distinguished ancestors and paraphernalia of many kinds pertaining to the family history. That branch of the O'Haras has belonged to the Church of England since the sixteenth century. At the Restoration of the Stuarts in the 1660s, families who remained Catholic lost their lands. It is evident the branch from which Theodore's father Kean descended had not abandoned their traditional religion, had lost whatever land they may have had, and emigrated during a time of great oppression of Catholics. Precisely how and why must remain for now only conjecture.[3]

This much is certain: at one point during this nationalistic turmoil and its consequences, which spawned its own haunting body of defiant ballad literature, Kean (sometimes spelled Kane) O'Hara came to this country in the company of his brothers, James[4] and Charles, and his sister Polly, along with their father, James, Senior. As one biographer has noted, this appears to be one of the few authentic instances of three brothers emigrating to America together, though many families carry such a tradition.[5]

Among the legends that surround this odyssey was that the departure of these O'Haras from Ireland occurred as a direct result of the infamous "rising" of 1798, the "year of the French," when rebellious Irish patriots under the leadership of Lord Edward Fitzgerald were prepared to assist in the invasion of Napoleon's agents on the western coast. This plot was discovered and a pattern of cruel reprisals ensued, resulting in widespread massacre. Lord Fitzgerald died of wounds in prison. Wolfe Tone committed suicide while waiting to be hanged.[6]

This matrix of violence seems a fitting romantic prelude to the career of Theodore, who was himself later to become so attracted to turbulent adventures and so evidently quite at home in the presence of patriotic gore; but such legends must be countered with more sobering elements. Kean O'Hara's grave marker, still present in the small cemetery of St. Pius Church (now St. Francis), in the village of White Sulphur, Kentucky, indicates these defining events:

> Born in Ireland, Nov. 24, 1768
> Emigrated to America in 1793
> A Citizen of Kentucky in 1798
> Married in 1800
> Died in Franklin County, Ky.
> December 23, 1851

One should note well: "Emigrated to America in 1793." Such tombstone reality, certainly based on the facts provided at the time of death—and in the parish records—can hardly now be refuted. What then are we to make of the many accounts of Kean O'Hara's involvement in the rising of 1798 and the urgent circumstances of his leaving his native country? Such stuff as legends are made of, the kind of exciting fiction that surrounds notable people. The vague approximation between the date of the emigration and the better known events that transpired in the old country would have made for a fine broth of a tale, especially about a teacher who was as colorful as Kean O'Hara seems to have become. One contemporary letter provides us this perspective: "He was a familiar figure of my childhood. He took part in the revolt against England in 1798, when he was compelled to leave and come to the U.S., reaching Kentucky and teaching a classical school until he bought a farm."[7]

Clearly this attribution is incorrect, on several points; but it illustrates how a legend accumulates and adheres. This heroic chapter received sanction with the publication of George W. Ranck's biography of 1898, *The Bivouac of the Dead and Its Author,* to wit: "The father of the poet was an Irish gentleman. . . . He had been a fellow rebel with Lord Edward Fitzgerald, in the Irish uprising of 1798, and when that chivalrous but ill-fated nobleman was betrayed Kane O'Hara escaped to America."[8] And so, despite the evidence of Kean O'Hara's death records—and his gravestone—almost all treatments of the O'Hara family's coming to America follow this line. While it is impossible at this juncture to dislodge these earlier interpretations, one may perhaps shed new light on the origins of them. The entire decade of the 1790s in Ireland was characterized by political, social, and religious agitation; but in the years 1792–93, Irish Catholics became especially demonstrative, because of a series of failed

expectations and proposals for reform. Secret societies, calling themselves
Defenders, and supposedly nondenominational, were mounting new attacks on the traditional targets of tithes, rent, and other taxes and dues.
In the winter of 1792, violent battles were waged in several eastern counties, with significant damage and loss of life. Official attempts to impli-
cate the United Irishmen failed, but in the spring of 1793, authorities
passed capital sentences on twenty-one Defenders and transported thirty-
seven others. War between Britain and Ireland had been declared in February of that same year, and by the summer of 1793 antimilitia riots were
raging in almost every county.[9]

It is highly likely that these and comparable events precipitated the
departure of the O'Haras. Certainly the circumstances would have been
similar to those of 1798, and misinterpretations of the dates could easily
have occurred, particularly several decades later among those who may
have known only the more publicized events of the failed insurrection led
by Tone and Lord Fitzgerald.

Another element in the saga involves a purported invitation to Kean
to come to Kentucky issued by the pioneering Isaac Shelby, who had
been the first governor of the state (1792–96); but again, this attribution was insubstantial—that is, "said to have been."[10] Because Shelby
would not have held office in the late 1790s, no specific authority would
have graced such an invitation; and at that time, Kean O'Hara had not
earned any reputation as a schoolmaster or any other distinction that
would have merited such a welcome.

The O'Haras ventured to Maryland after entering this country. We
can speculate that in County Sligo, James O'Hara, Sr., may have been
fairly affluent or had relatives who were. Those who departed from Ireland in the 1790s generally were. The massive waves of Irish immigrants,
peasants, mainly, and the urban poor—well over four million of them—
who came to the United States in the middle and late decades of the nineteenth century did not leave until they finally had no choice: flight or
starvation. Further, those who emigrated prior to 1830 seemed to have
come from the gentry—or those who were close to that status.[11] The fact
that the younger O'Hara men, Kean and his brothers, seem to have been
already reasonably well educated when they arrived in this country is
further testimony to their cultural background—and to their ability to
connect so well in Roman Catholic society in Maryland. Even so, the
crossing, as all contemporary accounts reiterate, would have been a major ordeal even for those able to pay for their passage before they embarked.[12]

One account of the family's background—a handwritten note by Mary
O'Hara Branham, a granddaughter of Kean and daughter of his son,

Battlefield plaque with "Bivouac of the Dead" at Gettysburg. T. C. Ware Collection.

Battlefield plaque with "Bivouac of the Dead" at Crown Hill. T. C. Ware Collection.

Battlefield plaque with "Bivouac of the Dead" at Petersburg. T. C. Ware Collection.

Charles—states that "tradition" in the family spoke of James O'Hara, Senior, as a "very tall large man of fine education and considerable . . . eloquence of speech." She goes on to identify his wife, "a small delicate woman," as Susannah O'Farrell. But in identifying their children (Kean, James, Charles, and Polly), this note provides a shocking and somewhat confusing extra element: "and an infant who died on shipboard while the family was crossing from Ireland in 1798 at the last day of her [Mrs. O'Hara] life. Can't say what became of it."[13]

This statement suggests that James's wife died during the crossing and that an infant of hers died the same day. Since no other, later mention of this matriarch may be found in family papers, such may have been the

Battlefield plaque with "Bivouac of the Dead" at Cave Hill. T. C. Ware Collection.

case. (But one may also note once more the attribution of the date of 1798.) Kean had been married, although information about his first wife seems at present nonexistent; and one may wonder if indeed the infant who died may have been his from that first marriage. In 1793 Kean, the eldest child, would have been twenty-five years of age; one could presume that his mother may have been past the age of childbearing.

While in Maryland, the O'Haras became closely allied with the Livers-Hardy family, noted as one of the most important Catholic households in that region. Branham's note further indicates that "Solomon Hardy was my great grandfather. He married Rachel Livers."[14] James, Jr., Polly, and Kean all married into this family. Kean wed Helen Hardy (sometimes spelled Hardie) after he had spent almost two years in Kentucky seeking gainful employment. For a time, he worked in a store in Frankfort, traveling back and forth over the Allegheny Mountains for supplies to be sold in that area.[15]

It appears that such enterprise brought him little. First listed in the state tax rolls of Jefferson County as a man with "no property," he was then living in Middletown, near Louisville, for the purpose of setting up a school. This was 1800, the year he married. Later that same year, November 1, his name is listed in the tax books of Woodford County; and in 1801 he is described in the rolls of Franklin County as owning "one black."[16] It was there, on a farm on Peak's Mill Turnpike, a few miles from Frankfort, that his fortunes as a schoolmaster began to jell, though he would stay in this place only five years. At the time, O'Hara's school was located on the farm known as "Oakley," where the trees were so thick, according to one recollection, that students "had to blaze a trail to find their way to school."[17]

Some time during this period Kean began to teach at Kentucky Seminary in Frankfort, and by 1812 he was president of this school. The curriculum emphasized the classical subjects of the trivium and quadrivium: instruction in rhetoric, mathematics, astronomy, composition, Latin, Greek, and so on. He remained in this position of authority for five years.[18] Continuing to thrive, he had amassed his holdings in 1816 to include property in the counties of Woodford, Scott, Franklin, and Anderson. He was also listed as the owner of two slaves and four horses. In 1818, he was listed as being taxed for property in Mercer County, as well as for six slaves and two horses.[19]

These items and the patterns they envision suggest the odd nomadic habits of the man, a manner of life which in many ways would later characterize that of his son Theodore, one great difference being Kean's steadily increasing prosperity, as opposed to the misfortune his son consistently experienced. But the older O'Hara's prosperity became a pressingly important element in that family's life when one recognizes his growing responsibilities. Kean and Helen O'Hara had eight children, starting in 1801—four daughters in succession, then two sons, Charles and James P., then Mary Helen, and Theodore, the youngest.[20]

Kean may have chosen the name for his youngest son because of his long, pleasant relationship with a missionary priest, a legend in the history of Catholicism in Kentucky, Father Stephen Theodore Badin. Father Badin, born and educated in France, came to Kentucky in 1793, where he was strongly instrumental in organizing parishes and ministering to those Catholic families who had emigrated from Maryland. Before this famed priest returned to France in 1819, Kean O'Hara had become one of his close personal friends and supporters, and at one point Kean translated Father Badin's Latin poem *Carmen Secrum*.[21]

As to the lingering controversy over where Theodore was born, some answer may be inferred from an advertisement which appeared in a principal Frankfort newspaper, the *Argus of Western America*, December 17, 1819, which announced Kean's intention of opening a school the following January.[22] With Theodore's birth occurring the following February, Kean's new school would have almost certainly demanded the presence of the family in that city. His taxable property was listed in the Franklin County rolls in 1820 and rather steadily there until at least 1834.[23] As late as 1839, however, Kean was still opening new schools—a practice he followed for much of his professional life, so that the range of his students was quite wide geographically. His advertisement which appeared in the newspaper *Commonwealth* in Frankfort on April 10, 1839, contained one key phrase—"paternal care"—that seems to have captured the essential philosophy guiding his life's work: "He begs leave to assure those who may become his patrons, that his best efforts will be continuously exerted to make this institution substantially useful and worthy of their confidence; and that his paternal care in forming the literary taste and moral habits of his pupils will never be intermitted."[24]

Indeed, from the perspective of the times, Kean O'Hara truly belongs with that rare breed of singularly effective teachers whose influence on others constitutes much of the folklore of American education in the nineteenth and early twentieth centuries. He would have been approximately thirty years old when he came to Kentucky; and when he died in 1851 at age eighty-three, he had been celebrated in and around the blue grass region of Kentucky for half a century. One historian recounts this impressive career in a succinct manner: "Among the large number of pupils of Kean O'Hara who rose to distinguished positions in life were several of the Marshalls and the Browns, Zachary Taylor (afterwards President of the United States), and Major George Croghan of the United States Army."[25]

Croghan, the nephew of George Rogers Clark, won fame and a congressional award for his defense of Fort Stephenson in the War of 1812. Only twenty-one at the time, Croghan made a triumphant return visit to O'Hara's school after his great achievement. In like manner, while on his way to Washington for his inauguration in 1849, General Zachary Taylor himself made a special stop at Frankfort to visit his old mentor: "It was an affecting scene when the great soldier, then an old man (of 65), bowed himself in grateful homage before the venerable preceptor of his youth, and in few but earnest words thanked him for the care bestowed upon his early education, to which he chiefly attributed all the achievements of his early life."[26]

The "venerable preceptor" would have been approximately eighty on this occasion, and hardly a prominent family in that section of Kentucky would not have been touched in some way by his endeavors. Shortly afterward, his odyssey was over. In a personal recollection of him, his granddaughter wrote that "in getting off a horse, he fell—was injured and died from the affects [*sic*]."[27] Quite apart from his collateral role as the father, and mentor, of the young man who would become such a notable poet, Kean O'Hara deserves continuing acclaim in the early history of education in this country—and particularly in Kentucky.

An attempt was mounted by John Wilson Townsend in the early 1930s to have what remained of Kean, along with his tomb marker, moved to the

State Cemetery in Frankfort to repose near the grave of Theodore.[28] Alerted to this endeavor, however, relatives refused the request; and so it is that Kean's grave may be found in its original site. On the side of his tombstone, still remarkably legible, are two mottos. The first is a personal statement about him, probably drafted by his son Theodore: "Beloved in all the relations of life, as husband, father, master, and friend. Faithful in all social and political duties, and distinguished as the great pioneer classical teacher of the west. His fame lives in the fame of his pupils, and his memory in their hearts." The second is a passage from Cicero, whom one would assume to be one of his favorite authors. It is quite possible that Theodore selected the passage: "Quid mumus [*sic*] republicae majus aut melius affere possimus quam si juventulem bene eradimus." It may be translated in this fashion: "What greater or better service to the Republic are we able to offer than if we spend our youth well."

In all, this may be seen as a highly appropriate sentiment about one who had been so long a model of service to youth, a model of honor, diligence, and prosperity. The social historian Dickson Bruce, Jr., has observed that "it has become almost a truism to assert that antebellum Southerners craved order and a stable, secure community life."[29] Such a mode of living was clearly a legacy the father attempted to pass on to his children, and especially to his youngest son, whose prospects for success seemed remarkably bright. Accompanying this legacy of care and mentoring from the well-traveled and accomplished paterfamilias, however, would have been an equally heavy set of expectations about individual achievement, expectations which were to trouble deeply Theodore's own quest for honor and prosperity during his formative years.

Chapter 2

The Formative Years

Although Kean O'Hara personally taught all of his children, being the youngest child seems to have been especially fortunate for Theodore, particularly in the development of his love of learning, which his father individually shaped and directed. For the duration of his life, Theodore O'Hara was noted for his broad range of knowledge and his refined taste in literature, as well as for his buoyant, gregarious disposition. But perhaps the extraordinary attention he received may have encouraged in him some other habits which were later to be detrimental in his several careers of teaching, law, journalism, and soldiering. He was, we are told, "the apple of his father's eye, educated by him with the greatest care."[1] His father would have been in his early fifties when Theodore was born and, one may judge from his landholdings and his two decades of success as a schoolmaster, reasonably prosperous by the standards of the time. One of the few specific anecdotes about Theodore's early years is both disturbing and deeply revealing about some major formative elements in his cultural environment, indicating a pattern that was later to be confirmed by contemporary accounts of his behavior as an adult. This incident involved a return to Ireland to visit relatives: "When a mere child he was taken by his parents to Ireland, where his father, Kane O'Hara, was born, and being rather precocious, was noticed a great deal by his relatives. He used to be given a good drink of Irish whiskey, and then placed on a table, where he would make speeches and recite, to the infinite amusement of his listeners. With true Irish love of fun he was cheered on, and generally carried the whole house with him."[2]

One may with some accuracy project from this episode the central qualities of the younger O'Hara's character, personality, and demeanor: daring, precocity, and a delight in being singled out as a performer. Although this story in its essential form became repeated several times in biographical sketches, this particular description by someone who knew O'Hara well, General Albert Brackett, is the only account of the visit which includes the detail about the "mere child" being given whiskey, and thus it carries with it something of the panache that could only have come from a studied retelling by Theodore O'Hara himself, recollecting the event in later life.[3] The fondness for whiskey—and its important presence in his daily life—remained an abiding characteristic, even in his military campaigns, adding to that conviviality for which he became well known and creating a cause of some of his major misfortunes.

Though little else of specific incident is recorded about his early education, we know that he began attending classes in Frankfort at his father's school, perhaps as early as 1824. A quick and diligent scholar, he reportedly aided other students in their lessons—"doing sums for them and helping in various ways."[4] Study, states one account, was not "the task, but the passion of his childhood, and fortunately [he was] trained by one who understood his nature." Nevertheless, he was also characterized as full of mischief, perhaps deliberately so in the presence of his strict, disciplinarian father, analogous to the proverbial preacher's son. That Kean O'Hara was a firm disciplinarian—a "stern preceptor"—there is little doubt. One charming but elucidating narrative gives special insight to his mode of teaching while at the Kentucky Seminary. His students rebelled against his firmness by locking themselves in their quarters until he relented and gave them a brief holiday from their studies. The account reads in part: "Our brave garrison put the teacher and trustees in a perfect rage, but at length they agreed to our terms. But the door was not unbarred till old Kean and his trustees reiterated that no penalty be exacted and then it took several hours to unfasten the barricades and draw out a profusion of nails . . . and we enjoyed our conquered holidays."[5]

Theodore's love of poetry and song, especially about heroic deeds— the verse of Sir Walter Scott, for example—was evidently nurtured early in his life and became one of his most striking intellectual traits.[6] As he grew to manhood, he seems to have sustained great proficiency and delight in reciting such verses in congenial company, holding an audience "spellbound." As Hugh Holman and other scholars of American cultural history have noticed, belletristic reading of the pre–Civil War South became deeply indebted to Scott and his imitators, especially in the creation of the image of a feudal order. Given also the nationalistic pageant in O'Hara's family background and the rugged topographical features of the Kentucky wilderness, one may recognize how the young Theodore would have easily assimilated such qualities into the conservative view of life which would have been his heritage from his father, both in his religion and in the classical literature he spent his life in teaching.[7] William Aytoun's *Lays of the Scottish Cavaliers,* principally about chivalry, insurrection, and tragedy in Scottish experience during the reigns of Tudor and Stuart monarchs, remained a special favorite of O'Hara, and one may find in some of those "lays" the qualities of the elegies he himself would later compose.[8]

In addition to this devotion to classical studies, at some point during this formative period of his life, he was taught to read music and to play the violin, becoming in time quite proficient. And the meticulous personal habits which were cultivated in him, such as his good humor, his excellent manners, his extraordinary neatness, his physical bearing, and his love of adventure, were recalled by a number of contemporaries.

After what was evidently intense academic preparation, he was judged fit to go on to higher education and was sent to St. Joseph's College in Bardstown, probably about 1836. His motivation for choosing college rather than an apprenticeship in some other occupation appears to have been a desire to follow his father's example, although as Bertram Wyatt-Brown argues, Southern ideals of education were scarcely different from others during that period about what best equipped young men to face the world: study of the classics and what would otherwise be considered great works.[9] At college Theodore apparently acquitted himself in an exemplary manner, although his academic prowess may be inferred principally from comments.[10]

Although it does seem true that most of the records of St. Joseph's College have been lost—or are at least inaccessible at this time—it is a striking coincidence that one ledger, and one only, still exists on the premises, attesting to this period of the poet's career. The ledger records the years 1838 to 1840 at the college: listings of the administrators, the faculty, the student body, and the curricular offerings. For the academic year 1838, Theodore O'Hara is identified as "Tutor of Latin and Greek," but not as a student.[11] Some accounts have him graduating in 1839, at the age of nineteen. He may have been a senior at that point, the fall of 1838, but he was not listed as taking classes. More likely he would have graduated in the spring of 1838 with distinction enough to earn appointment as tutor, but it is certain that he was never a professor of Greek, as is often stated.[12] The absence of his name in either the 1839 or 1840 roster in this ledger makes it clear that his tenure as a tutor was abbreviated, probably ending with the school year in 1839.

Although the distinction of being selected as tutor may suggest a dis-

tinct level of intellectual maturity and the beginnings of financial eman-
cipation for the young man, he would have remained under parental restrictions. Jon Wakelyn's study of the literature of antebellum college life
provides evidence that the fathers were both the sources of power and
the enforcers of "law and order." As he concludes, only the most able
and ambitious sons would have been sent to college, and the fathers would
have been expected to support them in this venture, obviously intending
for those youthful energies to be set to useful endeavor.[13]

To understand specifically the importance of this aspect of Theodore
O'Hara's school days and what it meant to him personally as well as pro-
fessionally, one must recognize that his father charged him for the cost
of his sojourn at St. Joseph's. Kean O'Hara's last will and testament became a complex document, involving as it did a sizable estate and several bequests to his wife, daughters, and sons. After disposal of certain
houses and pieces of property, Kean directed that all of his personal property and land be sold; and after the payment of his debts the residue was
divided into twenty parts. Theodore was willed four of "said parts." A
later stipulation by the father charges Theodore "one thousand dollars,
paid by me to and for him to enable him to acquire his college education
and his profession as a lawyer. Also with two hundred dollars paid to
him on his visit to New Orleans in the winter of 1850 and 1851."[14]

But by late 1839, just prior to his entering the study of law, Theodore
O'Hara's actions and his achievements had announced his qualities and
his mode of life, though not yet his direction. He had rejected an academic career, because apparently that kind of daily life, like the profession of law he would now attempt, did not present the levels of challenge
and adventure that could sustain his interest and commitment. As his
later military compatriot General Albert Brackett would assert, he was a
"singular man in some respects . . . and while he was undoubtedly a man
of genius, he did not appear to have that stability, which is necessary to
secure success." He also indicated that "it was necessary to know O'Hara
sometime before his good qualities were appreciated, and it is safe to say
that he had many of them." In several places, Brackett's observations give
us some further insights into O'Hara's later habits: he liked hotel life; he
worked into the night and was fond of getting up late (not a desirable or
even acceptable military habit). On one long march he took along a "negro
woman" for his personal cook; and he generally carried along some "supplies from Kentucky" (one assumes bourbon) which he hospitably shared
in his tent with fellow officers. He was content to let life run on, taking
little heed of the future.[15]

All this, of course, was seen from the vantage point of the 1890s, and
from that perspective the drama of O'Hara's life could permit General

Brackett's interpretations that no one could foresee when the young academician turned from tutoring in the classical languages to reading law. To suggest at that juncture, in 1839, that Theodore O'Hara would not succeed in any endeavors he chose would be to assert that intelligence of a high order, a deeply ingrained moral sense, a college education, talent abounding, and an attractive personality were not sufficient attributes for a young man in the brave new world of nineteenth-century America. In addition, he must have given the general impression of being rather a formidable, aristocratic person, as attested by several who knew him well. J. Stoddard Johnston, who was a contributor to the *Louisville Times* when O'Hara was editor, recalled his colleague in sharp detail:

> He was slightly below the medium height . . . being about
> five eight, with black hair and a deep hazel eye, and with
> a healthy peach-blow[16] complexion. His head was well-
> shaped and well set upon his shoulders, his features regu-
> lar, and his profile with its finely turned chin, classical
> and refined yet full of manly force. His figure was shapely and
> he bore himself so erectly yet gracefully that he seemed
> really taller than he was . . . he would have attracted attention
> in any company as a cultivated, intellectual gentleman of
> the best breeding, but with all those traits there was a certain
> aspect of reserve born of his military service, beyond which
> only his intimates could safely venture.[17]

Yet his restlessness, his convivial habits, and his need for new horizons—"the run arounds in his feet" as one observer called this affliction[18]—would work against his own winning characteristics. And though it may seem ethnic stereotyping to suggest that the aggregate of his Irish heritage included also a tendency toward melancholy and dreaminess, those qualities, in contrast to the gregarious habits, were frequently remarked as present in his complex nature. Unfortunately, much of the comment on this aspect of his genetic makeup often moved into romantic sentimentality, as in this neo-Wordsworthian interpretation by Jennie Morton: "Here [Frankfort] the embryo poet found in nature food for his soaring, singing poetry. The beautiful hills, the flower-embroidered dales, the bold, barbaric cliffs, the wild, dashing river, all had voices and messages for him. And in this genial atmosphere he began to touch the heart-chords which was to give to the world in tune and in time 'The Bivouac of the Dead.'"[19]

At some point in his youth, probably about the time he returned to Frankfort from St. Joseph's, he began the practice of spending hours in the State Cemetery grounds that overlook the Kentucky River. Musing in such picturesque spots had become a favorite pastime for aspiring young poets at that time, a vogue begun in England during the late eighteenth century by the "Graveyard School."[20] These poets, associated with the early development of the romantic movement, often wrote lengthy, melancholy works, speculating on the gloomy topics of physical decay, death, and immortality. The macabre elements generally present in old burial grounds held a fascination for them. In his treatment of "The Age of Beautiful Death," Phillipe Aries points to the power of the Rousseauian myth during this period: "the corrupt town as opposed to the innocent country, close to nature . . . ; and the desire to recover the old familiarity with death that characterized the country."[21] Also, for someone with Theodore's religious and cultural upbringing, and his military experience, the idea and the fact of death would never have been far away—and could well at this crucial period in his life have appeared, in the abstract, "beautiful."

Given both O'Hara's knowledge of literature and the nearby retreat of this attractive hillside plot, it is not difficult to see how he would have been drawn to such a practice. If one adds both his occupation at this period of his life—spending long days reading law—and his proclivities toward elegiac poetry, soon to manifest themselves in his two major works, then the final elements of supposition fall into place.

Reading law and entertaining poetical thoughts may seem antithetical, but during this period of his life the two processes seem to have come together. As one observer recognized, this spot of ground, the Kentucky State Cemetery, was to be "intimately associated" with his major literary productions. As Edgar Hume observed, "Always inclined to Celtic meditation tinged with sadness, he loved to walk here amid the solitudes and to allow his imagination free flight."[22] And it remained, at least until he was approximately thirty years of age, free-flying imagination without sustained literary production. The crystallizing of his thought into poetic utterance would later be prompted by two formal occasions which brought significant public attention to the little cemetery: the burial of Kentucky's dead from the Battle of Buena Vista and the reinterment of Daniel Boone. His literary responses to these events, about a decade away, would, ironically, bring him the enduring recognition which would otherwise elude him.

Another apt judgment, by Robert Burns Wilson, would conclude of him that "he was possessed of the impulsive spirit which induces one to stake all on the hazard of a die rather than to attain by painful and persistent effort." And further: "It may be that the Muses did haunt his every step, weaving about each scene the witchery of idealism and romance so enchanting to the poetic mind, but they certainly did not compel him to put into living verse the varied and picturesque experiences through which he must have passed. He wrote but little."[23]

Indeed, for public audiences, he wrote but little, or so it appears. One must lament the absence of any body of papers, such as juvenilia or other fledgling attempts at poetry writing. It may be that such items did exist. One of his sisters, Mary Helen Price, wrote to George Ranck this tantalizing recollection: "I do not know of any other poems of Theodore's. I remember of his taking away with him an old portfolio filled with all manner of pieces printed and in manuscript, but what there were I do not know. . . . I wrote to our friends in the South, in a vain endeavor to obtain the old portfolio. All went when we lost all. Oh, the sorrows! The sorrows! but let us draw a veil."[24]

Testimony by a Mr. Edward Hensley of Frankfort provides us this item: he personally heard O'Hara recite the following poem "a number of times," and he "was positive" O'Hara wrote it.

Second Love
Thou art not my first love,
I loved before we met,
And the memory of that early dream
Will linger round me yet;
But thou, thou art my last love,
The truest and the best,
My heart but shed its early leaves
To give thee all the rest.[25]

A quite respectable lyric, reminiscent of some of Robert Burns's work, and it leads one to wonder, if it is O'Hara's, whether it was a mere literary exercise or something born of a personal experience. O'Hara was never to marry, and though he was to travel much in the society of fashionable women, especially during his military career, there is no individual who may be clearly identified as a first or even second love, although Louisa McCalla, whom he met in Washington, may qualify. A letter from Marie O'Hara Branham, great niece of the poet, states that "he was in love with a young lady with an ambitious mother . . . Being a younger son he had no material wealth, which the mother wanted. So she separated them."[26] Implicit here, of course, is a subtle but real note of tragedy, one novelists have often developed. Being the youngest of eight siblings in the household of a schoolmaster could well have provided him a special urgency about choosing the wrong career. And the poignancy of losing irrevocably a lady he loved may account for his later lack of sustained interest in any given enterprise, as well as the acceleration of his intemperate habits. He would not have been the first nor the last to have demonstrated such a pattern of behavior.

Another item attested by Hensley as being O'Hara's work is this piece of doggerel, seeming to be a jestful toast, in a bawdy antiromantic spirit of the kind that young males would offer in riotous company:

> I'd lie for her,
> I'd sigh for her,
> I'd drink the river dry for her—
> But damned if I would die for her.[27]

The *Louisville Times,* and other newspapers with which O'Hara became associated, occasionally printed anonymous verse, and it is possible, indeed probable, that he wrote such items but did not wish to take credit for them. Or, as Hume has suggested, he may have emulated the practice of Sir Walter Scott, a favorite author of his, who was known to publish items under the guise of anonymity.[28]

Despite the brevity of the legal career which would follow these years of apprenticeship, the impact of his reading the law was to remain evident later in his life and in his writings, both private and public. His skills as an orator, earning him a strong reputation among his contemporaries, were shaped not only by that boldness and love of attention exhibited and encouraged in his childhood but also by the kind of legal rhetoric and declamatory patterning which were characteristics of American speech making since the days of the founding fathers. Only a few of his public addresses have survived, but one notable example remains in the obituary statement he delivered on the occasion of the burial of William Barry at the State Cemetery. It reads in part:

> The tribute we are here to pay is that which a people's cool
> sense of gratitude and justice . . . dispassionately renders to ex-
> alted merit and appreciated public service. It . . . has exacted
> from the still devoted subjects of its living sway. It is the tribute
> which an immortal eloquence, mingling its undying echoes
> in eternal harmony with her joyous anthem of freedom and
> peace and happiness, has won from the land. . . . It is the
> tribute which a burning patriotism . . . has extorted from the
> grateful memory of the country which now garners these
> sacred ashes to her bosom. . . . We are here . . . to execute
> upon these remains . . . that consecrating judgment of ancient
> Egypt, which, upon a severe trial of her greatest worthies after

death, and a cold scrutiny of their whole lives, admitted those
of spotless fame and of the loftiest worth to the sublime repose
of her everlasting pyramids.[29]

This oration has been credited as having influenced Lincoln when he
composed his Gettysburg Address,[30] but if so—and there can be only
conjecture—the differences between O'Hara's excessive formality of diction, phrasing, and allusion and the tighter parallel construction of the
Gettysburg speech suggest that the analytic eye of Lincoln permitted him
to cut down to the basic organization of O'Hara's eulogy. And quite
probably the comparison may owe more to the standard oratorical traditions of the time—especially in the legal profession—than to specific
influences.

O'Hara's later letters also strongly indicate his acquired sense of legal
diction and rhetoric, as well as his growing sense of merit unrewarded.
One in particular, to the Honorable C. C. Clay, a Confederate senator,
about O'Hara's removal from his rank of colonel with the Twelfth Alabama Regiment, demonstrates how his indignation was barely kept in
check in his command of legalese (emphasis added):

> I wrote to you last Spring claiming your *friendly and official*
> *exertions* as a Senator from my State to *obtain reparation for*
> me for a *gross wrong and injustice* which I suffered from
> this Administration. . . . The revoking of my appointment
> as Colonel of the 12th was wrong. And *notwithstanding*
> this, they permitted Jones to continue in a position which by
> their own acknowledgement *rightfully and legally belonged*
> *to me.* . . . In consequence of their own *blundering and un-*
> *righteous action.* . . . You must pardon this *ebullition of in-*
> *dignation* unto which I find myself betrayed. . . . I'll have sat-
> isfaction for it.[31]

The term "satisfaction," of course, evokes the concept of besmirched
honor associated with the tradition of dueling, if only symbolically.
Dickson Bruce, Jr., has explored that violent course of action as it continued in the South up to the time of the Civil War. Within the hier-
archical pattern of military service, such a recourse would have been
frequently desirable though always impossible; but the language of
O'Hara's letter indicates how deeply imbued in him that concept of a
Southern gentleman's honor had become. His sense of injury often found
outlet in this kind of violent rhetoric, which as Bruce has noted, was to
suggest not only that "things had fallen apart" but also that the threat

of violence—and directed violence itself—could and would result in desired change.[32] Such attitudes became increasingly more prominent in O'Hara's perspective as the frustrations in his life continued.

In sum, the years of his formal education, from the beginnings at his father's knee through his college years, his short tenure as a tutor of Latin and Greek, and culminating with his study of law, seemed an excellent preparation for the times. His reputation as an orator, already beginning to manifest itself in his youth, can doubtless be seen as a combination of natural eloquence and thorough grounding in the classical authors (such as Cicero) and the sometimes-ponderous rhetoric of the legal profession.

And yet with all of this apparent advantage, there were brooding elements in his manner, his behavior, his character that cannot truly be accounted for by reference to the comments about him at this point. At the end of the next decade of his life, in 1851 when his father lay dying, he would reflect on the matter: "I have been at home 3 or 4 weeks and have had some sport—although Frankfort is dull. I went up with Albert Johnson day before yesterday and returned yesterday on account of the severe attack of my father who I fear has a disease from which he will never recover. I am now at home assisting to wait upon him. Poor old gentleman. It grieves me to the soul to think how much I have done to disturb him in my life."[33] Beyond his plaintive lament he does not elaborate. He was then thirty-one; he had served in the War with Mexico, and at that point he had also written the elegy on which his fame would rest. But in 1839, while still at St. Joseph's, he had decided to turn from the profession that his father had pursued with vigor and success and seek a new direction, a new profession, a new way of life. The world, it seemed, lay all before him.

Chapter 3

The Muffled Drum Resound!

Theodore O'Hara resigned his position as tutor at St. Joseph's College after teaching there less than a year. No explanation seems to have been recorded. He would choose another path, turning his back on the academic way of life. Perhaps the son turned his eyes elsewhere because he did not wish to compete with his father, to be compared with his father. He may have considered the financial rewards too meager. Of course, it may have been that young O'Hara viewed the classroom as suffocating. He seems always to have viewed routine as his enemy and excitement as his special calling.

So Theodore O'Hara exchanged careers. He again borrowed money from his father to further his education, and he persuaded Kean O'Hara to write the necessary letters and make the arrangements so that he might study law under Judge William Owsley, a widely known and well-respected Frankfort attorney and sometime-member of the Kentucky Supreme Court. It is curious that the O'Haras, staunch Democrats, would have turned to Owsley, a leader of Kentucky Whigs. Joining O'Hara in Owsley's office at this time was nineteen-year-old John Cabell Breckinridge, the charming, capable heir of one of Kentucky's most powerful families. From the outset, it seems, Breckinridge, although a year younger, won the admiration, indeed the adulation, of his colleague. O'Hara believed, and the feeling would persist, that Breckinridge's physical presence and dignity and "capacity" could "cow" those who might oppose him. The two young men became friends for life.

Judge Owsley proved a taskmaster. Indeed, that quality may have led Kean O'Hara to choose him to educate and train Theodore in the law.

No one questioned Owsley's integrity, his sense of propriety, his diligence, or his ability, but most of those who knew him agreed he was cold and aloof, a driven man, hardly the type of teacher to inspire O'Hara and hardly the type to appreciate his student's gregarious, outgoing nature. Breckinridge reported that he and O'Hara read law for seven, sometimes eight hours a day. Blackstone had to be read twice, then the students progressed to Kent's *Commentaries.* To give context, their teacher also required that history and literature be studied daily. For Breckinridge the experience was exhilarating, and the "mist" of the law began to lift: "I begin to apprehend with some clearness, the leanings of one part of it upon another, and the great principles which govern the system."[1]

O'Hara reacted differently. Once admitted to the Kentucky bar in 1842, he quickly discovered the law to be little more than monotonous, passionless routine. He saw ahead of himself a career without fascination, without prospects for distinction. So, after practicing law less than a year, he abandoned the profession.

A man named William Tanner, a fervid Democratic publisher about whom little is known, lured O'Hara to the office of the *Kentucky Yeoman* in the spring or early summer of 1843. This Democratic weekly, which Tanner purchased in June 1841, had been established in Frankfort a year earlier, the successor to the old *Argus of Western America.* O'Hara helped Tanner edit the *Yeoman,* giving zest to its editorials. Tanner in return bestowed the title of assistant editor upon his colleague. In June 1843 the two men decided to found another paper, the *Tocsin,* evidently a special-purpose campaign sheet. They advertised their venture in the columns of the *Yeoman,* promising that it would be "devoted to Politics but will contain news, poetry and incidents of the Day." The *Tocsin* immediately endorsed Col. Richard M. Johnson, Kentucky's favorite Democratic son, for president and Jacksonian Levi Woodbury of New Hampshire for vice president. The *Tocsin,* printed on the press of the *Yeoman,* had a short life, with perhaps as few as half a dozen issues, and disappeared in the fall of 1843. Probably seeking independence from the constraints of Tanner, O'Hara ventured out again during the presidential campaign of 1844. He and Henry Clay Pope of Louisville, an intense young man with a short temper, established the *Democratic Rally* in Frankfort. It became "the organ of the Democratic party in Kentucky" during the exciting canvass or election of 1844 between Clay and Polk. The first issue of the *Rally* appeared in May of that year, coinciding with the opening of the Democrats' national convention in Baltimore. Although the *Rally* was also extremely short-lived, it stood as the "staunch advocate of the rights of the people." O'Hara's vigorous editorials, salted with sarcasm and sweetened with Irish wit, caught the attention of the Democratic faithful. O'Hara's contemporary, Richardson Hardy, considered the *Democratic Rally* "one of the most effective, spirited and popular campaign papers ever published in Kentucky."[2]

It became crucial for Theodore O'Hara to make political friends. He needed them. Although James K. Polk won the presidency in 1844, Whigs still held the upper hand in Kentucky. Judge Owsley, O'Hara's mentor, had won a grand victory as governor in 1844 over the popular Democrat William O. Butler. For O'Hara, there seems to have been little joy in Owsley's triumph, however, and as a trumpeter for the Democrats, he decided to leave Kentucky and seek his fortune in Washington.

O'Hara did have a patron, it seems. John Moore McCalla had taken an interest in the young partisan editor. A fervent Kentucky Democrat himself, McCalla had served as United States marshal under Jackson and Van Buren. Widely popular in Kentucky, McCalla opposed Owsley in the gubernatorial election but lost. With Polk's election, however, McCalla found he had gained a powerful voice in patronage and a claim on a position for himself. On March 31, 1845, McCalla became second auditor in the Treasury Department and invited O'Hara to join him in Washington. So, on July 3, 1845, O'Hara accepted an appointment as a clerk in McCalla's office and moved east, forsaking his two-year career in journalism.[3]

O'Hara joined sixteen other clerks, a messenger, and a chief clerk in McCalla's office. For his services he was paid $1,250 per year, a substantial salary for the times. The office of the second auditor was responsible primarily for expenses of the army—pay and allowances, military and hospital stores, and the like. It was humdrum work for the most part. Despite the salary, the plodding routine of the clerkship was hardly a fair exchange for the excitement of journalistic warfare. It provided little challenge for O'Hara's darting mind and proved stifling to his sociable disposition. He and McCalla, however, seem to have gotten along well, and there is evidence O'Hara may have developed an interest in McCalla's daughter Louisa, an intensely religious young lady. And there seems little doubt that Washington social life, although restrained by the temperance of the Polks, had great appeal for the young Irishman. The handsome O'Hara, conversationalist and storyteller supreme, was in demand. He added gaiety to dinner parties, camaraderie to boardinghouse life, and a diversion during stolid state occasions.[4]

At the time O'Hara was learning the ways of the national capitol, Kentucky decided to honor her most illustrious son, Daniel Boone. Boone had died in Missouri in 1820, but Kentucky wanted his remains and those of his wife Rebecca brought home. They were to be reinterred, amid great ceremony, in the Kentucky State Cemetery, high atop a cliff overlooking the Kentucky River and Frankfort itself. A beautiful spot, it was O'Hara's favorite.

The chairman of the committee on arrangements for the Boone funeral was O'Hara's former newspaper associate, William Tanner, and it is likely that Tanner made sure to include his friend in the grand occasion. Among the invited dignitaries were the present and past leaders of the state. The pallbearers included former vice president Richard M. Johnson; the funeral oration was to be delivered by Senator John Jordan Crittenden.

The thirteenth of September 1845 was a memorable day, and the Boone funeral promised to be an impressive event, a spectacle. O'Hara would not have missed it. The procession, a great line of citizens more than a mile in length, began from the capitol building in the center of Frankfort. The crowd accompanied the coffins up the limestone hill to the grave site, gathering there to listen to the distinguished speakers. The ceremonies deeply impressed O'Hara; five years later he would honor Boone himself by composing "The Old Pioneer," a poem that would gain him more than a local reputation.[5]

Following Boone's reinterment, O'Hara, profoundly moved by the occasion, returned to Washington and the great ledgers of the Treasury. General McCalla seems to have been sympathetic with the plight of his talented but frustrated young clerk. It seems plausible that it was McCalla, perhaps at this time, who gave O'Hara a vision of a career in the military. Kean O'Hara hardly would seem to have been an influence in this regard; and indeed, at this juncture of Theodore's life, his father seems to have become a remote figure. McCalla, at O'Hara's age, had been a member of the Lexington Light Artillery, an elite militia unit he joined for the usual political and social purposes. In the War of 1812, McCalla and his comrades found themselves ordered to the northern frontier, sent to the relief of besieged Frenchtown on River Raisin. When their commander, General James Winchester, surrendered his force to the British and their Indian allies, McCalla and his fellow Kentucky militia suffered brutal mistreatment and imprisonment. McCalla survived the disaster, however, and when he returned home continued to serve in the militia. In 1817 McCalla became major of the Forty-second Kentucky Volunteers and was elected brigadier general soon after. Using his militia position and his law practice as a base, McCalla became a political figure of consequence in Kentucky, a leader of the Democrats.

A grand opportunity for soldiering presented itself to O'Hara in the spring of 1846. Mexican forces crossed the Rio Grande and mauled a squadron of dragoons belonging to Zachary Taylor's army. The United States in a fury declared war and Treasury Clerk O'Hara immediately stepped forward. As a faithful Democrat, backed strongly by McCalla and probably by Kentucky's Gen. William Orlando Butler, O'Hara was rewarded by the Polk administration with a coveted commission as captain, not of Kentucky militia, but in the regular army itself.

O'Hara had had no military experience, of course, but in 1846 that fact mattered little to the powers in Washington. President Polk was concerned that the Democrats be well represented in the officer corps of the U.S. Army. After all, Polk reasoned, was not West Point, that center of supposed scientific military leadership, a Whig stronghold? Its influence needed balancing in the army's ranks with carefully positioned, faithful Democrats.

Once O'Hara had his commission safely in hand, he resigned from the Treasury Department on June 30, 1846, and headed west to find General Taylor's army. By the time he arrived, however, the battles of Palo Alto and Resaca de la Palma had been fought and won and the army established in camps along the Rio Grande awaiting the arrival of volunteer regiments from various states.

On the Rio Grande, late in the summer of 1846, O'Hara found himself assigned to quartermaster duty, probably because of his Treasury Department experience. Familiar with the procurement and disbursement of military stores, O'Hara busied himself forwarding supplies up river from Port Isabel, the great depot at river's mouth. Oceangoing vessels from New Orleans, heavily laden with equipment and ordnance and glory-hungry recruits, unloaded there. Their cargos were then placed aboard small river steamers for shipment up the narrow, twisting Rio Grande. Volunteers were placed in camps along the river; supplies were distributed rather haphazardly in dumps along the banks. River steamers were very few in number, as were wagons. The situation quickly became a logistical nightmare.

Zachary Taylor intended to move south against Monterrey, the enemy's strong point in northern Mexico. First, however, a staging area, a base, had to be located far upstream at Camargo. Taylor seized Camargo with his regulars on July 14, 1846, and relocated his headquarters there. Once the army had been concentrated at Camargo, Taylor started south toward Monterrey, establishing on August 19 another forward depot at Cerralvo, thirty miles closer to Monterrey. A month later Taylor, carefully keeping his force closed up, appeared on the plain before Monterrey itself. The Americans attacked on the twenty-first, and by the morning of the twenty-third had broken into the city. House-to-house fighting and heavy casualties followed. This was not what Taylor wanted at all. He quickly, and unwisely, agreed to an armistice.

O'Hara's role in Taylor's Monterrey campaign is not known. He is not mentioned in the battle reports, so it is reasonable to conclude that he was not involved in the assault on the city and remained either in Camargo or Cerralvo forwarding supplies. Nevertheless, because of Zachary Taylor's respect and fondness for his old teacher Kean O'Hara, the young quartermaster captain no doubt enjoyed a special relationship with the commanding general.[6] The nature of this association can only be inferred, although later O'Hara would express regret at being assigned to Brig. Gen. John A. Quitman's brigade and having to leave that part of the Army of Occupation directly supervised by Taylor.[7]

On November 16, 1846, O'Hara was stationed in Cerralvo, midway between Monterrey and Camargo, where he was engaged in stockpiling commissary goods and dispatching essential equipment, ordnance, and food to the front. From what his letters reveal, quartermaster O'Hara's greatest personal concern appears to have been the monthly checks he sent home being received by his father.

The Mexican army, badly disorganized by the capture of Monterrey in September, was now united under Santa Anna, who rapidly strengthened his forces and concentrated them at San Luis Potosi. General Taylor, ordered by the War Department to abrogate the Monterrey armistice, warned Santa Anna, then once again took the offensive. He advanced a force to Saltillo, but having seized it, grew cautious. He had proceeded deep enough into Mexico, he believed, so he dispersed somewhat his army of occupation with the intent to "settle down into garrison duty."

In the meantime U.S. naval forces had seized the port of Tampico on the eastern coast. When Taylor learned of this success, he decided to occupy Victoria, a midway point which would consolidate the American position and give him a string of bases stretching three hundred miles from Parras to Tampico.[8] En route to seize Victoria, Taylor was stopped suddenly at Montemorelos on December 17, 1846. Gen. William Worth, commanding the advance post at Saltillo, reported Santa Anna advancing upon him in great force from San Luis Potosi. Immediately Taylor turned back with Gen. David Twiggs's division, leaving Quitman's brigade to continue to Victoria by itself. Captain O'Hara, acting as a general supply officer, had accompanied Taylor's column to Montemorelos. The commanding general now ordered him to remain with Quitman and to take command of the expedition's large supply train. This decision did not suit O'Hara at all. He wanted action and believed his best chance would be to return to Saltillo with Taylor. "But I could not be spared," O'Hara wrote his father, "& I had to come hither."[9]

On December 19 Quitman advanced southeast from Montemorelos toward Victoria with his brigade, a Tennessee regiment, and a battery of artillery. O'Hara's wagon train was especially vulnerable. It was strung out two and a half miles and O'Hara struggled to keep it closed up. Partisans and small groups of Mexican cavalry lurked in the immediate countryside, waiting for an opportunity to strike, so O'Hara took the additional precaution of gathering his wagons in chaparral thickets each night. This maneuver he thought would hinder, if not preclude, any sudden cavalry attack by the enemy. It worked.

Quitman and O'Hara should be credited with a well-managed march from Montemorelos to Victoria. The column arrived before the city on December 29. They had not lost a man, nor had to fight a skirmish. The menacing enemy cavalry had chosen not to attack them, and the Victoria city fathers surrendered the town without a fight.[10]

On January 4, 1847, Generals Taylor and Twiggs rejoined Quitman. Worth's cry for help had proven a false alarm. A few hours after their arrival in Victoria, Generals Robert Patterson and Gideon Pillow appeared, leading a division of volunteers from Matamoras. Once again the Army of Occupation was concentrated in strength. It was no longer Taylor's army, however. A new commander, Gen. Winfield Scott, was on the scene. Scott took control of Taylor's troops and ordered them to proceed to the coast, to Tampico, where they would reassemble in preparation for an amphibious attack on Vera Cruz.

O'Hara arrived in Tampico on January 25, following a "dreadful march." He had remained with Quitman's brigade as quartermaster and now encamped with them on a lagoon outside of town. O'Hara and the others remained in these temporary quarters through the winter months, "eagerly expecting" the "imperial Maj. General" (Scott) "to put them in motion for their destination." O'Hara fretted about his quartermaster accounts. Business matters seemed to irk him anyway, and now this irritation was compounded by a "Despot Quartermaster" at Tampico, Capt. Edwin Burr Babbitt, a West Pointer and a stickler for detail. Being held personally responsible for his expenditure of public money made O'Hara nervous. He worried about settling his quarterly accounts and took the precaution of making copies of vouchers for expenditures and sending the originals to Washington, sealing the papers in Babbitt's presence. He then placed the documents in Babbitt's own mailbag and sent a "duplicate letter by different mail." O'Hara seemed to indulge himself sometimes, infuriating and goading superiors he regarded with scarcely concealed contempt.

O'Hara continued to send his pay back to the family. Kean O'Hara was ill, confined to his room with some undefined "affliction of the legs," probably sustained when the eighty-year-old fell from his horse. In a letter to his father of March 2, 1847, O'Hara related that he was sending him fifty dollars a month, which severely depleted his salary; in addition that month he was forwarding fifty dollars to his sister Theresa Ann and

one hundred dollars to his older brother James. He wanted the family to
know that he enjoyed having the regular income the army provided. His
health was "most excellent." It had been so since his arrival in Mexico.
The opportunity to pass the winter on the coast was a delight:

> Roasting ears and watermelons on our Christmas dinner table
> & then all the most delicious tropical fruits in the utmost
> abundance—the balmy skies of your June, with soft wind
> weighted down . . . with the burden of perfume wafted from
> circling groves of the orange, lemon, river apples, bananas in
> every stage of vegetation from the opening bud to the golden
> fruit while the air for miles around is made vocal with the
> gay notes of innumerable parrots and the many birds of gor-
> geous plumage. Indeed[,] this a beautiful place—abounding
> in scenery and enchanting as its fruits are luscious & its flow-
> ers fragrant. In possession of our people it would be an Eden.[11]

The last sentence of this letter to his patron McCalla reveals O'Hara's
conversion to the American expansionist impulse, dogma that would become central to his life in the following decade.

Rumor had reached O'Hara at Tampico that Congress intended to
create ten new regiments. Important things were happening back home,
and he felt "woefully behind the politics of the day," even the proceedings of the last Congress. General McCalla tried to keep him informed
and sent him political papers such as the *Nashville Union* as regularly as
possible. If the rumor of the new regiments were true, O'Hara asked of
McCalla, would he be so kind as to see the president and inquire about a
captaincy in the Voltiguer regiment or in the infantry: "Maybe I would
take one there if Mr. Polk would make it a personal matter."[12]

O'Hara shipped out from Tampico with Quitman's brigade on
March 7. They sailed on the "splendid steamer" *New Orleans,* intent on
overtaking Scott's fleet before the army landed at Vera Cruz. O'Hara and
his friends expected the Vera Cruz defenses to be "trifling . . . but[, he
added,] experience teaches us that we cannot rely upon the accounts depre-
ciating the preparations of the Mexicans for defence."[13]

Although the *New Orleans* was fast, the trip south was stormy and
the troops crammed aboard suffered greatly. They did rendezvous with
the fleet on time, nevertheless, and immediately were taken to an anchor-
age at Sacrificios Island, where they disembarked and got aboard surf-
boats. At 9:45 A.M., March 9, 1847, the landing force began to make for
shore, escorted by a mosquito flotilla of gunboats. Delays and confusion
and uncertainty and caution delayed the strike, however, and it was not

until 5:30 P.M. that the command "Land the Landing Force" was signaled. "It was an imposing magnificent spectacle," observed quartermaster O'Hara. "The landing was accomplished without interruption or ac-
cident, & by 8 o'clock P.M. the troops were all ashore & disposed in order
of battle."[14]

At dawn on March 10, Scott's three divisions advanced inland, and
within "the course of three or four days" the investment of Vera Cruz
was accomplished. Trenches were dug, running closer and closer to the
city's walls; batteries of heavy guns and mortars were emplaced. Then the
Americans opened fire: "The terrible work was continued day & night
& such whining, whistling & bursting of shot & shell around, above &
on all sides of us was sublimer than comfortable." Finally a very powerful naval battery was brought ashore and positioned. It quickly succeeded
in silencing Vera Cruz's biggest guns, and the garrison surrendered the
city to the elated Americans on March 29. Once the disarmed Mexican
soldiers departed, O'Hara and his comrades fell into ranks and marched
into Vera Cruz itself, passing in review before Winfield Scott, who stationed himself high atop a balcony on the plaza.[15]

Scott regrouped as quickly as he could. He wanted to push inland before the Mexicans had time to prepare their defenses in the mountains
and, of equal importance, he wanted to extricate his army from the low
coastal area, the yellow-fever belt, before disaster struck. Again logistics
posed an enormous problem. Inland with the army, for instance, must go
some two hundred thousand muleshoes and one hundred thousand horse-
shoes. To obtain cattle and horses necessary for this march into the mountains, Scott dispatched Quitman's brigade with O'Hara as its quartermaster to Alvarado. A poorly coordinated operation resulted, however. The
Mexican garrison at Alvarado was alerted and managed to destroy or remove the stores and livestock Scott needed so badly. The bungled expedition, however, worked to O'Hara's advantage in that it helped build a
trust relationship with Quitman, who would prove a powerful friend and
associate in the filibustering days that lay ahead.

Scott knew he must advance anyway. On April 2 the leading elements
of the army left Vera Cruz, with the rest of the army a day or two behind. Good fortune awaited them. A sharp but brilliant action was fought
on April 17–18 at Cerro Gordo resulting in a complete American victory.
Scott continued to push forward. He seized Jalapa, then continued on to
Puebla. The Mexican army melted away before him, but guerrillas began
to swarm on the American flanks and in their rear. Every day Scott worried more about the security of his lengthening line of communications.

Another matter complicated Scott's plan of campaign. Enlistments for
the volunteers, twelve-month men, were about to expire, and the War

Maj. Gen. Gideon J. Pillow, USA, 1849. Engraving by Henry S. Sadd.

Department decided to replace these state militia organizations with ten new regiments recruited for the duration of the war. Rather than continue his advance inland with the old volunteers, 90 percent of whom had refused to reenlist, Scott decided to wait for the new regiments and sent the old volunteers home. He thus lost about one-third of his effective strength. His army shrank to seven thousand.[16] The War Department also decided to reduce the number of volunteer staff officers. Captain Theodore O'Hara, however, was selected as the senior of twenty assistant quarter-

masters who would be retained in the army, for the duration at least. It
was certainly a vote of confidence in the young officer.[17]

O'Hara also received a grand promotion, at least in responsibility. In
June 1847 he was assigned chief quartermaster of Maj. Gen. Gideon J.
Pillow's division. O'Hara seems to have worked well with Pillow, who
appreciated volunteer officers, especially journalists who shared his political creed. Among O'Hara's duties early that summer was outfitting the
brigade supply trains. Col. Thomas Childs's brigade of Pillow's division,
for instance, required a train of 50 ammunition wagons, 16 supply wagons, 27 baggage wagons, 5 hospital wagons, and 30 forage wagons, 128
wagons in all. To gather these wagons, which were chronically in short
supply, and load them with the necessary supplies and ordnance was a
bedeviling assignment.[18]

For three months Scott waited in Puebla for the new volunteer regiments. Then, with the arrival of Gen. Franklin Pierce and his three thousand volunteers, Scott had about sixteen thousand men and decided to
press forward. On August 7, the advance began through the mountains
and into the Valley of Mexico. Scott bypassed Santa Anna's heavily for-
tified El Peñon position and struck out south of Lake Chalco. When the
army reached San Augustin, the main road they had followed turned
north through the towns of San Antonio and Churubusco to the south
gate of Mexico City itself. This obvious approach through San Antonio
looked extremely hazardous, so Scott sought a way to bypass the strong
point, having his engineers search for a route across the Pedregal, an almost impenetrable lava field some three miles square.

Directly across the Pedregal, unfortunately, was the Mexican General
Gabriel Valencia and a strong force posted on high ground at the village of
Padierna. Pillow's division, guided by Capt. Robert E. Lee, nevertheless
worked their way across the lava and confronted Valencia. The ensuing
battle, known by the American troops as Contreras, was fought August 19–
20, 1847, and directed by Pillow. While a frontal assault by General Twiggs
and several badly outmanned artillery batteries held Valencia's attention,
Pillow sent brigade after brigade north around the enemy flank in a bold,
risky envelopment. Pillow tended to employ all of his staff officers, including quartermasters, as aides-de-camp once fighting started. On August 19
at the Battle of Contreras, O'Hara and his fellow staff officer, Capt. Joseph
Hooker, were conspicuous as they moved back and forth through the sharp
lava rocks of the Pedregal, leading units into position and carrying messages. The result was a classic surprise attack: the morning of August 20,
Valencia was struck in rear, flank, and front by Pillow's detached brigades.
The Mexican troops were overwhelmed and fled with great loss.

Pillow's division pursued closely and advanced north against another
strong point Santa Anna established at Churubusco. This time Scott

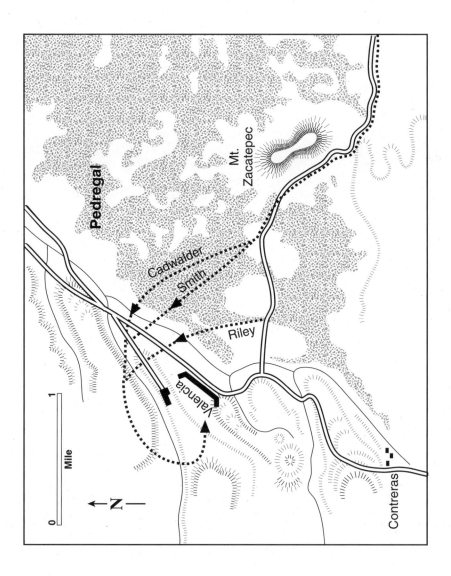

Battle of Contreras,
August 20, 1847.

threw all of his divisions against the well-fortified Mexican position and broke their ranks after hard fighting. Staff officer O'Hara again was most active, appearing here and there on the battlefield, exposing himself to Mexican musket fire in a reckless manner. Pillow was much impressed by the young officer's bearing and attitude. He complimented O'Hara's work highly and saw to it that the young captain won a brevet promotion to major for his gallantry.[19]

Back home O'Hara's deeds did not go unnoticed. The *Frankfort Yeoman* announced:

Major O'Hara

The readers of The Yeoman,—those particularly who recollect Major O'Hara as one of its editors in 1843–4,—will be gratified to see by the following official announcement in the list of brevet appointments lately published, that he has acquitted himself as handsomely in his military as in his editorial capacity.

'For gallant and meritorious conduct in the battles of Contreras and Churubusco, Mexico, August 20, 1847. . . .

To date from August 20, 1847:
Captain Theodore O'Hara, Assistant Quartermaster
(volunteer staff) to be Major by Brevet.'[20]

Major Theodore O'Hara was not done. Scott's army closed on the City of Mexico and prepared for the final attacks. O'Hara participated in Scott's ill-advised morning attack on Molino del Rey, a bastion of stone buildings guarding Mexico City. There the American army suffered terrible casualties, and a timely Mexican counterattack from the fortress of Chapultepec routed one of their advancing columns. The fighting was bitter, and rumors of Mexicans slitting the throats of wounded Americans made Scott's troops fight with even greater determination. By noon, despite their losses, Scott's troops had fought their way into the stone foundry. They blew it up and retired. The specifics of O'Hara's role in the fighting are unknown, but he undoubtedly served as he had at Churubusco, carrying instructions to Pillow's brigadiers George Cadwalader and Franklin Pierce, leading units into position, and gathering intelligence.

When the final assault on Chapultepec came on September 13, O'Hara is said to have been by the side of brigade commander Pierce, joining his staff after division commander Pillow was wounded and disabled.[21]

Once Mexico City had been secured, Scott sent units into the countryside to consolidate American control and to scatter guerrilla bands. By mid-October affairs were in hand and most American officers congre-

Maj. Thomas T. Hawkins, ca. 1860. From Anderson C. Quisenberry, *López's Expeditions to Cuba, 1850–1851* (Louisville, 1906).

gated in the city, looking for places to live. O'Hara had an early start and, once snipers had been cleared from the streets, found himself a choice residence. It belonged to Señor Batros, an official of the Mexican government, who had fled the city following Chapultepec. In the home of Batros, O'Hara found weapons, "doubtless of those who continued firing from houses upon our men after the surrender of the city." This discovery made him feel quite justified in occupying the home. Batros returned to the city in October, however, and demanded of Military Governor John

A. Quitman that O'Hara be "dispossessed." O'Hara stood his ground. He appealed to Quitman, reminding him that Batros "was up to the time our army entered here *General Treasurer of the Mexican Government.*" Furthermore, "to obviate any prejudices to his restoration to this office after our army leaves the country, he does not design to come to live in his house here, *while the American army occupies the city*—but intends only to send his family in." In all probability O'Hara had his way, remaining in his attractive quarters throughout the winter of 1847–48 and perhaps into the spring.[22]

About this time Scott's officers decided to form a club and looked about for a suitable location. Not far from army headquarters was the elegant residence of Señor José M. Bocanegra, former minister to the United States. This mansion suited the needs of the American officers nicely, and there, on October 13, 1847, they established the Aztec Club. O'Hara was a founder of this organization, which modeled itself on the Society of the Cincinnati and would become hereditary.[23] The 160 founders included future presidents Davis and Pierce, future generals Grant and Lee, and a host of well-known military and political figures.[24]

In Mexico O'Hara had made valuable friends—Quitman and Pierce, of course, but there were others as well. Lt. Col. Joseph E. Johnston would write sixteen years later, "We served together in the Mexican War in the same division. . . . My observation in these various circumstances, has given me full confidence in . . . [his] capacity, skill & courage."[25] Also with O'Hara in Mexico were his old friend Breckinridge, major of the Third Kentucky Regiment; William Preston, lieutenant colonel of the Fourth Kentucky; and a very close friend, Thomas Theodore Hawkins, adjutant of the First Kentucky Mounted Volunteers.[26]

Gideon Pillow also appeared to be a promising contact. Extremely well positioned politically, Pillow wrote President Polk privately that O'Hara was "a brave and Gallant officer," "your warm friend and mine." Pillow seems to have encouraged O'Hara to remain in the army and did what he could to effect O'Hara's transfer from staff to line officer, thus enhancing his chances for a permanent commission once the army of occupation was demobilized. Pillow also attempted to help O'Hara by securing an exchange with O'Hara's newspaper friend, Capt. Henry C. Pope of the Mounted Rifles. Pillow did not hesitate to use the good offices of the president, but this highly irregular ploy floundered because Pope prematurely resigned. It seemed Pope had been to the home of a good friend (unidentified), and on the way back to his barracks he "stopped to take some refreshment & drank a little wine." For this indiscretion, according to Pope, his superior officer disciplined him, and, either in a huff or to avoid a court martial, Pope resigned his commission.

Back in Washington the prickly adjutant general, however, was wary of such Pillow tactics and haughtily disposed of O'Hara's request for an exchange: "Capt. Pope was out of the army before the receipt of this application—his resignation having been accepted to take effect the 31st of Dec. 1847. Of course he cannot exchange from the M. Riflemen with the *Volunteer Staff!*—if such an exchange were under any circumstances allowable."[27]

Gideon Pillow felt indebted to his young Irish quartermaster. Perhaps it was because of O'Hara's faithful and effective service on his staff, perhaps it was because he was a faithful Democrat and master of the sharp phrase. More likely it was because O'Hara appealed to his friend Breckinridge to act as Pillow's counsel in a crucial Court of Inquiry, defending the latter officer against charges brought by Winfield Scott. This high profile but most undesirable assignment would involve Breckinridge, just having arrived in Mexico City from Kentucky, in the shameful controversy that would split the army of occupation and result in the recall of America's commanding general from Mexico. O'Hara did his friend John C. Breckinridge no favor.[28]

Moreover, close association with Pillow, while deeply reinforcing O'Hara's Jacksonian biases and ingratiating him with the Democratic establishment, fatally damaged his military career. Pillow's protégés, who, for the moment, bathed in the warmth of presidential attention and preferment, would remain consistently suspect in the eyes of the professional military establishment, in the eyes of a Robert E. Lee, a Braxton Bragg, and a Samuel Cooper.

Chapter 4

Cuba Libre

Theodore O'Hara's activities, not to speak of his whereabouts, from the winter of 1847 in Mexico City until the spring of 1855, have remained unusually difficult to establish. This lively young adventurer was on the go—involving himself and his friends in grand schemes, traveling frenetically along a triangle from New Orleans to Washington to Frankfort, checking in and out of hotels, undertaking responsibilities and shedding commitments at a startling rate. Much of the time he was engaged in secret negotiations and missions for aggressive expansionist groups such as Young America. He also seems to have involved himself in the effort to build a railroad across Mexico's Isthmus of Tehuantepec, yet another instance of his unbridled passion for the doctrine of Manifest Destiny. Some of this time he invested in journalistic endeavors, although he himself seems never to have regarded his role as newspaper editor as more than partisan spokesman. O'Hara probably returned to the law for a while in Washington, or at least made the pretense, and he edited one book during this period.

Again and again O'Hara would find himself returning to Kentucky, to the State Cemetery, wandering among the silent graves of the eminent. It is easy to imagine O'Hara there, looking up through the arms of the giant oaks, standing at the edge of the cliff, and gazing down at Frankfort, its tiny red buildings lining the river bank like toys. He would find a grassy spot and sit for a while, brood and grieve. Then, with a start, he would get to his feet again, pacing with measured strides and talking out loud to himself. When the sun turned blood red in the West and lost its heat, O'Hara would come down from the cliff.

O'Hara had left the army with regret. He enjoyed the security and the freedom which regular pay afforded him, the camaraderie of the officer corps, the adventures and dangers of war. He had been mustered out officially on October 15, 1848, but he had returned to Kentucky on terminal leave months before. In Frankfort O'Hara was approached by a young veteran, John A. Scott, who asked if he would help him publish a journal he had kept while a captive of the Mexican army. O'Hara agreed, and over a number of weeks worked hard editing Scott's account. The result was the *Encarnaciòn Prisoners,* published in Louisville in 1848 by the house of Prentice and Weissinger.

It is the story of a group of Kentucky soldiers, under the command of Capt. Cassius Marcellus Clay and Maj. John P. Gaines. All were members of Col. Humphrey Marshall's First Kentucky Cavalry. In January 1847, as a prelude to the Battle of Buena Vista, Clay and Gaines had been sent out by Gen. William O. Butler to determine the enemy's strength. When this patrol encamped at Encarnaciòn on the night of January 22, they carelessly failed to post sentries. The next morning they found themselves surrounded by a host of Mexican lancers and surrendered without a fight. A party of American cavalry sent to their aid also was swallowed up by the Mexicans.[1]

O'Hara took full liberty as editor of *Encarnaciòn Prisoners.* He embellished Scott's account, bringing descriptions of landscape to full flower, darkening and intensifying the suffering and gloom of the prisoners. The book stands, however, as a valuable firsthand account of the Kentucky volunteers and their adventures. The task must have appealed to O'Hara greatly. It enabled him to help a fellow Kentuckian "tell his story to the world," and it gave him a chance to jab Cassius M. Clay, antagonistic emancipationist Whig and O'Hara's rival editor in Lexington. O'Hara's role as editor of *Encarnaciòn Prisoners* went unnoticed, however. His name is not even mentioned.[2] Replete with faults, O'Hara seems to have been modest in the extreme about self-promotion and was perfectly willing to settle for the role of ghostwriter. It was one of the qualities, in all probability, that drew men and women to the handsome, fashionable Irishman and turned many of them into loyal friends.

It appears O'Hara left Frankfort later in 1848 and returned to Washington. The Polk administration was in its last days, and O'Hara may have attempted to secure another federal position. He had entree to the president through the good offices of McCalla and Pillow, but the days of Democrats' ascendancy were numbered. Zachary Taylor came to office March 5, 1849, and began removing Democrats, appointing Whigs in their stead. Despite Taylor's close relationship with Kean O'Hara, Theodore had distanced himself from the president because of his activity on behalf of the Democratic Party. He could not hope for an appointment. According to several sources it was at this time and in this city that O'Hara again attempted to practice law. In any event, he was unsuccessful in establishing himself in Washington, so he left and returned to Frankfort in early 1849.[3]

Back home, O'Hara renewed his association with William Tanner and rejoined the *Yeoman*. Together, using the press of the *Yeoman*, they edited a Democratic weekly which they called the *Campaign Yeoman*.[4] In January 1850, O'Hara proposed assuming control of the *Champion of Reform*, a single-purpose paper supporting the adoption of the new Kentucky constitution, but changed his mind in a published statement of February 4, 1850.[5]

Newspaper work in Kentucky, however, could well have been a cover. O'Hara was on the move—New York, New Orleans, Washington. He now had a new cause: Cuba. When he had gone to Washington in late 1848, following his discharge from the army, he had spent a great deal of time with an attractive, bright Kentuckian named John T. Pickett. O'Hara returned to Washington in the winter of 1849–50 and renewed his association with Pickett. Son of diplomat-soldier-newspaperman James Chamberlayne Pickett and Ellen Desha, daughter of the former governor of Kentucky, the twenty-five-year-old Pickett, thanks to a childhood in South America, had developed a "perfect knowledge" of French and Spanish.[6] He had wanted to be a soldier like his father and tried West Point, but young Pickett discovered he could not tolerate the routine. So he turned to the law, but like O'Hara, found it sterile. Pickett had the good fortune, however, to be appointed U.S. consul for the Turks Islands (Jamaica jurisdiction), British possessions lying between the southern tip of the Bahamas and Hispaniola. He spent the Mexican War period at that diplomatic post. While at Turks Islands he "began to think about the project of revolutionizing Cuba." When he returned to Washington, Pickett made Theodore O'Hara a quick convert.[7]

It all seemed to fit. In 1848 liberal political revolutions convulsed Europe. Constitutional government and representative democracy were the battle cries. The two young Kentuckians particularly sympathized with and admired Louis Kossuth and his followers in Hungary. Indeed, the restless John T. Pickett had joined Kossuth earlier and even been given the title of "general" in the Hungarian patriot army. Pickett, who would influence O'Hara as much as Breckinridge, perhaps more, convinced the romantic, impressionable Kentuckian that they too should raise the banners of freedom.[8] So together with many others, Pickett and O'Hara became members of Young America. This idealistic group backed the ef-

Lt. Col. John T. Pickett, ca.
1850. Courtesy of the Filson
Club Historical Society.

forts of European liberals in their battles against repressive government.
Young America, which flourished from 1848 to 1852, favored free trade
and tended to be highly nationalistic, aggressively expansionistic, and
overwhelmingly Democratic. Stephen A. Douglas of Illinois was its shin-
ing star and its voice was the *Democratic Review*. Kindred groups were
Young Germany and Young Ireland. Reform on an international scale
had enormous appeal for idealistic young adventurers such as O'Hara
and Pickett. It could divert them and their nation from divisive, destructive sectionalism, and, with the leadership of the Democratic Party, return the United States, perhaps, to Jacksonian purity.[9]

The possible acquisition of Cuba had enormous popular support
among Americans, particularly in the South, and had had since the days
of Jefferson. As editor J. D. B. DeBow put it, the possession of Cuba was
"indispensable to the proper development and security of the country."
Many Americans, North and South, believed it the mission of revolutionary America to give help to an oppressed people seeking political liberty.
The corrupt captain general of Cuba enjoyed almost unlimited authority
and openly exercised his power to suppress and imprison political oppo-

sition and to censor the press. O'Hara was outraged. Whether or not he, like many Southerners, also wanted Cuba as additional slave territory is not known, although his actions in the 1850s would indicate he shared this view.[10]

The leader of the Cuban independence movement was fifty-year-old Narciso López. A native of Venezuela, López had fought in the Spanish army against Simon Bolívar in 1814, and when Spain was driven from Venezuela, López fled in 1822 first to Cuba then to Spain, where he won distinction fighting to suppress the Carlists.[11] He was credited with helping place María Cristina on the throne, then joined with a group of "enlightened army officers" who wanted to install a republican form of government and who succeeded in deposing the regency of María Cristina in 1840. López was rewarded for his loyal service with the governorship of the central province of Cuba. When he returned to the island, López married a Cuban and became allied with several of Cuba's most powerful families, but he was deposed as governor in 1843 in "a reign of persecution against liberals and freemasons."[12]

From this point, it seems, López grew dedicated to the cause of Cuban independence. He began working secretly with some of the "most enlightened and wealthy" citizens to bring about revolution or intervention by the United States.[13] In 1848 he opened communication with the Polk administration but was betrayed and had to flee from Cuba. Polk's attempt to purchase the island from Spain failed, and López, making New York City his headquarters, determined to raise an army and forcibly free his adopted country.[14] With five other prominent Cuban exiles, López founded a junta in New York. These men proclaimed the independence of Cuba and adopted a flag with a lone star on a red field, which López designed himself.[15] Spanish officials in Havana retaliated by condemning López and his associates to death.

In 1849, with the aid of young John T. Pickett and others, López managed to fit out an expedition, but the wide publicity given their enterprise proved their undoing.[16] As they gathered their men and supplies near New Orleans in the summer of 1849, President Taylor, under heavy pressure from Spain, stepped in and broke up the scheme. He captured the men assembled on Round Island and confiscated their munitions. Taylor called upon all Americans to uphold the Neutrality Law of 1818, which, he declared publicly, he intended to enforce.[17]

The failure of this "Round Island" expedition served only to make López more determined. In late 1849 he announced in several newspapers the organization of the Junta Promovedor de los Interéses Politíos de Cuba with headquarters in Washington and openly sought financial backing from friends of Cuban liberty. The Spanish ambassador, of course, was infuriated and protested strongly to U.S. Secretary of State John M. Clayton in January 1850.[18]

All this talk about freeing Cuba proved quite heady for Theodore O'Hara in the winter months of 1849–50. When Pickett took him to meet López in Washington, O'Hara was captivated and inspired by the patriot. He was not alone. López biographer Portell Vilá lists O'Hara specifically as encouraging López in the company of former Mississippi senator John Henderson, "los senadores Davis, Foote [Henry S.][19] y Douglas [Stephen A.], el coronel Theodore O'Hara, y otros."[20] After discussing possible schemes with the Cuban revolutionary, O'Hara, T. T. Hawkins, and Pickett traveled to Washington soon after Christmas and met with Ambrosio J. Gonzales, López's chief of staff and translator.[21] They told Gonzales that they would raise a regiment of Kentuckians and place them under López's command. They offered to equip the regiment and have the men transported to New Orleans at their own expense. The three Kentuckians then left Washington and proceeded by stage to Louisville, where Gonzales, acting in the name of the liberation front on February 27, issued a commission as colonel to O'Hara.[22] The latter would undertake recruiting the Kentucky regiment at once. Gonzales and López continued south, down the Ohio and Mississippi, stopping at points to meet with parties interested in the venture. The most significant meeting took place in March 1850 in Jackson, Mississippi, between López and John A. Quitman. López offered Quitman command of the military forces of a freed Cuba while López would head the civil government.[23] Quitman eventually would refuse the offer, however, believing that the revolutionary movement should originate on the island itself. Once it had begun, he then would accept the command.[24]

López had more success with Chatham Roberdeau Wheat. This high-spirited Louisiana adventurer and Mexican War veteran wanted badly to share in the expedition. He pledged to raise a skeleton regiment of Louisianians and obtain money from his friends to charter transportation for his men.[25] The doings of López and O'Hara and Wheat were no secret, however. Spanish ambassador Calderon de la Barca wrote Vincent Antonio de Larrañaga, Spanish consul in Charleston, that López was going south and appeared to be transferring his headquarters from Washington to New Orleans. They must watch López's movements with the greatest care.[26]

It proved a most successful journey south, despite Quitman's reluctance. Word of López's mission spread throughout the South. New Orleans proved enthusiastic; Mississippi would provide a third regiment. The owner of the *New Orleans Delta*, Laurent J. Sigur, arranged for a supply of weapons.[27] Former senator John Henderson of Mississippi and others undertook to secure financial support.[28] López issued 6 percent bonds pledged in the public lands and property of Cuba, and Henderson sold these bonds mostly to speculators, some five hundred thousand dollars worth, at ten cents on the dollar. With sixteen thousand dollars of the proceeds Henderson purchased the steamer *Creole*.[29]

Meanwhile, O'Hara and Pickett, aided by O'Hara's close friend Thomas T. Hawkins, set to work recruiting the Kentucky regiment. They sought about 250 men, a skeleton force, which would be expanded by Cuban volunteers into one or more full-sized regiments of a thousand each. Unlike Wheat, who drew his Louisiana regiment from the streets of New Orleans, "wretched tatterdemalion indifferently scraped up in a hurry," O'Hara sought "the best quality of young, adventurous *Americans*. No Dutch or foreigners of any kind, and as many Kentuckians as possible."[30] They raised the Kentucky regiment quickly, greatly assisted by William Hardy in Ohio, who recruited over a hundred men from the Cincinnati area.[31] Some of the Kentucky regiment were revolutionaries fired by O'Hara's idealistic appeals. More of them, of course, were lured by the hope of a bonus of four thousand dollars and a land grant in Cuba. For their efforts and risks the officers were promised ten thousand dollars and high rank in the future army of Cuba.[32]

The Kentucky regiment began assembling in Cincinnati. On Thursday afternoon, April 4, 1850, Hardy's men from Ohio boarded the *Martha Washington* and crossed over to Covington, Kentucky, where a company of Kentuckians embarked. On they went to Louisville, where forty more came aboard. They met O'Hara in Evansville. He had a company of men from Frankfort with him, and also Hawkins, whom some of the men from Ohio mistook for López—because of his dark complexion and black mustache. "Though of a slight and delicate frame, [Hawkins's] bright black eye strikes one at the first glance, reflecting high spirit, pride, and cool courage." He appeared "quite military." Hawkins's reputation for a quick temper and for being "the highest living authority on the code duello" followed him.[33]

The united Kentucky regiment now sailed downriver, most of them aboard the *Martha Washington,* some with O'Hara on the *Chancellor,* still others on the steamer *Saladin*. They traveled unarmed, masquerading as goldfield emigrants and adventurers bound for California. As proof each man was given a steerage ticket to Chagres, Panama. They fooled no one. At Vicksburg a curious onlooker remarked with disbelief, "Cuba, by G——d! No such men as these go to California to dig. Did you ever see such a body of men! D——d if they ain't all gentlemen! What fire, intelligence and energy glows in every countenance!"[34]

These men were to be led into battle by Colonel O'Hara. John T. Pickett, whom one man described as being able to "tramp his forty miles without taking the starch out of his shirt-collar," would be lieutenant colonel. Hawkins would be major of the Kentucky regiment. This last appointment caused a problem among the men of Ohio, for O'Hara, in a letter of April 1, had promised William Hardy, who had recruited half of the Kentucky regiment, that commission. O'Hara changed his mind, however, and insisted on Hawkins as major. Hawkins was "the most intimate friend and adviser of Col. O'Hara, who received, with great respect, his suggestions." Outstanding among the company commanders were Captains Jack Allen and John A. Logan of Shelby County, Kentucky.[35]

On the afternoon of April 11, 1850, the loosely organized Kentucky regiment reached Freeport, Louisiana, just west of New Orleans. The trip down the Mississippi had been lively—"at night great hilarity generally prevailed—singing, dancing, &c." Most of the regiment crowded into the boardinghouses of Freeport and there learned that they had arrived two weeks early! The price of lodging in Freeport was exorbitant and a two-week stay was out of the question, so O'Hara had the men moved to Lafayette, where he ordered them to remain. While the two hundred young men endured their exile from the glitter of New Orleans, O'Hara and most of the officers were quartered at the St. Charles and Verandah Hotels in the city, where they "drank Juleps at Hewlet's, visited the theatres, masked balls, etc." This discrepancy would not do at all, and of course men began to slip into the city. One night, for a lark, nearly two hundred of them marched arm-in-arm into New Orleans. O'Hara met them in the street, reminded them that they might jeopardize the expedition by their foolishness, and sent them back to Lafayette. The incident revealed little that New Orleans did not know. "We had been the subject of several newspaper notices," explained filibuster Richardson Hardy, "and the Cuba expedition was the bar-room conversation all over the city."[36]

At last transport was arranged. So, on April 25, 1850, the regiment left Lafayette and crowded aboard the bark *Georgiana*.[37] A tug came alongside about 9:00 P.M., and cheered on by a large crowd lining the pier, pushed the *Georgiana* free. Narciso López, Ambrosio J. Gonzales, and John Henderson waved good-bye as O'Hara and his Kentuckians floated out into the channel of the Mississippi and vanished into the darkness.

The men awoke the next morning and found themselves looking "over the blue expanse of the Gulf of Mexico." A small fishing boat appeared. It hailed the *Georgiana*, but as it approached, a U.S. revenue cutter began to circle the bark. The fishing smack disappeared. Three times the cutter sailed around the *Georgiana*, which was anchored, but after a final hard look, pulled away. Then the little boat reappeared: L. J. Sigur and Major Hawkins could be seen aboard. The craft moved in beside the

Georgiana and quickly began shifting its cargo of "splendid" muskets and ten thousand rounds of ammunition to the *Georgiana*. O'Hara, at this point, bade Sigur farewell and made a speech to the regiment, explaining their mission in general terms and informing the Kentuckians that in a few days, López in a steamer with more men would rendezvous with them at an island in the Caribbean. Any who wished to go home, he indicated, should leave now.[38]

The morning of April 27 the steam-powered towboat pushed the *Georgiana* out to sea. Sails were hoisted and she sailed south, toward the coast of Yucatán. For five days fair winds carried her along, so fast that the captain kept shuffling his charts, trying to reckon their position. Sprawled about on deck, the volunteers suffered from seasickness and longed for sight of land. O'Hara's orders were to land on Mujeres, an island just off the coast of Yucatán. There he was to organize his recruits into a skeleton regiment and drill them until López arrived with the balance of the command.

Finally they sighted the Mexican coast, but the strong winds had blown them far off course—almost a hundred miles south of Mujeres. Turning about, the *Georgiana* fought against the wind for four more unhappy days. O'Hara knew his men had had enough of confined shipboard life. He ordered the discouraged captain of the *Georgiana* to put them ashore at Contoy, a desolate, uninhabited little island twenty miles short of Mujeres, about ten miles from the coast of Yucatán, some eighty miles from Cuba.

O'Hara now took active control of the regiment. He appointed officers for the six companies and gave the men a choice as to which company they wished to join, although he insisted that the companies be evenly distributed numerically—some forty men in each.[39] They landed on Contoy early on the morning of May 7. While Hawkins supervised the men making camp, O'Hara, accompanied by the mate of the *Georgiana,* took a small boat and circled Contoy, then explored an adjoining island.

Thus Camp Pelican, as the encampment on Contoy came to be known, was created. It was grim: "Contoy is nothing but rocks and sand, the only specimens of vegetation being immense prickly pears, some bushes, long grass, a few dwarf trees, and numberless *lizards!*" There was a lake of sorts in the middle of the island, and although large fish could be seen below the surface, the water was salty and unfit to drink. Already men were becoming sick.[40]

By night O'Hara had the men build large signal fires to attract the attention of López and the *Creole*. The signal fires, as feared, drew unwanted visitors, flying Spanish flags, but these fishing smacks, although

Narciso López, ca. 1850. Courtesy of
the Filson Club Historical Society.

they made the men nervous, proved harmless. The enterprising O'Hara
turned the presence of the Spanish fishing boats to his advantage by en-
gaging one of the sailors as a pilot for the sail to Mujeres. By day the regiment reboarded the *Georgiana* and tried to reach Mujeres using the "flat-
bottomed . . . old bark." Four days O'Hara tried. One day the winds
would be too high, the next there would be no wind at all. The pilot became exasperated with the *Georgiana,* "saying she sailed like a crab."
Each day the pilot and the bark's nervous captain would give it up and
return to Contoy.[41]

The regiment grew restless. Sullen faces and actions undercut O'Hara's
insistence on daily drill on the beach. The men from Ohio still resented
Hawkins's authority and his orders, and to them Theodore O'Hara himself seemed to "affect a supercilious dignity." A crisis developed on May
12. With no sign of the *Creole* and disgusted with their miserable existence
on the sandbar of Contoy, the men became mutinous. Two or three ring-
leaders found support from the captain of the *Georgiana,* Captain Rufus
Benson, who was sick of the whole affair. Benson told the would-be mutineers if they got the signatures of the majority of the men on a petition
to quit the expedition, he would make sail and return them to New Orleans. Encouraged by Benson, a group of the volunteers decided to capture their officers and seize the weapons. Their attempt came within an
inch of succeeding, and the officers in alarm turned to O'Hara, who assembled the regiment on the beach, dramatically broke open his orders,
and in a long speech explained their mission carefully and in great detail.
He admitted the grave complications brought about by the delicate tim-

ing of the expedition, but he strongly believed their prospects for success were excellent. Then he continued, appealing to their patriotism in the highest terms, reminding them of the glorious nature of their enterprise, the credit they could bring upon themselves and their states, and assuring them of his belief in López and all he represented. In closing, he further disarmed their fury by promising to lead them back to New Orleans himself if López and the *Creole* did not appear in eight days.

To the utter frustration of Captain Benson and the mutineers, and to the great relief of the edgy officers, O'Hara's speech was "received with great and almost unanimous enthusiasm, and responded to by three cheers for López, three for Cuba, and three for '*annexation.*'" The next morning O'Hara had an oath drawn up "for every true Liberator to sign, pledging himself to obey the orders of his officers" and submit to the regulations of the U.S. Army. If a man refused to sign, and fifteen did, he would not be permitted to go with the regiment to Cuba. In a fortunate turn of events, Indians appeared about this time, bringing in their canoes large turtles, vegetables, and melons, which gave relief from the diet of salt meat and hard crackers. The night of May 13, O'Hara and Hawkins gathered the men in the stern of the *Georgiana*. The men sang—good Methodist hymns at first, then "in full chorus parodies on old familiar hymn tunes." One went:

> Oh! *Cuba!* oh! Cuba!
>   I'm bound for the land of Cuba!
> Oh! Cuba is my happy home—
>   I'm bound for the land of *Cuba!*[42]

On the fourteenth men awoke to cries of "Steamer! steamer!" O'Hara, spyglass in hand, studied the smoke in the distance, then shouted to the men that it was the *Creole*. As the ship drew closer, the Kentuckians saw for the first time the beautiful "*Free Flag of Cuba*" flying from its masthead. The *Creole*'s captain saluted the soldiers on the beach, "'General López's compliments to the Kentucky Battalion,—the Colonel [O'Hara] will please come aboard.'" O'Hara went aboard and met with López and Gonzales. It was decided that the *Creole* would sail for Mujeres for water, then return on the fifteenth; in the meantime the troops aboard the *Creole* would disembark and drill with O'Hara's men on the beach.

The Kentuckians were disappointed. Wheat's Louisiana regiment turned out to be only 175 strong, "the privates men of degraded character." They also had heard great things of Col. William J. Bunch's 500 Mississippians, but discovered that "flower of chivalry" regiment consisted of about 160, "very few of them Mississippians at that." The spirits of the liberators were raised, however, when López's address was distributed. In lofty rhetoric the document reminded them of glories won at Palo Alto and Churubusco. The Cuban revolutionary called upon them "to strike from the beautiful limbs of the Queen of the Antilles the chains which have too long degraded her, in subjection to a foreign tyranny, which is an outrage upon the age; to do for your Cuban brethren what a Lafayette, a Steuben, a Kosciusco, and a Pulaski are deathless in history for having aided to do for you; and eventually to add another glorious Star to the banner."[43]

This printed address, although signed by López and presented in the common declamatory diction of the time, bears clear signs of the work of Theodore O'Hara—its imagery, its pitches and rolls of language and emotion. The speech had its intended effect. It stirred the patriotism of the men, increasing their confidence in López. Officers then called the men forward and began distributing the uniforms of the liberators—red shirts and black caps adorned with a lone star cockade. The star, of course, was to evoke the successful independence effort of Texas; the red shirt, the 1848 European struggles at the barricades; and the cockade, revolutionary France.[44]

López returned from Mujeres on May 16. He handed a Cuban flag to O'Hara, and the latter gave Lieutenant Colonel Pickett the privilege of presenting it to the regiment. Then all the liberators, 521 of them, came aboard the *Creole*.[45] At midnight they sailed from Contoy—men jammed in every corner of the old steamer, many of them "almost smothered in the hold," others "scorched on the deck." They fought to keep the *Creole* trimmed for the first two days out as she ran against waves as high as "mountains." "Her wheels would not half the time touch water."[46]

The first day out López called a council of war and briefed his officers. The liberators would land at Cárdenas before dawn, pass through town quickly and seize its railroad depot on the far side, then proceed rapidly by rail to Matanzas, thirty miles away. They would establish a recruiting center there, but, as a precaution, one hundred men would be sent ahead to break communications with Havana to prevent a sudden retaliatory strike by the governor general. Then the liberator force, strengthened by the enlistment of thousands of Cubans, would move from Matanzas on Havana itself. López expected to appear before Havana with a force of at least five thousand, hopefully thirty thousand, within a week of the landing.[47] López also settled during that council the delicate question of which unit would land first. The honor would go to O'Hara's Kentucky regiment.[48]

On the afternoon of May 18, 1850, the *Creole* passed Nassau. She dodged fifteen sailing ships that day. If a ship ventured too close, the troops would tear off their red shirts and scurry below deck. About sundown, López assembled the liberators on deck and reviewed them. Then

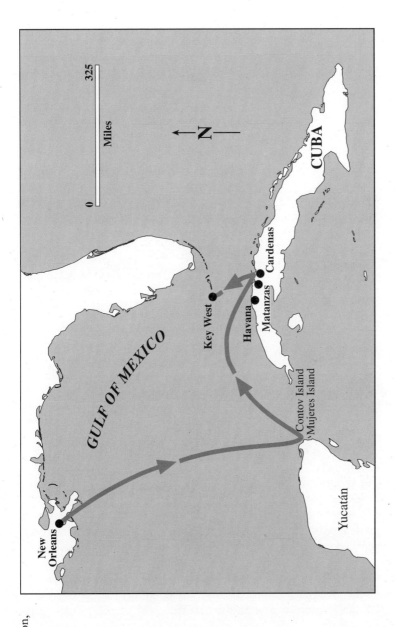

López Expedition,
May 1850.

he "addressed the troops warmly in Spanish," telling them they "were about to strike the *first blow* in a glorious revolution." The general's inspiring words were carefully translated and delivered to the liberators by Colonel O'Hara, López's second-in-command.

Ammunition boxes were broken open and sixty rounds issued to each man. Officers were armed with the sword and carried a Jenning's patent repeating rifle, capable of fifteen shots per minute. López gave the regiments their choice of weapons. Wheat's Louisianans chose muskets, Bunch's Mississippians chose the Yager,[49] and O'Hara's Kentuckians chose rifles. Most of the troops also had bowie knives and "five shooters" sticking from their belts.[50]

When all was ready, O'Hara gathered his Kentucky regiment around him on the boiler deck, in the best position for speedy debarkation. They stood silently and waited. They listened as the leadsman called out the depth—dangerously shallow. At ten o'clock the *Creole* passed the lighthouse at the head of Cárdenas Bay, fifteen miles from the city. A brilliant full moon shone, giving odd shapes to the small islands and sailing vessels scattered over the bay. About one o'clock the lights of Cárdenas itself came into view, "the city lay sleeping in beauty . . . the Sabbath had just begun."

Suddenly the *Creole* ran aground. They were in sight of the pier, so the ship's mate, Callender I. Fayssoux, put a line between his teeth and swam from the ship.[51] He fastened the rope to the pier, a heavier line was next run out, and the *Creole* hauled in. Once the ship was secure, a single plank, twenty feet long and ten inches wide, was laid from the deck to the pier. O'Hara then led his Kentuckians ashore single file. He assembled them as quickly as he could just beyond the wharf. The landing had seemed an eternity.[52]

Running aground and the incredible expedient of a single narrow plank for disembarking cost López the element of surprise and the hope of taking Cárdenas without a fight. Guards fleeing from the pier sounded the alarm, and the small Spanish garrison awoke and prepared themselves. Messengers raced toward Matanzas to report an American invasion but not before taking up a stretch of track "to contain the invaders."

Meanwhile John T. Pickett took two companies of Kentuckians and made for the railroad station on the run. The depot lay almost a mile outside of Cárdenas, and a mile and a half from the *Creole*. Fortunately Pickett seized the station, a locomotive, and several cars without a fight.[53]

O'Hara waited on the pier. López had changed the plan at the last minute. Instead of O'Hara taking the remainder of the Kentucky regiment, moving "rapidly through the town and dispos[ing] them in its rear, in such a manner as to cut off all communication from the place," López directed O'Hara to march into the center of Cárdenas using the main street and seize the Spanish barracks.[54] Wheat and Bunch with their regiments would advance along parallel streets, Wheat to the east, Bunch to the west.[55] Rather than being guided by one of López's aides, as was the plan, O'Hara had to find a man on the street. This Cárdenas citizen, "either from fright or stupidity, proved unequal to his task" and took O'Hara and his men "some distance out of [his] way." Exasperated, O'Hara countermarched his command up a side street, seizing other citizens and asking directions, but they "were so terrified they could not speak." At last he encountered López and the general gave him a guide, yet another man picked up on the street. O'Hara took up the march again, but this second guide proved worthless also, and "stupefied with fear, could give me but a confused idea of the position of the barracks."

When a Spanish sentinel startled the column with his cry, O'Hara deployed his men. The sentry fired his musket and fled. The Kentuckians raced forward two blocks toward the plaza. Then came more shouts from soldiers stationed in the stone jail house dead ahead. "Alto! Quien vive? quien vive?"

O'Hara halted the column and yelled back in English, "Friends and López."

The Spanish opened fire. O'Hara, at the head of the column, was struck twice in the legs. He shouted, "Column forward!" and "scrambled" to the side of the street. His Kentuckians rushed past. Major Thomas T. Hawkins stooped for a moment over his fallen friend, then ran forward to take command of the column and lead the attack in person.

Rob Wheat heard the volley that felled O'Hara, and believing it to be a salute to López, marched at the double-quick into the plaza at the head of Louisianans. The Spanish opened fire, wounding Wheat and driving the Louisiana regiment back. Steadily, however, the Kentucky regiment, now supported by Bunch's Mississippians, neared the jail. Wheat's Louisiana regiment reformed and kept up the fire from the rear of the enemy garrison. About dawn, as the Americans closed on the jailhouse and battered down the door, the defenders surrendered. Other Spanish soldiers continued the fight stubbornly from the Governor's Palace, but López had his men fire the lower floor and the building was soon ablaze. However, "even after the roof had fallen in, a party of soldiers kept firing from one corner, killing and wounding several men." Finally they were subdued by the bayonet. By 8:00 A.M., Cárdenas belonged to the liberators. Fighting had been bitter, particularly at the Governor's Palace, and losses high. The Spanish casualties were lower, but among those captured were the lieutenant governor, three civil officials, and several dozen soldiers.[56]

López established his headquarters in the captured barracks and presented himself in the plaza, making speeches to the people and the Spanish prisoners. Thirty-four Spanish soldiers tore off their uniforms and joined the liberators, but no Cubans. Most of the civilians melted away into the hills. Those remaining on the streets argued that the five hundred liberators would be set upon the next day by five thousand Spanish soldiers, and if they joined López it would mean their destruction, certainly the loss of their property. So the Cubans either fled or contented themselves by "merely walking about, bowing and scraping to the red shirts." The Americans meanwhile scattered through the streets of Cárdenas and consumed a great deal of liquor, but it seems civilian property was protected scrupulously. While his troops celebrated, the wounded O'Hara was brought first to the boardinghouse of Mrs. Wergener Woodbury in Cárdenas, then soon after carried back to the *Creole* and placed in a cabin.[57]

Throughout the morning the expedition's quartermaster hurried forward supplies and equipment from the *Creole* to the railroad depot, believing, as did the liberators, that the advance upon Matanzas would begin at any moment. Indeed, Pickett had three locomotives ready. López, however, was profoundly discouraged. The lightning attack on Matanzas that he envisioned had been utterly frustrated by the unexpected resistance of the Cárdenas garrison. Of greater importance, all three of his most important subordinates, O'Hara, Wheat, and Gonzales, had been wounded. Furthermore, rumor spread through the back streets of Cárdenas and into the countryside that the Spanish were closing in. Three thousand of them, it was said, would arrive by midnight. More concrete reports reached López of Spanish lancers lurking about the outskirts of Cárdenas. The nervous liberator commander worried also that a Spanish warship might show up in the bay at any moment. The situation was perilous.

Late in the afternoon López announced his decision to reembark and attempt to land elsewhere on the Cuban coast. He ordered baggage, coal, water, and the captured Spanish arms to be moved to the pier and placed aboard the *Creole*. He pulled back the Louisiana and Mississippi regiments and had them reembark. O'Hara, from his cabin, sent a message forward to Hawkins: send back a company to the pier as a working party and help load the precious coal and water.

The rest of the Kentuckians remained at the lower side of the plaza as a rear guard, and Hawkins took the precaution of deploying a company across each of the side streets leading to the wharf. Presently, Spanish infantry appeared on the opposite side of the plaza, where they formed a line of battle. Three times they charged Hawkins's position, and each time they were driven back. Hawkins then retired his Kentuckians a block closer to the *Creole*. This sign of weakness enticed the Spanish lancers to "come thundering on in gallant style." Hawkins repulsed them handily

with a well-aimed volley, but they came on again, determined to overrun
the handful of Kentuckians. Just in time Pickett returned from the depot
with his men. He rushed them forward and lined up alongside Hawkins,
and together they repulsed the determined lancers, with sharp losses.
About 8:00 P.M. Hawkins was ordered to pull back closer to the ship. He
gathered his dozen wounded and retreated to the pier, where he had his
men build a breastwork or barricade of sugar hogsheads. "There they
waited for more than an hour for the order to come aboard."[58]

At 9:00 P.M. López called Hawkins and the Kentucky regiment aboard
and the *Creole* cast off. Immediately the pier was alive with Spanish soldiers. Musket fire ripped the ship. Major Hawkins and two other officers
were wounded, but the *Creole* escaped. Losses had been heavy for the liberators at Cárdenas. The *Creole* now held about fifty wounded, including O'Hara, Hawkins, Wheat, and Gonzales; about twenty liberators had
been killed. Losses in O'Hara's Kentucky command totaled fourteen killed,
twenty-six wounded.[59]

The *Creole* carefully retraced its passage out of the bay, but suddenly,
five miles from the pier, a shudder went through the ship as she struck a
reef and went hard aground. The liberators became frantic as they envisioned Spanish warships closing in on the helpless steamer. Again and
again Capt. Armstrong I. Lewis of the *Creole* attempted to warp the
steamer off. He tried fastening a line to a rock or to an anchor and haul-
ing away, but every effort failed. O'Hara lay in the cabin helpless, listening to the ominous scraping of the *Creole* and the shouts of the men
on deck.

In desperation the captain ordered all heavy equipment tossed over the
side. Yet the *Creole* "would not move an inch." López then began to jet-
tison precious ammunition, but still the steamer remained stuck fast. Finally, two hundred liberators disembarked on a small island in the bay.
This expedient, with the help of a rising tide, worked. The *Creole* floated
free. The two hundred liberators were picked up, and once again the
steamer felt her way toward sea, the lighthouse coming into view at day-
light. Stopping the *Creole*, López put off the Spanish officials he had captured, then set a course up the Cuban coast.[60]

López was in high spirits. He intended to attack again with the *Creole* and his liberators—this time at Mantua at the western end of the island. They would capture Havana from the blind side. López had many
friends in Mantua, and he believed that the capture of Cárdenas had
served to pull the Havana garrison away from the capital "on a fool's
chase." Mantua should be easy. In a hastily called council of war,
Wheat, Hardy, Jack Allen, and others supported López. O'Hara,
propped up on a cot and weak from the loss of blood, on the other hand,

made loud noises in opposition. He would have none of the second invasion. He stunned López by attacking the Mantua plan as madness. The officers, now hopelessly divided, turned to the men, and the decision went overwhelmingly against López. Infuriated and staggered by this rejection, López resigned command and asked to be put ashore. This request was refused, and the *Creole* sailed for Key West, the only port close enough to be reached with the short supply of coal on board.[61]

The evening of May 20 the *Creole* anchored in shallows, forty miles east of Key West. The next morning the captain commandeered a pilot from a fishing boat and set out. About thirty miles from Key West, López spotted the smoke of another steamer. It was the Spanish warship *Pizarro,* and she began to close rapidly. When Key West was ten miles distant, the interval between the two ships tightened to two miles. The *Pizarro* was much faster, though the *Creole* had the advantage of a head start and light draught. But the coal taken aboard at Cárdenas, "miserable black dust," produced a speed of barely five knots against the *Pizarro*'s twelve or thirteen. Coal ran short on the *Creole.* When the lighthouse at Key West came into view, "the last shovel full was thrown upon her fires." Now into the furnace liberators furiously tossed barrels of rosin, bacon meat, and red shirts.[62]

Circumstances favored the filibusters, however. The *Pizarro* stopped to take on a pilot and lost fifteen minutes. With a mountain of smoke billowing from her stack, the *Creole* steamed into the harbor of Key West and anchored under the guns of the USS *Petrel.* The *Pizarro* turned away, just a "cannon's shot astern."

The liberators abandoned the *Creole* quickly. Customs officials, accompanied by a boarding party from the *Petrel,* seized the old steamer but made no attempt to stop the party of filibusters from dispersing. To appease the raging Spanish commander of the *Pizarro,* United States authorities surrendered seven slaves who had escaped Cuba with the liberators.[63]

O'Hara, wounded and discouraged, made his way back to Frankfort, probably by way of Columbus, Georgia, probably in the company of the faithful Hawkins. There at home during the summer and fall of 1850 he recuperated. For emotional therapy he would venture out again and again to the Frankfort cemetery, that lofty land of heroes that never failed to comfort him, to inspire him. He would not give up the cause of Cuba and revolution, ever, he swore to himself. There in the cemetery, he began to turn his thoughts to poetry. Perhaps the magic of meter and rhyme could help him make sense of this disappointing world, help him discover a new direction for himself and a proper way to honor men who had sacrificed so much, so unselfishly, for political and religious liberty. He would try.

Theodore O'Hara's determination and suffering during this dark summer of 1850 would result in "The Old Pioneer" and "The Bivouac of the Dead."

Chapter 5

While Fame Her Record Keeps

It may be argued that the two elegiac poems which Theodore O'Hara wrote when he was approximately thirty years of age—"The Old Pioneer" and "The Bivouac of the Dead"—especially the latter work, became capstones, poetic commemorations to the life and career of a man whose adventures had already included direct participation in some of the major events of the mid-nineteenth century in the United States. His occupation as an attorney had been brief and to him boring, even in the capitol city of Washington. His efforts as a journalist had been sporadic and, while politically strident, generally aimless. His service in the war with Mexico had crystallized some of his loose energies and had earned him some distinction; but at its end he returned, halfheartedly it appears, to Frankfort and to journalism. Whatever possibilities that had existed of a fulfilling relationship with Louisa McCalla had apparently vanished. Subsequently, the daring adventures as a filibuster in Cuba would end inconclusively and leave him wounded in body and spirit. And his two attempts to build a military career, one in the regular U.S. army, the other, later, with the Confederacy, would end in humiliating circumstances.

The year 1850, however, would turn out to be his *annus mirabilis*. Like 1839, it was a moment of great decision, although it would at the time appear to be just the opposite: an exhibition of lethargy and indecision. During this period, though neither he nor those around him fully recognized the importance of the fact, he would write two elegiac poems which would ensure his fame: one ("The Old Pioneer") would bring

O'Hara personal honor and fame within the state of Kentucky; the other ("The Bivouac of the Dead") would earn the poet a wide measure of national recognition—and the poem itself would secure an enduring place in our military pantheon.

"The Old Pioneer"

A popular conception that prevailed for a time in much of the English-speaking world held that Daniel Boone was made famous by the poet George Gordon, Lord Byron. Byron's mock-epic poem *Don Juan* (1819) was unquestionably one of the most widely read poems of its kind and time, perhaps the most popular long poem in English since *Paradise Lost*. In canto 8 of the work, stanza 61, Byron begins a description of Boone which carries over the next seven stanzas, a total of fifty-six lines. In a heavily autobiographical work which is characterized by comic rhymes and ironic allusions to all manner of places and people, this view of Boone is quite a sustained portrait, one which romanticized the pioneer as a happy, bold creature, enviable in his oneness with nature, shunning the degrading cities, and consequently living to the age of ninety. (Actually he lived to almost eighty-six, dying in the same year, 1820, Theodore O'Hara was born.)

Boone as a "natural man" would have appealed greatly to the romantic British poets; his life story, highly mythicized, would have come to Byron through the accounts of Gilbert Imlay, a man who fleeced Boone of some valuable land and later fled to Europe. Imlay became a lover of Mary Wollstonecraft, whose daughter, wife of Percy Shelley, was part of the Byron circle for a time in Italy.[1]

Even in the Kentucky of the 1840s, when the controversial decision to remove the remains of Daniel and his wife Rebecca from Missouri to Kentucky became final, the Boone story had become an archetypal frontier myth, made current by a number of biographies capitalizing on his fame.[2] And so, on September 13, 1845, the bodies had been brought to Frankfort for reinterment in accordance with the wishes and directions of the Kentucky legislature. A distinguished group of pallbearers had been selected; and the principal speaker of the occasion was the Honorable John Jordan Crittenden, the U.S. senator who had replaced Henry Clay in that capacity. The glorious proceedings must have been without precedent in the history of the region.

Significant questions have existed, however, about whether Theodore O'Hara was present for this event—and about the order and the circumstances in which he wrote his two elegies. Major Hume has asserted that O'Hara was present at this ceremony: "it is almost sure."[3] He also asserts, correctly it appears, that "Pioneer" was the first of the two poems—and incorrectly, it appears, that it was written shortly after the reinterment ceremony. Although Hume made no mention of the original publication of the work at this point, he strongly argues that the ultimate raising of a suitable monument at the Boones' grave site in 1850, by action of the legislature in February 1849, was mandated as a direct influence of O'Hara's lines about the absence of "a stone above him here":

> O'Hara's lines about no monument being raised in Boone's memory, ultimately produced its effect, though but slowly. The Frankfort *Yeoman* for August 31, 1848 . . . says that in the previous May and June the committee to solicit funds for the Boone monument had sent letters to many state and county officials "had not yet received a single response!" Finally the Legislature ordered that a suitable monument be placed over the two graves . . . here again is a parallel between O'Hara's two elegies, for the lines in the *Bivouac of the Dead* about a monument to Kentucky's dead had something to do with in-suring the erection of the "marble minstrel."[4]

Despite this line of reasoning, no evidence exists that either of these main assertions has validity. First, no connection whatever can be made between O'Hara's poem and the erection of the monument to Boone; second, the very mention of "yon marble minstrel" in "Bivouac" strongly indicates that the shaft honoring the Kentucky veterans had already been raised when he composed that elegy.

Another scholar, Monroe Cockrell, has argued that it would have been "improvidence personified" for O'Hara, having been out of work for months, so soon after his new employment in Washington to have traveled so far to attend the funeral of someone "of no personal interest to himself and who had been buried 25 years in Missouri."[5] While Hume's arguments provide us no substantiation, this latter assertion by Cockrell leaves out of consideration such elements as O'Hara's lifelong admiration for honor and heroism, his sense of Kentucky history, and his recognition of the special place reserved for Boone in that history. At that time Boone would have become apotheosized as the embodiment of Kentucky itself. Further, one must acknowledge that O'Hara's new employer, General McCalla, almost certainly would have been present—indeed, would probably have been expected to be present—at such an auspicious ceremony.

Cockrell, however, has raised the interesting point as to why, if it were written in 1845, O'Hara's first printing of his poem honoring the "old Pioneer" would have been so long in gestation, appearing for the first time in the *Kentucky Yeoman* for December 19, 1850. He offers the in-

terpretation that O'Hara wrote the poem in Frankfort some time during
the fall of 1850 while recuperating from the injuries occurring in the
López expedition to Cuba. The poem most likely was submitted from
New Orleans, where O'Hara was standing trial for the Cuban expedition.

The prospects—first, that O'Hara attended the reinterment ceremonies
in 1845, and second, that he completed the poem during a somewhat lei-
surely convalescence in 1850—are not contradictory, but highly likely.
(The publication in the *Yeoman* indicates "Written at the grave of Daniel
Boone in the Frankfort Cemetery.") This is the text of that first publication:

The Old Pioneer

A dirge for the brave old pioneer!
    Knight-errant of the wood!
Calmly beneath the green sod here,
    He rests from field and flood;
The war-whoop and the panther's screams
    No more his soul shall rouse,
For well the aged hunter dreams
    Beside his good old spouse.

A dirge for the brave old pioneer!
    Hushed now his rifle's peal—
The dews of many a vanish'd year
    Are on his rusted steel;
His horn and pouch lie mouldering
    Upon the cabin door—
The elk rests by the salted spring,
    Nor flees the fierce wild boar.

A dirge for the brave old pioneer!
    Old Druid of the West!
His offering was the fleet wild deer;
    His shrine the mountain's crest.
Within his wildwood temple's space,
    An empire's towers nod,
Where erst, alone of all his race,
    He knelt to Nature's God.

A dirge for the brave old pioneer!
    Columbus of the land!

Who guided Freedom's proud career
    Beyond the conquered strand;
And gave her pilgrims' sons a home
    No monarch's step profanes,
Free as the chainless winds that roam
    Upon its boundless plains.

A dirge for the brave old pioneer!
    The muffled drum resound!
A warrior is slumb'ring here
    Beneath his battle ground,
For not alone with beast of prey
    The bloody strife he waged,
Foremost where'er the deadly fray
    Of savage combat raged.

A dirge for the brave old pioneer!
    A dirge for his dear old spouse!
For her who blest his forest cheer,
    And kept his birchen house,
Now soundly by her chieftain may
    The brave old dame sleep on,
The red man's step is far away,
    The wolf's dread howl is gone.

A dirge for the brave old pioneer!
    His pilgrimage is done;
He hunts no more the grizzly bear,
    About the setting sun.
Weary at last of chase and life
    He laid him here to rest,
Nor recks he now what sport or strife
    Would tempt him further West.

A dirge for the brave old pioneer!
    The patriarch of his tribe!
He sleeps, no pompous pile marks where,
    No lines his deeds describe;
They raised no stone above him here,
    Nor carved his deathless name—
An empire is his sepulchre,
    His epitaph is Fame.

Certain details in the imagery of the poem lend some credence to Hume's argument that the poem was written early, earlier, that is, than the placement of the monument. Such elements are to be seen specifically in stanza 1, line 3, "the green sod," and in the last stanza, in a reference to the absence of a "pile"—"no lines," "no stone," "Nor carved his deathless name."

The original monument currently at the tomb was erected July 1, 1850, just before O'Hara would have returned to Frankfort from Cuba.[6] So the physical characteristics of the grave site, as described in the poem, would have come from a visit earlier than the date. But several considerations, especially the poetic elements, point to the composition of the elegy about the time O'Hara returned to Frankfort, probably in early June 1850, about the same time "Bivouac" was composed.

Both poems are, of course, elegiac in tone and purpose; both emphasize fierce winds on broad plains and the irrevocable yet modest end of heroic endeavors. Both feature that necessary element of military funerals, "the muffled drum." In "Bivouac," it is "din and shout" which are past. In "Old Pioneer" it is the "pilgrimage" which is done. As one would expect, both mention euphemistic terms for death, variations on "rest," "sleep," "slumber," and "dream." In both instances, the phrase "no more" is prominent in the first stanzas. The image of "rust" is central: in "Bivouac" it is on the "shivered swords," suggesting the ferocity of close combat; with Boone it is the old pioneer's "rifle," his "rusted steel," on which the "dews of many a vanish'd year" now appear. The color red, however evanescent, appears in both: in "Bivouac" it is the blood stains which "tears have washed" away; with "Pioneer" it is the "red man's step" now far away. In both, one sees the notion that no secular intrusion of the place of honor can ever distract from its sacredness. In "Bivouac," "No impious footsteps here shall tread"; in "Pioneer," "No monarch's step profanes."

In short, the diction, the patterns of imagery, and the phrasing reveal a poetic matrix which strongly links the two and suggests that they may have been and probably were written about the same time by a poet in his leisure, drawing on literary genres which he had favored since childhood, drawing on painful battlefield experiences of its own, and celebrating the rituals attending the death and burial of heroes.

When one compares what can be called the "music" of the two works, however, there are a few striking differences as well as strong similarities. "The Bivouac" consistently followed an iambic rhythmic pattern throughout, eight syllables and four beats to the first line, six syllables and three beats to the following one, in what has sometimes been called "hymn meter," or more traditionally, "common measure" or "common meter." This venerable stanzaic form may be traced to medieval times and was used by sixteenth-century translators of the Psalms into English. Thus in "Bivouac," the opening lines:

> The muffled drum's sad roll has beat
> The soldier's last tattoo:

For the rest of the poem, in all of its revisions, this rhythm is unvaried.

With the opening of "Old Pioneer," however, one hears and sees not the subdued and traditional meter but a rousing exclamatory call, as if to signal a desperate need for attention:

> A dirge for the brave old pioneer!
> Knight errant of the wood!

While the rest of the six-line stanza exhibits the common meter, each of the following seven stanzas opens in the same fashion as above, with each of the first lines shifting to an anapest with the second metrical foot, and each of the first two lines ending in exclamation points, except for the second stanza.

While it cannot be certain that O'Hara would have read Byron's *Don Juan*, it is readily apparent that the Boone of this depiction follows the "natural man" tradition, even to the point where O'Hara has him first as a "Knight-errant," then a "Druid," whose "offering was the fleet wild deer" and whose

> . . . Shrine the mountain's crest
> Within the wildwood temple's space
> . . . .
> He knelt to Nature's God.

Then shifting from the worshipper of nature to the explorer of uncharted territory, the poet sees his character as the "Columbus of the land," who not only "guided Freedom's proud career" but also "gave a home to her pilgrims' sons."

In all, the poem, especially read aloud, as the poem was intended to be, leaves its reader with a sense of detached admiration for one who clearly had become larger than life; and from all indications, O'Hara was highly satisfied with the work as it originally appeared in the *Kentucky Yeoman* in December 1850. Once struck, this elegy was never revised. It was as if the poet knew that it was an act of noblesse oblige, a preliminary effort, anticipating the other elegy forming in his mind. And yet despite its declamatory qualities, it is in many ways a personal poem, in the sense that the best examples in the long tradition of the pastoral elegy in European and American literature have always been both conventional and personal; and as both scholar and poet, more than he was anything else in his lifetime, he would have known that body of writing. This tradition is usually dated back at least to the third century B.C., to the *Idylls* of Theocritus. Some of the best examples of the personal mixed with the conventionalized treatment within this genre include Milton's "Lycidas" and Shelley's "Adonais." O'Hara would doubtless have known both of the latter works as well as the long Greek and Latin traditions. He would also have been conscious of the power of persuasion in the structure of what was in effect a public ovation. As Dickson Bruce, Jr., has argued, Southern oratory was not meant merely "to whip up the crowds"; Southern orators expected their speeches to have some influence.[7]

O'Hara would have known also only the mythicized Boone, but in that regard his work belongs perhaps in company with Walt Whitman's dirge for Abraham Lincoln, "When Lilacs Last in the Dooryard Bloom'd," though "The Old Pioneer" is clearly a lesser poem and never had or deserved the popularity or currency of "The Bivouac," a work whose generalized Victorian era sentiments and metaphoric structuring gave it more universal appeal, much in the manner of Tennyson's *In Memoriam*.

Nevertheless, O'Hara's address to Boone was a fitting tribute to the courageous and controversial man who had explored the Kentucky wilderness so thoroughly and with such delight; and the work has truly earned a special place in the history of the region.

"The Bivouac of the Dead"

On July 20, 1847, a crowd estimated at twenty thousand gathered in Frankfort to witness the reburial of those killed at Buena Vista, a startling victory won by General Zachary Taylor, but at great cost to the Second Kentucky Regiment of Foot Volunteers. Among those at Buena Vista, for example, was Lt. Col. Henry Clay, Jr., son of the great statesman, and so the ceremony of reburial seemed especially somber and momentous. Theodore O'Hara was not present, however, being still in Mexico serving with Scott's army as it prepared to enter the Valley of Mexico. He would not be discharged until October 15, 1848. Yet among the legends which surrounded the composition of O'Hara's poem was that he was invited to read during the ceremony and that he worked all night and into the morning of the funeral in order to read the elegy.[8] And like so many incorrect assertions about both Kean and Theodore O'Hara, the legend took root.

According to George Ranck, the poet was composing his elegy during

August 1847 for the dedication of a monument for those fallen Kentuckians to be raised in the State Cemetery at Frankfort, and even Ranck incorrectly lists O'Hara at that time as editor of the *Kentucky Yeoman*.[9] It
was not until February 1848 that the Kentucky legislature appropriated
money to pay for the monument, which was not completed and erected
until June 25, 1850, shortly before the placement of the Boone monument.

And so "The Bivouac of the Dead," as the poem later became titled, was
certainly not read at this dedication, although specific questions of when it
was completed and where it was first delivered remain to this day unan-
swered. A story that came third hand to Major Hume, who had close access to the sources of the O'Hara family tales, indicates that Theodore first
read the poem aloud to a cadre of young friends in a saloon across from the
state house in Frankfort.[10] This episode would seem to have been quite consistent with what we know of the poet's carousing habits at the time. Because O'Hara did not return from Mexico until late in 1848, one may at
best place only the origins of the poem in this period, though Hume declares
that the first publication was in 1858 in the *Mobile Register*, where and
when O'Hara had assumed editorship. This assertion has its critics, valid
ones. A document now in the archives of the Filson Club in Louisville, for
example, testifies otherwise. This is a newspaper printing of the elegy,
headed by the title "A Beautiful Poem," which states, "The following beautiful poem was written on the occasion of the burial of the gallant Kentuckians who gloriously fell at Buena Vista in the cemetery at Frankfort Kentucky. The author, Colonel Theodore O'Hara, gallant as a soldier as he is
gifted as a writer, is now in our city. At our earnest solicitation he has con-
sented to its publication in our columns."

This version of the "beautiful poem" is composed of ninety-six lines,
in twelve stanzas of two quatrains each, in the traditional hymn meter,
essentially the same as in portions of "The Old Pioneer." The article con-
tinues: "We, the undersigned, do hereby certify that the above is the ex-
act photographic copy of the famous lyric by Colonel Theodore O'Hara
now called 'The Bivouac of the Dead'—as it appeared in print in the year
1850, in the Frankfort (Kentucky) *Yeoman*. Date of month not known
by Mrs. [Mary] Branham in whose scrapbook, a family relic, this clipping is preserved."

This comment about the publication of the poem is dated February
11, 1901, and signed by several people, including Susan Bullitt Dixon
and Mary O'Hara Branham, identified in the article as niece to the poet.
The statement adds that the original was destroyed by fire soon after this
publication.[11]

Whether this story—all or any part of it—is true, it certainly places the original publication at some unknown month in 1850, but certainly before the appearance of the "The Old Pioneer" in a December issue. It is well documented that O'Hara continued to revise his poem repeatedly over the years. In the Filson Club collection, for example, are several other newspaper clippings which address the issue of revisions and a disputed final version. One such item, "Mutilation of a Great Poem," dated August 1, 1900, by the same Susan Bullitt Dixon who presented the "original" item mentioned above, attacks in detail the work of Ranck, who had published an edition of the poem the prior year. As this article states, many different versions of the poem had already appeared but none so "unjust" as the one by Mr. Ranck, according to Bullitt. She particularly laments the alterations and omissions by which this editor had attempted to rid the work of "local" references and to make the elegy more "universal."[12] But whatever conclusions may be reached about the merits of the versions—both by O'Hara himself and by Ranck's editing—and Dixon's criticism notwithstanding, portions of the poem in that earlier version already belonged to the ages. On February 22, 1867, Congress passed an act "to establish and to protect national cemeteries." With this act, the project of official recollection of the Civil War dead—and in particular the Union dead—began; and shortly afterward "The Bivouac" became officially selected as the language of that memorialization.

One source, a newspaper article at present unidentifiable, provides information about what appears to be the absolute origins of this entire project. The article quotes the *Brooklyn Daily Eagle* in its citation of a letter which Gen. Horatio C. King of Brooklyn received from Gen. Anson G. McCook, who had just returned from Gettysburg Cemetery, where together they had evidently seen the poem but could not discover the name of the poet. In this letter, General McCook attributes the authorship to O'Hara. This article goes on citing the letter to this effect:

> Gen. McCook writes that the *National Tribune* at Washington published that on June 29, 1865, Quartermaster M. C. Meiggs [*sic*] directed that the poem be copied in the fly-leaf of the bound copy of the roll of honor of the names of soldiers who died in defense of the American Union, interred in the National Cemeteries at Washington, D. C. from August 3, 1861 [*sic*], to June 30, 1865. Afterward, in June, 1861 [*sic*], he directed that certain verses from the poem be inserted and distributed to the National Cemeteries as the wooden tablets were decaying.[13]

Perhaps the most intriguing aspect of this account is the offhand reference to the decaying wooden tablets. What this statement suggests is that in some fashion, a relatively primitive one, O'Hara's poem had been selected and displayed in at least Arlington if not a number of other battlefield cemeteries as early as 1861, with the implications clearly present that these "wooden tablets" had been there long enough—probably a decade later—to start decaying.

In addition, excerpts from the elegy were selected—one assumes also by Quartermaster General Montgomery C. Meigs—to grace the archways of both sides of the McClellan Gate, the original entrance to Arlington Cemetery. Construction of this impressive gate, which rises twenty-four feet above the roadway, was begun in 1870 but not completed until 1879 because of the difficulty of obtaining suitable quantities of the red sandstone which had been chosen for its composition.[14]

It was not until the 1880s, however, that the elegy was established with the memorial status it has now occupied for well over a century. These official memorials took the form of cast-iron tablets, originally ordered from the Ordnance Office by the quartermaster general on June 10, 1881, with an enclosed draftsman's sketch of the specifications, one foot six inches by three feet, for mounting on posts measuring four by four inches. The order, for five hundred castings of the tablets, was sent to the Rock Island Arsenal, Illinois. Now in the National Archives, the authorizing letter reads: "To be cast in the solid, with socket fitted on the back by which they can be secured to wooden posts. They are desired to replace the present wooden tablets at the cemeteries which are rapidly decaying."[15] On June 27, 1883, the arsenal sent the total bill for the completed work and the shipping: $2,002.57.[16]

This letter inaugurating the project was signed by the quartermaster general at the time, Bvt. Maj. Gen. Montgomery Meigs, an officer who enjoyed a long and distinguished career in that capacity. His selection of O'Hara's poem provides not only an insight to the level of Meigs's own cultural refinement but also an index to the contemporary popularity of O'Hara's lines—and indeed of the concept of public poetry honoring those who fought in the war. And though one cannot now determine where Meigs may have encountered this work, it is a testament to its popularity that it was so readily handy to him, so well known a poem in slightly over a decade from its first appearance, almost certainly in 1850. Ironically, Meigs took a poem about the fallen Kentuckians of the Mexican War and applied its lines to the Union dead of the Civil War, and thence to all soldiers in death's tenting grounds. These plaques may be seen today in various arrangements in such cemeteries as those commemorating some of the bloodiest battles of that war: Antietam, Gettysburg, Fredericksburg, Shiloh, Stone's River, Vicksburg—and at

others which officially honor the Civil War dead and those veterans who
were later buried in these plots: Crown Hill in Indianapolis and Cave Hill
in Louisville, for example, and in the Custer Memorial Battleground at
Little Big Horn, Montana. And reading these somber passages—especially aloud—as they appear among starkly ranked lines of gravestones,
one senses how the somber lines aesthetically reenforce the notion of col-
lective and unrelenting military order, an order which follows even the
disintegration of the individual soldier by death. A highly effective work
for the purposes to which it was appropriated, it is a distinctly neoclassic
elegy, exhibiting characteristics of late-eighteenth-century British poetic
diction and versification. It is, in truth, an exemplar of its kind, unsur-
passed in American literature. (The full text of the elegy in its original
form appears at the end of this chapter.)

Often compared to Thomas Gray's "Elegy Written in a Country
Churchyard," "The Bivouac" is notably less sentimental, less introspec-
tive, and less philosophical than Gray's poem, which has at its core a
speaker who refers to "me" and who reflects on the mysteries of fate and
the democratic "levelling" of death. O'Hara's elegy also relies much less
on pastoral conventions, such as the bucolic imagery which has characterized the lyric tradition encompassing the elegies of Edmund Spenser,
Milton, and Shelley—and even of Whitman. Instead, O'Hara's work
evokes the trappings of military finality, the calming sense of relief when
the day's battle is over, the reestablishing of the discipline when every individual takes his place within the evening's campground—but the campground is the final resting place where the uninitiated cannot intrude.

Though the poem demonstrates certain rhetorical devices and other
technical elements which root it in the main lines of the elegiac tradition,
it was that central metaphor and the tone of proud weariness that doubtless recommended the work to General Meigs. In the sequence in which
the lines were selected from within the context of the poem, these are the
quatrains he chose: the first two for one hundred castings each; the next
four, fifty castings each; and the last one, one hundred castings.

> The muffled drum's sad roll has beat
>   The soldier's last tattoo;
> No more on life's parade shall meet
>   That brave and fallen few.
> On Fame's eternal camping-ground
>   Their silent tents are spread,
> And Glory guards with solemn round
>   The bivouac of the dead.
> No rumor of the foe's advance
>   Now swells upon the wind;

No troubled thought at midnight haunts
       Of loved ones left behind;
No vision of the morrow's strife
       The warrior's dream alarms;
No braying horn or screaming fife
       At dawn shall call to arms.
The neighing troop, the flashing blade,
       The bugle's stirring blast,
The charge, the dreadful cannonade,
       The din and shout are past.
Your own proud land's heroic soil
       Shall be your fitter grave;
She claims from War his richest spoil,
       The ashes of her brave.
Rest on, embalmed and sainted dead!
       Dear as the blood ye gave!
No impious footstep here shall tread
       The herbage of your grave;

These lines, aptly chosen from the heart of the poem, stress not so much the final isolation of death and the exile from family and friends as it does the manly sublimation of grief, and the abiding satisfaction with the performance of the day: "the rapture of the fight." The solace, then, comes from the poet's own knowledge and stoic acceptance of the major hazards and minor comforts of the soldier's life.

The immediate responses of the public displays of these plaques must have been electrifying. The National Archives contain a number of letters written from the 1880s to about 1910 from all manner of citizens and prominent officials, requesting the War Department to provide or sell comparable tablets to honor deceased veterans buried in plots in several northern and midwestern states. This, from one of the more prominent of those officials, a senator from Michigan, to "Quartermaster General, U.S.A.":

United States Senate
Committee on Privileges and Elections
September 9, 1902

My Dear General:
    I very much desire to secure, if possible, four of the marker tablets such as are in use in the National Cemeteries, containing four of the verses of the famous Elegiac Poem of O'Hara. These tablets are desired for a large memorial Lot

in Riverside Cemetery in the City of Three Rivers, Michigan, and the dedication and beautifying of the site is in the hands of the G.A.R. Post at that place. It would seem that it would be especially desirable to furnish these if it can be done, as there are over one hundred soldiers buried in the Cemetery, many of whom are in the immediate vicinity. . . . Please make special effort to provide these tablets, and advise, Mr. M. H. Bumphrey, Three Rivers, Michigan at as early date as is possible, upon what terms four can be procured. . . . I enclose a copy of the verses specially desired. Trusting that the request can be complied with, and appreciating any special effort in their behalf, I am,

Sincerely yours,

J. C. Burrows[17]
[chairman]

And the answer to this high-level request, as to all of the others, was an unequivocal and resounding NO: "The cast iron tablets referred to, were provided exclusively for use in the National Cemeteries of the country in August 1882. There are none now at hand and there is no law under which they could be supplied as requested either by gift or sale."[18]

So the many appeals for extending such further official public display of the poem to state and community cemeteries went not unheard but ungranted. Nevertheless, the poem itself would continue to receive a high degree of popularity throughout much of the following century. Indeed, despite the fact that the name of the author of those lines was not on the McClellan Gate nor on the plaques, nor in any capacity, it was apparently general knowledge that Theodore O'Hara had written those lines. Later, newspapers across the country established a practice of citing passages in editorials on Memorial Day. The question of copyright or public domain had probably never entered in the selection and use of the elegy, and no evidence exists that anyone in O'Hara's family received any monetary compensation or even formal acknowledgment from the federal government.

And so in several regards those elegiac lines have transcended the poem itself—and certainly the poet, his place, and his times. And in many regards the idyllic period during which he wrote the two poems represented an uncharacteristic lull in what was to become an even more turbulent career. One may only speculate on what kind of poetic production may have resulted had he concentrated on that aspect of his abilities.

The Bivouac of the Dead
(Original version in twelve stanzas)

I.   The muffled drum's sad roll has beat
                The soldier's last tattoo;
        No more on life's parade shall meet
                That brave and fallen few.
        On Fame's eternal camping-ground
                Their silent tents are spread,
        And Glory guards, with solemn round,
                The bivouac of the dead.

II.   No rumor of the foe's advance
                Now swells upon the wind;
        No troubled thought at midnight haunts
                Of loved ones left behind;
        No vision of the morrow's strife
                The warrior's dreams alarms,
        No braying horn nor screaming fife
                At dawn shall call to arms.

III.   Their shivered swords are red with rust
                Their pluméd heads are bowed;
        Their haughty banner, trailed in dust,
                Is now their martial shroud;
        And plenteous funeral tears have washed
                The red stains from each brow,
        And the proud forms, by battle gashed,
                Are free from anguish now.

IV.   The neighing troop, the flashing blade,
                The bugle's stirring blast,
        The charge, the dreadful cannonade,
                The din and shout are past;
        Nor war's wild note, nor glory's peal,
                Shall thrill with fierce delight
        Those breasts that nevermore may feel
                The rapture of the fight.

V.   Like the fierce northern hurricane
                That sweeps his great plateau,
        Flushed with the triumph yet to gain,
                Came down the serried foe.

Who heard the thunder of the fray
    Break o'er the field beneath,
Knew well the watchword of that day
    Was "Victory or death."

VI.   Long did the doubtful conflict rage
    O'er all that stricken plain,
For never fiercer fight did wage
    The vengeful blood of Spain.
And still the storm of battle blew,
    Still swelled the gory tide—
Not long our stout old chieftain knew
    Such odds his strength could bide.

VII.   'Twas at that hour his stern command
    Called to a martyr's grave
The flower of his own loved land,
    The Nation's flag to save,
By rivers of their father's gore
    His first-born laurels grew,
And well he deemed the son would pour
    Their lives for glory too.

VIII.   Full many a norther's breath has swept
    O'er Angostura's plain—
And long the pitying sky has wept
    Above its mouldering slain.
The raven's screams, or eagle's flight,
    Or shepherd's pensive lay,
Alone awakens each sullen height
    That frowned o'er that dread fray.

IX.   Sons of the Dark and Bloody Ground,
    Ye must not slumber here,
Where stranger steps and tongues resound
    Along the heedless air.
Your own proud land's heroic soil
    Shall be your fitter grave;
She claims from War its richest spoil—
    The ashes of her brave.

X.   Thus 'neath their parent turf they rest,
    Far from the gory field,

Borne to a Spartan mother's breast
    On many a bloody shield;
The sunshine of their native sky
    Smiles sadly on them here,
And kindred eyes and hearts watch by
    The heroes' sepulcher.

XI.   Rest on, embalmed and sainted dead,
    Dear as the blood ye gave,
No impious footstep here shall tread
    The herbage of your grave;
Nor shall your glory be forgot
    While Fame her record keeps,
Or Honor points the hallowed spot
    Where Valor proudly sleeps.

XII.   Yon Marble Minstrel's voiceful stone
    In deathless song shall tell,
When many a vanquished age hath flown,
    The story how ye fell;
Nor wreck, nor change, nor winter's blight,
    Nor Time's remorseless doom,
Shall dim one ray of Glory's light
    That gilds your deathless tomb.

Chapter 6

The Fine Gentleman and Gallant

While Theodore O'Hara regained his strength and created the poems that would gain him immortality, his former commander, President Zachary Taylor, sought to punish him and his fellow liberators. In the early summer of 1850, once he had received details of the Cárdenas attack, Taylor took prompt action, directing the U.S. district attorney in New Orleans to arrest and prosecute the leaders of the expedition for violation of the neutrality laws.[1] Judah P. Benjamin of Louisiana agreed to assist with the prosecution. The grand jury at New Orleans on June 21, 1850, found true bills against sixteen of the liberators for violating of the Neutrality Law of 1818. The filibusters indicted included López, Quitman, Gonzales, Henderson, Sigur, O'Hara, Pickett, and Hawkins. The trial began on December 16, 1850. Three successive juries, however, failed to convict "in the face of the overwhelming pro López feeling in New Orleans." The government finally grew weary and dropped the cases. Similar efforts to convict in New York and Ohio also failed.[2]

O'Hara, of course, had to be present in New Orleans during the late fall and winter of 1850–51.[3] He perceived the trials and his treatment at the hands of his government, indeed, the frustrations of the Cuba Libre movement, as evidence of a larger issue—the sectional struggle to redefine the nature of the American union. These sentiments are revealed in a speech O'Hara made in New Orleans on March 14, 1851:

> I cannot but thank Mr. President Fillmore for the good turn
> he has done me in detaining me in your city long enough to

> witness a demonstration of sentiment worthy of the great
> metropolis of the South. Sir, I have ever regarded the cause
> of Southern rights in the great struggle which has been tran-
> spiring for years in our national councils as no less than the
> cause of liberty itself. If the South yields one step to North-
> ern aggression, her liberty is gone forever, and the great prize
> which she assisted so gloriously to win in the revolution of
> 1776, is ignobly forfeited . . . [and we are to] exist as a mere
> colony of the Northern States.[4]

Actually, the prosecution by the government backfired, at least in the South. The trials and their attendant publicity helped popularize López and the effort for Cuban independence. The Battle of Cárdenas was fought and refought during the summer and fall of 1850 in the columns of the *Delta,* the *Mobile Register,* the *Tallahassee Sentinel,* the *Savannah Georgian,* and of course the highly sympathetic *Democratic Review* and *Kentucky Yeoman.* The filibuster trials during early 1851 also were given full and highly sympathetic coverage. López took advantage of this groundswell of favorable public opinion, assuredly, and even as the trials progressed, was making preparations for another try in 1851.[5]

This attempt would be known as the *Cleopatra* expedition. It would prove to be "the best organized and equipped enterprise of the Cuban junta." The invasion force would be assembled and embark from several points. One of these assembly areas was on the St. John's River at Jacksonville, Florida. O'Hara was there. His leg healed and ready to do battle with the Spanish, O'Hara registered at a Jacksonville hotel. He and perhaps a hundred other adventurers had gathered there awaiting water transportation. It was planned that other contingents would depart from New Orleans, South Florida, and Savannah. This time they would assault the Cuban coast with adequate force. A reporter for the *Newark Advertiser* observed in Jacksonville warehouses, "cannon, gun carriages, rifles, muskets, ammunition, and the furniture of an army equipment[6] to a very large amount."[7] A Savannah newspaper reported a Cuban invasion force of six hundred men at Jacksonville, including O'Hara.[8] The ambitious *Cleopatra* effort, however, was doomed. Spanish spies had penetrated the organization and U.S. authorities, alerted just in time, seized the steamer *Cleopatra* in New York harbor in late April 1851, before she could rendezvous with the filibusters gathered in Jacksonville and along the Florida coast.[9]

The leader of the eastern Florida assembly was Henry Theodore Titus (1815–1881), a shadowy figure of intrigue who had participated in the Cárdenas expedition with O'Hara and who "owned large property and sawmills" near Jacksonville. O'Hara had been the guest of Titus while filibusters from Georgia, New Orleans, and western Florida were making their way to the coast.[10]

Although there was great frustration among the Cuban exiles and their American friends over four years of repeated failure and even greater dissatisfaction on the part of many with the apparent incompetence of Narciso López, nothing, it seemed, could daunt López himself. It was not too late, he believed. The men and munitions had been assembled; all that was needed was a suitable vessel. Therefore, in May 1851, he and Laurent Sigur decided to try yet again and the latter purchased the steamer *Pampero*. Once more they secured the services of the trusted Armstrong I. Lewis, who had been captain of the *Creole*.[11]

In July 1851 López and Sigur were aided and invigorated by an uprising in Cuba—the Agüero insurrection. When news reached New Orleans there was an outpouring of support which greatly encouraged López. Filibusters rushed into the city and their presence, of course, helped fan the excitement. Impatient for additional information and eager to assist the Agüero rebellion, López hastened plans to invade the island using the *Pampero* as the troopship. He alerted O'Hara and his friend Henry T. Titus in Jacksonville to stand ready. Meanwhile John T. Pickett and T. T. Hawkins were raising volunteers in Kentucky once again and hoped to have their troops downriver in time to sail with López's first contingent.[12]

They were too late. López impetuously had sailed on August 9 with fewer than five hundred men and landed in Cuba on the twelfth.[13] He then dispatched the *Pampero* back to Jacksonville to pick up Titus and O'Hara and Gonzales.[14] They, as the first contingent of reinforcements for López's force, were to make a landing at Puerto Principe. Misfortune dogged the enterprise, however. The *Pampero*, plagued by engine trouble, reached Key West on August 13, picked up a few recruits, then labored on to Jacksonville, arriving there on Sunday the thirty-first.

This tardy run for reinforcements doomed López. Theodore O'Hara did not know this. Indeed, the previous Friday night O'Hara had spoken at a rally at the courthouse in Jacksonville. "Thunders of applause" had greeted his address as well as those by other "liberators." The audience not only passed resolutions endorsing the enterprise but also donated funds to help defray the expedition's expenses.[15]

Finally, on September 2, the *Pampero* sailed from Jacksonville, carrying "about 120 men, and a large quantity of arms and ammunition, including several cannon. She will touch along the coast," reported the *Jacksonville News*, "and take in a full complement of men, and then sail for Cuba." This portion of the expedition, reported the *News*, will be under the command of Cárdenas veterans Col. Henry T. Titus and Lt. Col. Theodore O'Hara.[16]

All was in vain. While the *Pampero* played hopscotch along the eastern coast of Florida, López fought for his life and met with disaster. His invasion force was dispersed and he was captured. Then, as a clear message by Spain to would-be Caribbean freebooters, filibusters, liberators, and annexionists, López was garrotted in the plaza at Havana on September 1.[17] News of the calamity must have reached the *Pampero* as it touched shore below Jacksonville, perhaps at Key West, for by September 11 the steamer had turned about and returned to Jacksonville.[18] There during the next few days the stunned Laurent Sigur, John L. O'Sullivan, O'Hara, and others pondered the fate of López's followers in Cuba and the prospect for future expeditions. There would be no more.[19]

Titus and O'Hara brought the *Pampero* back to Jacksonville, barely escaping the clutches of a U.S. cutter which fired upon them but, following eloquent protests by Titus and O'Hara, allowed them to proceed into the St. Johns River. There Titus stored the arms and provisions and would sell them to the U.S. government a year later for use in the anticipated campaign against the Seminoles. Titus would grow wealthy supplying the American army, then leave in April 1856 for Kansas, where he would earn an unenviable reputation as a "border ruffian" fighting John Brown and his men. He wrecked Lawrence, Kansas, then in turn was set upon by John Brown, who burned his home and hauled the badly wounded Titus back to Lawrence to be hanged. Titus, however, lived to fight another day, as he was freed by the governor of Kansas and made an aide-de-camp.[20]

O'Hara appears to have gone to Columbus, Georgia, remaining there during most of the early fall of 1851, with side trips back to Jacksonville and to New Orleans.[21] He associated closely with his old friends Pickett, Quitman, Gonzales, and John L. O'Sullivan, editor of the *Democratic Review*,[22] a journal to which O'Hara would contribute from time to time. The Spanish, of course, regarded O'Hara as a troublemaker, and their legations in the United States monitored his movements as best they could, reporting anything suspicious not only to Madrid but through Minister Angel Calderon de la Barca to American secretary of state Daniel Webster.[23]

O'Hara returned to Frankfort late in the fall. The *Kentucky Yeoman* reported that "Col. O'Hara was received with enthusiastic demonstrations of approval, all along his route through Tennessee and Kentucky."[24] Once they had arrived back home, O'Hara and his friend John T. Pickett made a special point to call on Mrs. Murray, the mother of Col. William L. Crittenden. Crittenden, who was to have commanded a regimental backup force in the *Pampero* or Bahía Honda expedition, had recruited instead a company of eager New Orleans young men and embarked on the *Pampero* with López. Crittenden, like López, had been captured and executed. As they expressed their sympathy to Murray, the thoughts of Pickett and O'Hara inevitably turned to Cuba. They told the grieving mother that López and her son had been betrayed by a supposed friend of Cuban liberty in whom he had confided. O'Hara shook his head sadly. He pledged to Murray that William L. Crittenden had not died in vain and that he and Pickett would not give up the cause.[25]

The anguished dreams of Cuba had to be suppressed, however. That fall Kean O'Hara had become seriously ill and Theodore O'Hara upon his return from Georgia and Florida spent a number of weeks with the old man, nursing him and keeping him company.[26] These days, as one might expect, were "dull" for the adventurer, so for diversion he went to Nashville, Tennessee, for a fortnight. He found the town "perfect clover," eager to entertain and honor Kentucky's poet and Cuba's would-be liberator. Nashville society impressed O'Hara: "Certainly the most delightful city I have ever yet visited—more wealth, style, elegance, high aristocratic refinement and social cultivation & more clever wholesome fellows & more rich & beautiful women than I ever saw any where else in all my life." Nashville turned O'Hara's head with its attentions:

> I was actually *lionized*. The newspapers announced my arrival with distinction—numbers of old Mexican friends called on me & all sorts of attentions & hospitalities were crowded on me. I was in a most felicitous state of health, spirits, dress & looks, and soon became very popular & sought after. At the theater, the hotel, on the street & at parties I was the observed of all observers & c & c. I bore myself accordingly in my best taste. The belles & fashionably married & single, all were curious & anxious to know me. I launched out among & played the fine gentleman & gallant very successfully.[27]

While in Frankfort O'Hara also approached S. I. M. Major, publisher of the *Yeoman*, and sought to purchase the paper, apparently presuming an inheritance from his father.[28] As O'Hara explained to Pickett, he wished to use the *Yeoman* to launch a campaign in support of Stephen A. Douglas's nomination in the 1852 Democratic Convention. O'Hara expected to be appointed a delegate to the convention himself, and he planned to use the opportunity to advance the cause of Douglas. "I am a Douglas man up to the handle," he confessed to Pickett. Although O'Hara was elected by the Democrats of Franklin County, Kentucky, as a delegate to the state convention, it was his friend Breckinridge who was named to be a delegate to the Democratic National Convention in Baltimore, not O'Hara.[29]

Franklin Pierce was O'Hara's acquaintance from Mexican War days, an intimate of General Pillow. Already Pierce's name was being mentioned seriously within important Democratic circles. But Douglas was the darling of Young America, a magnetic spokesman who articulated O'Hara's beliefs in a proud, aggressive America, free trade, and sympathy with the European revolutions of 1848. On a given day, Douglas could sound like a revolutionary himself. The annexation of Cuba fit nicely with his rhetoric, at least in the minds of O'Hara and Pickett.

And George N. Sanders: this combination of energy, intrigue, and revolution, originally from Lexington, was at the heart of the Young America movement and seems to have influenced O'Hara greatly, drawing him into his political and international schemes. Douglas, Sanders believed, was the best chance for political leadership that could bring about the spread of democracy and freedom throughout the world. In 1851 Sanders purchased the *Democratic Review* and made it the "mouthpiece for exuberant nationalism of the period."[30]

Kean O'Hara died just before Christmas 1851, and with an advance on his share of his father's slave and real property, Theodore again entered the newspaper business. Rebuffed by Major in his attempts to purchase the *Yeoman,* he turned to Louisville, combining resources with Walter W. Stapp and Matthew Howard, and purchased the *Louisville Times.* Little is known of Howard. Stapp, on the other hand, had prior experience in the newspaper business, having been editorially connected with the *Yeoman.* He was the nephew of a well-known Kentucky Democrat, William Shannon, a saddler of Frankfort and outspoken Jacksonian.[31]

The *Times* announced its editorial position boldly. It would, of course, support the commercial and social interests of Louisville. Politically the "complexion of THE TIMES will be essentially DEMOCRATIC, believing as we do that the doctrines of the DEMOCRATIC PARTY are best calculated to promote the welfare and prosperity of our country; and that, in its well proven attachment to 'the Constitution as it is,' and its cardinal maxim of 'equal rights to all—exclusive privileges to none,' exist the only elements which can harmonize conflicting sectional interests, or which can oppose an effectual barrier to any attempt on the part of factionists, or others, to disturb the stability or tranquility of the Union."[32]

The *Times* offered a breath of excitement—a Louisville newspaper promoting revolution. In its columns O'Hara paid lavish tribute to Louis Kossuth and memorialized the fallen Col. William L. Crittenden. He echoed the sentiments of the *Democratic Review* in its insistence on American expansion in the Caribbean. Not only was the seizure of Cuba in the interest of the United States, it was morally right. O'Hara's call to Manifest Destiny sounded almost evangelical.

In the spring of 1852, John T. Pickett returned from a diplomatic mis-

Kean O'Hara's gravestone, St. Pius Cemetery, White Sulphur Springs, Kentucky. T. C. Ware Collection.

sion and joined O'Hara at the *Louisville Times*. Howard disappeared from
the masthead in June, and in his stead William Tanner, O'Hara's old newspaper friend and financier from Frankfort, was listed as publisher. Pickett
moved on in late summer—for Santo Domingo to resume his diplomatic
work. There he proved to be a "fomenter of revolution" while he worked
tirelessly to lay the foundation for another strike at Cuba. O'Hara, with
cash from Kean O'Hara's estate in his pocket, bought out Pickett's interest
and that of Stapp. By September 1852 the *Times* had been reorganized—
Tanner as owner and publisher, O'Hara as sole editor, and William B.
Tremere, who had married Theodore's niece Ellen, "in charge of the desk
and business generally." Fancifully, but inaccurately, the *Times* of the early
1850s has been designated as the daily "brilliantly edited by the six fighting
Colonels," referring to O'Hara, Pickett, John C. Noble, T. T. Hawkins,
John O. Bullock, and Walter W. Stapp. Several sources have O'Hara also
editing the *Louisville Sun* during 1852–53, but this attribution appears to
be incorrect as well. Perhaps O'Hara would contribute a column now and
then, or as a correspondent, write a lengthy letter to the editor. That appears to have been the extent of it.[33]

O'Hara's *Louisville Times* also was known for its militant stand
against the powerful Know-Nothings. This intensely anti-Catholic, anti-
immigrant political faction, the old nativist American Party impulse of
the 1840s, had revived in the election year 1852. The immigration of so
many Germans, particularly German Catholics, to the Louisville and Cincinnati areas helped ignite latent prejudices. The *Louisville Morning Courier*, a Whig paper owned by Walter N. Haldeman, fought with the *Times*
over the issue. There was talk of excluding Roman Catholics and immigrants from political office and of making U.S. citizenship much more difficult to obtain. The entire Know-Nothing enterprise was, as John Tracy
Ellis observed, a "dreary tale," one that involved a steady publication of
books, pamphlets, and newspaper articles, capitalizing on the suspicion
and dislike of Catholicism which had become deeply rooted in the American heritage.[34] O'Hara struck back time and time again; "glowing sentences flashed like jewels from his gifted pen." Having learned to hate
Winfield Scott from his association with Democratic partisans Gideon
Pillow and Franklin Pierce in Mexico, O'Hara had little trouble linking
Scott with the Know-Nothing resurgence, and he attacked Scott in editorials as "no friend" to the Catholic Church or to the Irish. Perhaps the
death of Kean O'Hara stirred Theodore to adopt an even more radical
political stance and become an outspoken defender of his church.[35]

Once Pierce had been nominated by the Democrats in June 1852, in
preference to Douglas or Lewis Cass of Michigan,[36] O'Hara threw the

Theodore O'Hara, ca. 1850. Courtesy of the Filson Club
Historical Society.

Times in solid support behind his old friend. When Pierce triumphed that
fall, O'Hara was happy; by inauguration day, he became ecstatic:

A National Thanksgiving Day
. . . On this day cease the degrading sway of craven counsels,
and the dull stupor of ignoble conservatism [the administration of John Tyler]. The unterrified Democracy man the ship
of State. A pilot is at the helm who knows the importance of
the great voyage that awaits her, and who will loosen her
from the moorings where an ignoble predecessor detained
her, and send her forward on her proud march on the waves,
reckless of the billows and triumphant over the storm.

Alter erit nunc Tiphys, et altera quae vehat
Argos Delectos heroas; erunt etiam altera
bella Atque iterum ad Trojan magnus mittetur Achilles.[37]

It is interesting to note that O'Hara's and John McCalla's roles reversed in the spring of 1853. O'Hara wrote President Pierce urging that McCalla be reappointed to the Treasury, citing McCalla's faithful services to the Democrats over the years and reminding Pierce that McCalla had been rudely dumped from office when Zachary Taylor and the Whigs came to power in 1849. Things did not work out, however, and McCalla remained in Washington as a lawyer while his 1849 successor, Philip Clayton, stayed on, keeping the second auditor's position throughout the Pierce administration.[38]

O'Hara could not stand in place for long. Although the *Times* had succeeded financially and was well received in Louisville, and although he had complete editorial control, he felt compelled to move on. Perhaps it was the confrontation between O'Hara and a Lieutenant Cummings that spring, although the Jacksonville *Florida Republican* reported in late April that there had been a reconciliation between the two men rather than the anticipated duel.[39] In any event, sometime during the summer of 1853, he left Louisville. Although he continued to write as a correspondent, sending back reports and editorials now and then from New York and Washington, his interests had shifted. The *Times* announced in late October 1853, with regret, that "our friend and recent associate, Colonel O'Hara, retires this day from his editorial connection with this paper, having determined to go into business elsewhere."[40]

From the summer of 1853, when he left the *Times*, to the spring of 1855 O'Hara worked to organize another strike against Cuba. He and Pickett had conspired to this end since Bahía Honda. Much of this time he spent in New Orleans, New York City, and Washington, usually in the company of his old friend Col. Thomas T. Hawkins and often Pickett. The quiet and deadly Hawkins, who viewed himself—and was viewed—as a soldier of fortune, was involved in several plots and seems to have spent a good deal of the period 1851–54 in Mexico and in the company of William Walker, America's most notorious filibuster.

The election of Franklin Pierce had encouraged John A. Quitman as it had O'Hara. Advocates of Manifest Destiny (strategically placed in the diplomatic corps) and public statements by the president himself led Quitman to accept the offer of the New York Junta Cubana to become head of the planned revolution. Once the revolution began and the invasion came, Quitman would wield supreme military and civil authority until "in his judgment" Cuba had become a de facto independent nation. Quitman qualified his acceptance, however. He required the support of all Cuban exile factions in the United States, and he demanded adequate financial support. O'Hara wanted a substantial role in the coming venture and not only approached Quitman himself but had Pickett emphasize to Quitman that his comrade O'Hara was committed to the undertaking and anxious to fight for "a cause in which we have all hitherto suffered so much."[41]

In the summer of 1853, Quitman met with O'Hara, Pickett, and Rob Wheat in New York City. The Cuban invasion force would include them and Mexican War veterans Mansfield Lovell and New Yorker George Bolivar Hall, son of the former mayor of Brooklyn.

The days passed with agonizing slowness. Quitman would suspend preparations, then renew them suddenly. All manner of infuriating problems arose. A recruiting effort in which Hawkins and O'Hara were involved during the summer of 1853 was aborted. The men, many of whom had paid their way to a preliminary rendezvous, had to be sent back home.

In the spring of 1854, O'Hara wrote to Quitman through naval officer William Nelson. Based on his experience in the López fiasco and the discontinued invasion plot of July 1853, O'Hara urged that recruits be paid and not be expected to bear the expense of their own transportation. He estimated that the cost of raising one thousand men and transporting them to New Orleans would be twenty-five thousand dollars. He recommended that the men be gathered at once and that the recruiting effort be carried out in *the greatest secrecy*. Try earnestly, he urged, to raise a force of picked men. With a barely disguised slap at Rob Wheat's Louisiana battalion, O'Hara added, "The experience of Cárdenas impressively demonstrated the fatal consequence of an indiscriminate enlistment of men." Although acknowledging that assembling good men would take time, O'Hara argued that this delay might work to the advantage of the mission and dissipate the dangers of preliminary disclosure. "There will be time for any newspaper reports of our expedition being on foot to blow over & finally cease to arrest the attention of the public or parties abroad." Let the work begin, O'Hara advocated. Hawkins signed his concurrence at the bottom of O'Hara's letter, based on "my experience in the raising of men for Cuba and other expeditions for three or four years past."[42]

Quitman made significant progress during the late spring of 1854. He informed the Junta Cubana that he intended to attack Cuba with three thousand men and had laid the necessary groundwork. The junta provided him with $220,000 and momentum picked up—steamers were secured, weapons and supplies stockpiled. Cuba itself appeared on the verge of revolution. According to Quitman biographer Robert E. May, "what changed everything was the Kansas-Nebraska Act" of May 1854. Franklin Pierce and Stephen A. Douglas cautiously backed the act as the grand sectional panacea, and because of political necessity turned against Quitman's venture.[43] Indeed, the president issued a proclamation against filibustering and promised that the federal government would prosecute "with due energy" individuals involved in a Cuban expedition. Soon a federal court summoned Quitman, John Henderson, and a host of Cuban filibuster leaders to New Orleans for a hearing, but once again a grand jury found insufficient evidence to indict. Quitman counterattacked, publicly criticizing the federal judge, and was put under bond by the court for his action.[44]

For O'Hara affairs drifted in the early fall of 1854. In November he was in Frankfort again, again at the State Cemetery. The occasion was the reinterment of the remains of Kentucky heroes Gen. Charles Scott, Maj. William Taylor Barry, and Capt. Bland Ballard. Veterans of the War of 1812 and the Mexican War paraded. As a crowd of several thousand gathered, "a living stream of people," the bands played stirring patriotic airs. On the speakers' platform, Governor Lazarus W. Powell opened the proceedings, welcoming the assembled Kentuckians who had come to honor their own; Col. Thomas L. Crittenden delivered an oration about Scott; the bands played; then came O'Hara with remarks about Barry, followed by Col. Humphrey Marshall, who eulogized Ballard. To participate in this ceremony was an honor in itself, but for O'Hara it represented more. William T. Barry was a beloved Kentucky figure who had befriended him. Barry's career had been extraordinary: service in the Kentucky House of Representatives and Senate and speaker of the house in the Kentucky legislature; member of Congress and U.S. senator; aide-decamp to Governor Isaac Shelby in the War of 1812 and present at the Battle of the Thames; U.S. circuit court judge; professor of law and politics; chief justice of Kentucky; and President Jackson's postmaster general, 1829–35. Appointed minister to Spain in 1835, he had died in England en route to his post and had been buried there.

Kentucky had brought home her son Barry by act of the General Assembly, and it was a great distinction to be chosen to deliver his funeral oration. O'Hara's address, considered a model of the type of oratory then so popular, was carefully preserved.[45] O'Hara, much in demand as a speaker, prepared carefully, and his delivery struck like sharp flint against the emotions of nineteenth-century audiences. "It was always pleasant to hear him speak," wrote Union general and professional soldier Albert Brackett, "as he was never loud, harsh, or unkind. He believed in several things with the utmost intensity, but never wished to push his views upon the minds of others where they were not wanted. In fact, he was a Christian gentleman, and showed that he had been reared with great pains."[46]

In all, O'Hara's performance, on such a notable occasion, heightened what was already a wide reputation as a distinguished orator.

In December, however, O'Hara put all public appearances aside. General Quitman suddenly had refired the Cuban plan. "The announcement . . . has somewhat taken me by surprise," wrote O'Hara to Quitman on December 22, 1854. O'Hara, assisted by the faithful Hawkins, threw himself once again into the work of recruiting men. Temporary confusion existed, in Kentucky at least, as another recruiter, Domingo Goicouria, went through the state attempting to raise men for a Cuban expedition of his own. Goicouria seems to have abandoned his effort promptly, but the on-again, off-again nature of Quitman's expedition created many problems. Agents in Nashville, in Alabama, and elsewhere reported disappointing results. O'Hara, however, proved a marvel, securing about one thousand Kentuckians. Quitman, encouraged by O'Hara and after receiving good responses from Texas, Pennsylvania, and Arkansas, issued orders establishing points for rendezvous and embarkation.

All their hopes and plans exploded in January 1855, however. Spanish agents discovered that the junta planned to assassinate Cuba's new captain general, José G. de la Concha, on February 12. They also notified U.S. revenue agents that one of Quitman's invasion ships was anchored off the New Jersey shore. A quick raid in January by these American officials uncovered thousands of muskets and quantities of military stores aboard. The vessel was confiscated. Quitman used as much influence with the Pierce administration as possible, but to no avail. Frustrated and embittered, Quitman sent word to O'Hara and the others waiting throughout the country that he was through; they should disband the army of liberation.[47]

When O'Hara received Quitman's message, he realized all realistic hope for another expedition was gone. Still, he had these men he had recruited standing by, ready for action. Displaying imaginative initiative, he immediately dispatched letters to Secretary of War Jefferson Davis offering the services of his Kentucky volunteers for frontier duty. A week later a letter reached Davis from Kentucky congressman James S. Chrisman recommending O'Hara for a commission in the U.S. Army. Davis endorsed Chrisman's letter, "Note well."[48]

Chapter 7

Hard Fortune

O'Hara's timing was opportune. The U.S. Army was stretched thin in the West. Domestic troubles in Kansas and the need for security along the new route to Oregon had drawn regulars north from Texas. The few left behind confronted an enormous extent of territory to defend. Kiowa and Comanche raids became more frequent; pressure from the white man's land hunger grew in intensity. Texas called out volunteers to supplement the reduced regular army forces and pleaded with the War Department and Congress for assistance: troops were needed in Texas at once. Winfield Scott, commanding general of the U.S. Army, and Jefferson Davis, secretary of war, prodded Congress—the responsibilities of the army had doubled, they argued, without a proportionate increase in manpower. Congress reacted on March 3, 1855, authorizing four new regiments.[1]

Two of the regiments were to be cavalry, and, to O'Hara's immense pleasure, he received a commission as captain in one of them, the Second Cavalry. As an officer in the regular army, he would rank from March 3, 1855. O'Hara responded at once from Frankfort, accepting his commission and returning his oath. Curiously, he listed his age as thirty-two.[2]

Davis gave command of the Second Cavalry to his old friend Col. Albert Sidney Johnston. The executive officer was Lt. Col. Robert E. Lee; the senior major, William J. Hardee; the junior major, George H. Thomas;[3] the adjutant, Maj. Don Carlos Buell; the quartermaster and commissary, Capt. Richard W. Johnson. Of the senior officers only Johnston and Hardee were experienced in western Indian warfare.

O'Hara's fellow company commanders were an unusually able group, several having won distinction in Mexico: Earl Van Dorn, Edmund Kirby Smith, James Oakes of Pennsylvania, Innis N. Palmer of New York, George Stoneman, Jr., William R. Bradfute of Tennessee, Charles E. Travis of Alabama (son of the hero of the Alamo), Albert G. Brackett of New York, and Charles J. Whiting of Massachusetts.[4]

Early April 1855 found O'Hara at work in the Louisville area, recruiting.[5] Each company commander faced this challenge. Van Dorn, for instance, was ordered to raise his Company A from the Mobile area. On June 28 O'Hara had his ranks filled, many of his men being those he had recruited for Quitman's Cuban expedition. The adjutant general pulled O'Hara away from his company, however, and assigned him to a board of officers from his regiment to purchase horses for the Second Cavalry. In this duty O'Hara worked closely with Major Hardee and Lt. Charles W. Field in the Cincinnati area, then they expanded the search to Indiana, Kentucky, and Tennessee. They acquired approximately eight hundred mounts, paying an average of $150 for each. These horses were later divided according to color among the companies of the regiment. O'Hara's F Company, for instance, received bays; A Company, grays; K Company, roans; E Company, sorrels.[6]

O'Hara, Hardee, and Field completed their task on September 16, 1855 and left Cincinnati for Jefferson Barracks in St. Louis, where the regiment was being assembled. Johnston and Lee were ordered to court-martial duty, so Major Hardee took charge. He drilled the men strenuously. Hardee "was thorough in his knowledge of the tactics," Quartermaster Richard W. Johnson remembered, "and seemed to take great delight in teaching others. A position under him was not a sinecure, for when the officers were not drilling their own troops, he had officers drill."[7]

The Second Cavalry was to be a unique regiment. Davis, Johnston, and Hardee badly wanted to test new arms and equipment adopted by a cavalry equipment board that summer, so the War Department decided to experiment and allow field service to determine practicability.[8]

O'Hara arrived at Jefferson Barracks on September 21 and assumed command of Company F.[9] On the twenty-seventh, the War Department ordered the Second Cavalry to march to Fort Belknap, Texas. There Colonel Johnston would distribute the ten companies among the various frontier posts. A month later the regiment, consisting of 35 officers, 675 men, and 800 horses, set out. Accompanying them were Mrs. Johnston and three other officer's wives, riding with a train of 29 wagons and a single ambulance stretched out behind the main column.

As the Second Cavalry moved southwest through Missouri, the roads became wretched, the wagon train struggled to keep up. Over the Ozark Mountains they rode, and by November 14 they reached Springfield. Johnston reported at this time that a large number of men were sick, that there had been nine desertions, and that a large proportion of the horses had been incapacitated by distemper. The country, furthermore, provided virtually no forage, and the regiment was rapidly devouring its supplies as it moved torturously through "exceedingly rough country, covered almost everywhere with hickory, post oak, [and] black jack."[10]

Although the march proved an ordeal to recruits who had never experienced camp life, or who lacked proficiency in horsemanship, it toughened them. Captain O'Hara seems to have enjoyed the march thoroughly and did much himself to lift the spirits of the regiment. As his compatriot Captain Brackett recalled,

> O'Hara was at his best on the march, and thoroughly enjoyed the invigorating out door exercise. He was a good horseman, as becomes a true son of Kentucky, and was almost tireless. No fatigue seemed too much for him, nor did he lose his temper. . . . He generally kept some supplies from Kentucky, and after a long march sat down in front of his tent to enjoy himself and entertain such acquaintances as might favor him with a call. . . . On the march O'Hara's tent was always an attractive place where everybody was welcome. The wits and wags loved to assemble there, and the captain was ever ready to entertain to the best of his abilities. Nothing offensive ever occurred. There was a plain interchange of views, an airing of such news as was at hand, and a free play given to innocent mirth.[11]

The regiment journeyed on, following the boundary of Missouri to Maysville, Arkansas, then swung more to the southwest into the Indian Territory. The country became beautiful, the prairies dotted with trees. One evening a great grass fire broke out, threatening the tents and wagons. O'Hara organized a body of troopers to fight the fire and save the camp. According to Albert Brackett, he met the threat impressively, winning commendation from Colonel Johnston and "many compliments on his good behavior": "Some of his men did not move forward as promptly as he thought they ought to do, when he went after them with a will, and gave some of them a complete overhauling. He was naturally quick and industrious, and infused some of his life into his men."[12]

On November 27 the winding column of the Second Cavalry reached Tahlequah, capitol of the Cherokee Nation. O'Hara and his men were astonished to see homes of brick, "a fine seminary," and the Indians "well advanced."[13] The weather changed for the worse, however, when they entered the country of the Creeks. Nights became cold and camp life uncomfortable. O'Hara still entertained in his canvas salon. He played his violin frequently and was becoming quite proficient. He would sing, and when urged, and it required little urging, he would stand, Kentucky whiskey in hand, and "hold an audience spell-bound." "He could recite remarkably well, and generally chose some scene from Aytoun's 'Lays of the Scottish Cavaliers.'"[14] O'Hara's black cook, whom he had brought along, labored at her tasks, openly griping all the while in a loud voice about her fate and her master, "affording great amusement to her listeners, and no one could help hearing her, as her cooking place was only a short distance off."[15]

Sometimes the curious would get O'Hara to talk about Cuba. Usually this topic made him sad, then angry. He mourned for Crittenden and his lost friends, and he had come "to look upon it as a hare-brained scheme, which had little chance of success from the start, most of the members of it having been completely duped by its leader, General Narciso López."[16]

As the regiment entered Texas, they encountered a "succession of northers interspersed pleasantly with snows and sleets." Captain Kirby Smith complained, "The Department has been experimenting upon us as new and picked troops. . . . We are to subsist upon the country passed over." The march "has been very severe upon the command and indeed in the whole course of my military experience I never have seen men suffer more."[17]

They crossed the North Fork of the Canadian River, passed large settlements of Seminoles and Choctaws, and on December 12 arrived at Fort Washita. Capt. Braxton Bragg welcomed them with an artillery salute, and Colonel Sidney Johnston treated the officers to an "elegant" dinner party. O'Hara's company executive officer, Lt. N. R. "Shanks" Evans, challenged the officers of the post to race against his beloved Bumble Bee, the greatest horse in the Second Cavalry, he believed. Leaving Fort Washita, the regiment crossed the Red River on December 15, and on the twenty-second, about fifty miles northeast of Fort Belknap, was struck by a terrible norther at the close of a warm, pleasant day. The mercury plunged below zero and ice formed, six inches thick. Rain, hail, snow, and sleet followed. Several horses on the picket line froze to death, and Johnston had to abandon the march and encamp. Troopers huddled in their blankets to avoid freezing.

"Christmas Day we laid by, somewhat protected in a ravine . . . , the mercury six to eight degrees below zero." Yet this day was the "brightest, clearest day imaginable." Whiskey was shared liberally, and Captain Whiting made eggnog with frozen eggs. First Lt. Richard W. Johnson, the regimental quartermaster, recalled, "We were fifty miles away from any settlement, alone in the plains, and gave ourselves up to the moment, if not forgetting others, forgetting our troubles."[18]

Johnston started the column again, although the temperature still read below zero. They arrived at Fort Belknap on December 27. There Johnston divided the column, taking six companies with him to occupy Fort Mason on Rio Llano while sending Hardee with the remaining four, including O'Hara's Company F, to establish a camp close to the Comanche reservation on the Clear Fork of the Brazos, some forty miles west. At this location they could control the Comanches and protect the El Paso–Red River trail. Hardee's command arrived at their destination on January 3, 1856, and encamped one mile above the Comanche village. Hardee named the desolate place Camp Cooper, in honor of the adjutant general.[19]

At Camp Cooper, O'Hara and Company F passed the winter in tents. It was miserable, one of the worst winters in Texas history. Shelters could not be erected because of the lack of timber, horses were found covered with frozen sleet. "The horses had *no shelter,* and *no forage,*" one captain wrote, "so that when corn *was* procured, they *died by hundreds* of *blind staggers,* and on the first appearance of grass they *continued dying* of *scours.*" Among the charms of Camp Cooper were the wolves, which would "run through the camp in numbers every night, howling like fiends of the lower world."[20]

Despite the weather Hardee kept the command busy. Out they went on patrols along the Clear Fork. Out they went to hunt, hoping to discover sufficient game to relieve the monotony of their bacon and bread (corn crushed in a mortar) diet. These ventures served as a show of force to the restless Comanches and familiarized troopers with the area, much of which had never been mapped. Patrolling, particularly, provided "an excellent school in which to teach horsemanship." When he returned to Camp Cooper from patrol, O'Hara faced many empty hours. He read a great deal, continuing his practice of keeping abreast "with the literature of the day" as well as primitive frontier circumstances permitted.[21]

O'Hara was fine while active, seemed to function well under Hardee's direction, and led Company F effectively. "The men under his command were very fond of him, and he treated them with uniform kindness." But camp life bored him: "He was far from many things which make life agreeable, and had few companions to his liking. He went out on one or two scouts, but the whole thing was too tame for him; there was no excitement, no enthusiasm about it. The tales of the frontiersmen did not interest him, and he could not exult greatly over an uninteresting victory."[22]

Relief came on March 4, 1856. O'Hara was ordered to appear as a witness before a court-martial at Fort Mason. Capt. Charles E. Travis, commanding Company H, was to be tried for an offense that occurred earlier at Jefferson Barracks. Although O'Hara's role in the incident is unknown, he was regarded as a crucial witness. So he turned over command of Company F to Shanks Evans and traveled to Fort Mason.

En route to the fort, O'Hara and his small party encountered a crowd of buffaloes crossing their front. An excellent marksman and always hungering for excitement, O'Hara unslung his rifle and chased one for some distance. As he moved in for the kill, "he realized that some one else was after the same animal." It was a Comanche warrior, and together they killed the buffalo. O'Hara graciously bade farewell to the Indian brave and to the fallen buffalo, leaving his share of the kill behind, and thus "made his way back to his companions with a whole scalp."[23]

The adventure ended, O'Hara traveled on to Fort Mason. The Travis trial would drag on for weeks and ultimately result in that officer's dismissal from the army. While he was on this detached duty at Fort Mason, O'Hara also became involved in a sharp little action. Indians murdered a settler and his young slave, and Company I went after them. O'Hara, who would not miss a fight, tagged along, and helped lead the charge into the Indian camp. The troopers of Company I killed several braves, recovered much stolen property, and pursued the Indians relentlessly. Upon their return O'Hara turned newspaper correspondent and wrote a sparkling account of the attack for B. Gratz Brown, editor of the *St. Louis Democrat*, complimenting Capt. Albert Brackett of Company I for "having so handsomely performed one of the most successful and brilliant exploits which the annals of our border warfare with the savages record." O'Hara did not mention himself.[24]

When O'Hara returned to Camp Cooper in May, he found a new commanding officer, Lt. Col. Robert E. Lee, who had arrived on April 9. Hardee had been assigned to Fort Mason. This was Lee's first field command in his twenty-six year military career, and he itched for an opportunity to lead the four companies at Camp Cooper into action. Initially Lee had hoped to "humanize" the Indians, but after a series of talks with the Comanche chief Catumseh proved futile, the disillusioned Lee found the one thousand Comanches north of camp "in no mood to be humanized." Life at Camp Cooper, on the edge of a human and geographic furnace, was "stern, sad reality."[25]

Lee's opportunity came on May 27, when he received orders from Col. Persifor F. Smith,[26] commanding in the absence of Johnston, to lead an expedition against bands of renegade Comanches, apparently members of hostile Chief Sanaco's Penatekas, who were molesting border settlements in the vicinity of Fort Chadbourne. For the mission Lee chose two squadrons—one composed of the companies of Kirby Smith and Bradfute from Fort Mason, the other Van Dorn's A Company and O'Hara's Company F from Camp Cooper. O'Hara left Camp Cooper on June 12, Lee a day later. It took four days to march about ninety miles southwest to Fort Chadbourne, where they found the Fort Mason squadron awaiting them. Lee planned for the combined force to leave early on the eighteenth and march for the headwaters of the Brazos and Colorado Rivers, where they would fan out and begin their search deep into Texas for the marauding Indians.[27]

Shortly after reveille on June 18, Lee's united column of two squadrons, about 160 strong, prepared to move out, accompanied by the celebrated Indian guide Jim Shaw and his Delaware scouts. Capt. Theodore O'Hara, however, was not to be seen. He rode up some time later, before 7:00 A.M. but after reveille, and, with the help of Lieutenant Evans, got most of F Company on the trail. There was straggling, however. The company was obviously disorganized. For some terrible, self-destructive reason, O'Hara, "without authority or permission," had left his sleeping company, sometime after ten o'clock the night of the seventeenth, on the eve of their departure on campaign. Presumably he had ridden off to the sutler's store at Fort Chadbourne, where he stayed all night, returning after reveille as F Company was being formed for the march.

Lee confronted O'Hara on the trail. What the militarily proper Lee said to his subordinate is unknown, but he ordered him to collect the F Company stragglers and rejoin the column. Then Lee and the others rode off. Instead of following Lee's instructions, O'Hara rode back to Fort Chadbourne that morning and proceeded to get drunk. Late that afternoon, some instinct of duty or fear prompted him to return to his command. He found his mount and rode out in pursuit of the column, catching up with Lee about nightfall. He was still intoxicated.

The next morning Lee prepared formal charges against O'Hara for "conduct prejudicial to good order and military discipline" and "Drunkenness on Duty." He collected signatures of witnesses—Van Dorn, Evans, Lieutenants Walter H. Jenifer and Robert C. Wood, Jr., the sutler at Fort Chadbourne, George H. Leigh, and his son. Although infuriated, Lee did not relieve O'Hara of his command on the spot. He would bide his time.[28]

At Jim Shaw's suggestion, Lee headed west on June 19 toward mysterious wisps of smoke far in the distance. Four days of riding, however, brought them no nearer to the elusive Indians—the smoke turned out to be a prairie fire. Spreading his command, Lee swept as much area as possible to the northeast, then turned and made a sweep toward Double Mountain. They searched two days, and although they discovered Indian

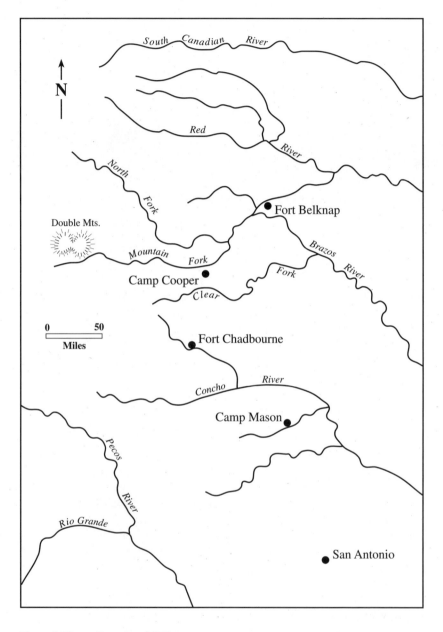

Texas Military Frontier, 1855.

trails and campfire ashes, the Delaware scouts reported them to be too old. Game apparently had also "abandoned the country." "Water grew extremely short," and what they did come across was "salt." Diarrhea and dysentery caused men to fall out. Ravines appeared in endless succession, blocking their path, capriciously, it seemed. The troopers wore themselves out, dismounting and helping push and pull the wagons up sharp grades.

Lee halted his command and stripped it down. He sent back the wagons, the weaker horses, and all sick troops to the Clear Fork of the Brazos. Tents went back with them and all supplies, except a minimum of ammunition and seven days' rations. Now Lee pushed faster. He struck the trail of a small group of Indians. Soon the Delaware scouts reported smoke to the west, about fifteen miles away. Lee divided his column, sending Van Dorn and O'Hara ahead, and took the remaining troops and headed south for the Brazos itself, positioning himself to intercept if the Indians retreated before Van Dorn and O'Hara.[29]

Van Dorn, being senior, commanded the squadron. On June 29 they marched west up Double Mountain Fork along parallel lines. Van Dorn and Shaw spotted the Indians first—a column of smoke. At sunset Van Dorn sent a Delaware scout with a penciled message to O'Hara giving his position and telling him that he would attack. Then Van Dorn waited. Presently the Delaware returned, saying he could not find Company F. Van Dorn thought the Indian had not exerted himself, but rather than send another messenger and risk delay, he determined to strike alone. At dawn on the thirtieth, Company A blasted into the Indian camp. It was over quickly. Two braves lay dead and one ran away, and an Indian woman was captured, along with twelve horses.

Off in the distance O'Hara heard the firing and ordered Company F to race toward the sound. They arrived just as the affair ended. O'Hara and Van Dorn had the Indian woman questioned and learned that this party of Indians was all that remained of a raiding party that had made its way into Mexico during the spring. White men had attacked the marauders on their return trip and made off with their booty, except for the horses.

Companies A and F scattered and combed the area for other members of the raiding party, but found none. Then they retraced their trail back to the Double Mountain and rejoined Lee, who organized more sweeps in the searing heat. On July 9 the companies of Van Dorn and O'Hara, again acting in concert as a squadron, deployed over a wide front and encountered an immense prairie fire south of the Colorado River. They also found the site of a large Indian camp near the head of the Concha River, but no Indians. Lee sent them out again—down both banks of the Concha. Van Dorn searched the right bank, O'Hara the left. Nothing.

On July 18, 1856, satisfied that the area was empty of Indians, Lee broke up his command. Kirby Smith and Bradfute headed back to Fort Mason, while Lee rode with Van Dorn and O'Hara to the Colorado River, which they crossed, then passed east of Fort Chadbourne, then north again to Camp Cooper, which they reached on the twenty-third, concluding a scout that had lasted forty days and had covered sixteen hundred miles.[30]

Colonel Johnston, who had returned to command replacing Persifor Smith, redistributed the regiment. Van Dorn and O'Hara were sent to Camp Colorado, a station near the point where the road from Fort Mason to Fort Belknap crossed the Colorado.[31] In early August, Johnston summoned O'Hara to regimental headquarters in San Antonio. In a painful interview, Johnston, known for his tolerance of shortcomings in subordinates, informed O'Hara of the charges preferred by Lieutenant Colonel Lee. Although they were old friends, the kind Johnston, in his role as regimental commander, put his personal feelings aside. O'Hara must resign from the army or face a court-martial. O'Hara suggested several alternative punishments and implored Johnston to consider them. Twisting and turning, desperate in his attempts not be disgraced, O'Hara handed Johnston his resignation, dated August 11. Pocket this, he bargained, and activate it immediately in the event of a reoccurrence of the offense. Having made this singular request, O'Hara returned to Camp Colorado. On August 13, however, Johnston informed O'Hara that his decision stood—resign or face court-martial.[32] On August 18, 1856, O'Hara resigned his commission unconditionally. This was probably the most agonizing decision of his life.

When he returned his resignation, O'Hara attached a letter asking Johnston to grant him a leave of absence until December 31 and that his resignation not be accepted formally until that time "or at least the 1st of that month, inasmuch as, should it take effect at an earlier date, I happen to be so situated that I should be greatly embarrassed & distressed. . . . Considering the severe decision of the Colonel Commanding in my case, and the hard fortune which has involved the forfeiture of my commission, I think I have right to expect from the liberality & magnanimity of the Colonel Commanding a ready compliance with the wishes expressed . . . herein." Johnston forwarded the pertinent documents to the War Department, supporting O'Hara's request. Jefferson Davis endorsed the request on September 10, "accepted to take effect as proposed in an accompanying letter Dec. 1, 1856."[33]

Humiliated and desperate for funds, O'Hara left Camp Colorado and headed east. His reputation as a soldier was ruined. Later, apologists would downplay the incident and attempt to camouflage it as a "misunderstanding with the lieutenant colonel." O'Hara's friend and fellow company commander, Capt. Albert Brackett, explained his hard fortune in these terms:

> He was contented while in the army with doing his duty
> well, and cared more for that than anything else. . . . The
> surroundings of Camp Cooper did not suit him, and he
> sighed for the good things to be found in Louisville. He liked
> hotel life, where all the luxuries are easily attainable, and
> was fond of getting up late, after working well into the night
> before. He was a natural soldier, and took kindly to duty,
> but the restraints of the regular army were not so much to
> his fancy. . . . Military life was no new thing to him, and he
> liked its excitement, but he did not like the monotony of a
> frontier post, and grew very restless under it. There was not
> novelty enough about it.[34]

Brackett was drawn irresistibly to O'Hara, so gentle and so elegant, a man who could look danger in the face and laugh, a man who would dress for dinner in the Texas wilderness as though at the Willard in Washington. Brackett treated the Fort Chadbourne incident with great charity, minimizing the grave nature of the incident, which disgusted Lee and the old army officer corps.

Brackett passes over, with a brush stroke, the lack of direction, the self-destructiveness, in O'Hara's life which caused him, like a vagabond, to wander from home to home, city to city, job to job. From 1850 to 1856, opportunities afforded few men—chances for distinction in politics, journalism, the military, and literature—passed through O'Hara's hands like water.

This troubled soul, this gifted Irishman, with his bright eyes and his love of life, was beset by a demon. No one who loved him, and very many people did, could bring themselves to give O'Hara's demon a name. Alcoholism, probably; or at least intemperance of a grievous order—no other explanation makes sense. The incident on the frontier with Lee seemed merely to crystallize elements which had already been noted by others, and which could not have come at a more inopportune time in O'Hara's life. The consequences of this indiscretion would prove disastrous for O'Hara's military ambitions. Perhaps Shelby Foote put it most succinctly: "Few people ever got on the wrong side of Lee and recovered."[35]

Chapter 8

Mobile

Where was Theodore O'Hara from October 1856 until November 1857? Correspondence has not been discovered which would establish a location. Even the U.S. Army lost track of him.[1] Most of his nineteenth-century biographers connect him with William Walker and his adventures during this time and even earlier. The Walker-O'Hara relationship has never been substantiated, however, and O'Hara has never been placed in Nicaragua. For that matter, none of the studies of Walker and his expeditions even mention O'Hara.[2] This omission has led twentieth-century O'Hara biographer George H. Genzmer to dismiss the Walker connection as apocryphal. Another writer, Maj. Edgar E. Hume, believes "it is very doubtful."[3]

It is possible, nevertheless, that O'Hara could have been involved, at least in the recruiting of men, in Walker's inglorious Sonora expedition to lower California, November 1853 to February 1854. Certainly O'Hara could not have accompanied Walker on his first Nicaraguan expedition in June 1855, for he was on duty with the Second Cavalry at the time. It also is conceivable, indeed plausible, that O'Hara could have joined Walker in the fall of 1856, following the former's resignation from the army. O'Hara does not appear in Frankfort or in Louisville in 1856–57, and when he next surfaces, it is in Mobile in November 1857. Walker's first Nicaraguan adventure had collapsed shortly before this time. He had been captured in May 1857 by the U.S. Navy and taken to New Orleans.[4]

O'Hara's friend Henry T. Titus had made his way to New Orleans in December 1856, with about a hundred men, and joined Walker in this

first Nicaraguan expedition. It proved a fiasco, with Titus being imprisoned by the British for insulting remarks about Queen Victoria and later
imprisoned by American authorities who informed the infuriated Titus
that "filibusters had no rights as citizens."[5]

It is certain that O'Hara sympathized deeply with the dreams of his
fellow filibusters, and it seems reasonable that he gladly would have assisted Walker in planning and recruiting, or would have participated actively in the earlier Nicaraguan expedition itself. So would have O'Hara's
shadow, Thomas T. Hawkins. The four men, Walker, Titus, O'Hara, and
Hawkins, often veiled their movements in secrecy and guarded what they
wrote, preferring word-of-mouth communication for security purposes.
Their few written messages were often coded and accompanied with instructions to destroy. Thus attempts to trace their movements and document their involvement are frustrated and historical investigation yields
finally to speculation.

It seems unlikely O'Hara was an important actor in the Walker dra-
mas, but, as a fully committed revolutionary, with his Nashville contacts,
with his friend Pickett's acute awareness of affairs in Central America,
and with his established connection with the principal players of the
Young America and aggressive Manifest Destiny movements, it is likely
O'Hara was involved in some manner with William Walker.[6]

What is known is that following his arrest by Commodore Hiram
Paulding, Walker was sent back to the United States and set up headquarters in Mobile, preparing for a third expedition to Nicaragua.[7] O'Hara was
there and actively assisted him. In January 1858 he served as a vice president of a Walker rally, and in December of that year, Walker wrote another
lieutenant, C. I. Fayssoux, that O'Hara was in Columbus, Mississippi, seeking "means and men." O'Hara, Walker confided, "will go as far as Aber-
deen [Mississippi]. There will be little difficulty, I imagine, in procuring a
clearance for a vessel hereafter."[8] Another year was to pass, however, before Walker managed to set sail. By October 1859, O'Hara was at his favorite New Orleans haunt, the St. Charles Hotel, and from there wrote
Fayssoux that "you will be in charge of the emigration" and gave Fayssoux
the name of a trusted Mississippi friend who "will come down with the earliest reinforcements & will prove an efficient man."[9]

There seems to be no doubt that O'Hara actively, openly, and enthusiastically supported Walker's Nicaragua enterprises from 1857 to 1860.
There is no evidence, however, that he accompanied Walker on any of
his expeditions.[10]

Equally tantalizing are references by nineteenth-century sources linking O'Hara to the Tehuantepec Railroad Company. This venture repre-
sents a continuing American effort from 1846 to 1861 to shorten the

shipping route to California by building a railroad across the waist of Mexico. Once again, no proof of O'Hara's participation has been uncovered. Yet such a connection seems logical.

O'Hara's friend, John Forsyth, Jr., of Mobile, was minister to Mexico and John Slidell, editor of the *New Orleans Delta*, was deeply involved as a promoter. The *Delta* had consistently supported American expansion into the Caribbean and Central America, the ventures of López and Quitman. The idea was to build a railroad across the narrow Isthmus of Tehuantepec in southern Mexico. Unfortunately for O'Hara, Forsyth would take a position opposing Slidell and side with Slidell's competitor, Col. A. G. Sloo. President James Buchanan and Louisiana senator Judah P. Benjamin would ally with Slidell.

Throughout the 1850s both Democrats and Whigs supported opening a route across Central America that would "integrate California and Pacific commerce" into the economic mainstream of America. Benjamin, who was the spokesman for the Tehuantepec route, saw it as a natural extension of the new railroad running south to New Orleans from Jackson, Mississippi, and points north. "What have we before us? The Eastern World!" Benjamin argued in the Tehuantepec prospectus. "Its commerce makes empires of the countries to which it flows. . . . That commerce belongs to New Orleans."

Things went smoothly in the early 1850s. The Louisiana legislature cooperated, a survey was made, a prospectus was printed. Secretary of State Daniel Webster negotiated a treaty with Mexico granting rights to the Tehuantepec Company. A new Mexican government, however, undid everything, and relations grew strained between the two nations. The Tehuantepec Company was reorganized, but to compound difficulties, John Forsyth, in Mexico City, opposed issuing a charter to Benjamin's company. Buchanan squelched this opposition by recalling Forsyth. Another Mexican government would prove pliable, but failure of a key banking house in 1859 set everything back. Then, as Benjamin scrambled to refinance the company, the Civil War intervened in devastating fashion.

How was Theodore O'Hara involved in all of this? The *Louisville Courier-Journal* in 1874 reported that "he was frequently, during Democratic administrations, called by the government to conduct negotiations with foreign governments, and his services were particularly valued in the Tehuantepec business." Three other writers, within twenty-five years of O'Hara's death, repeated the assertion. Some weight should be given this contemporary testimony, albeit vague and unspecific.

It is probable that O'Hara was active in the Tehuantepec affair in 1850–52 or during the 1856–57 interval. Once the break between Forsyth and Buchanan occurred, doubtless O'Hara would have sided

Judah P. Benjamin, ca. 1860.
National Archives.

with Forsyth, and that would have ended his association with the enterprise, dominated as it was by Benjamin. For the reconstruction of
O'Hara's life and activities, it is regrettable that his activities on behalf
of the Tehuantepec railroad cannot be documented. It would have provided yet another novel subcareer.[11] The only concrete evidence connecting O'Hara with a Mexican railroad enterprise is one puzzling frag-
ment—a report ten years earlier in the *Daily American Star* (Mexico
City), December 5, 1847, stating that O'Hara chaired a meeting in
Mexico City (at the height of the occupation) to establish a railroad between Vera Cruz and Mexico City.[12]

O'Hara's nomadic existence ended temporarily in late 1857. He sold
his remaining interest in the estate of Kean O'Hara to his brother James
P. O'Hara of Franklin County, Kentucky, for twenty thousand dollars.[13]
This settlement gave him some degree of financial independence. Furthermore, the Democrats of Alabama invited him to come to Mobile and edit
the *Mobile Daily Register,* a long-established (1821) and respected journal. The publisher and editor, John Forsyth, had accepted appointment
by the Buchanan administration to become minister to Mexico. Elated,
O'Hara wrote Gen. John A. Quitman on November 25, 1857, that he
was "just about entering upon my duties. I wish to say that if in this po-

sition, it shall ever be in my power in any way to serve your views, nothing will afford me a more sincere & perfect pleasure."[14]

The *Mobile Daily Register* had been purchased by Forsyth in April 1857, seven months before O'Hara's arrival. Forsyth had held part interest in the *Register* since 1853 and served as its editor. He also had edited the *Register* earlier, from 1837 to 1841. Forsyth was highly energetic, a talented newspaper man with strings of powerful friends across the South. He was O'Hara's patron and would continue to be.

Forty-five years old, son of the former governor of Georgia and Jacksonian secretary of state John Forsyth (1780–1841), he was refined, well educated, and ambitious. He had been admitted to the Georgia bar in 1834 but decided to locate in Alabama, settling in Mobile in 1835. Forsyth became U.S. attorney for the southern district of Alabama and, in 1837, editor of the *Register*. When his father died in 1841, Forsyth returned to Georgia, where he simultaneously practiced law, edited the *Columbus Times,* and acted as postmaster and president of the Columbus Gas Light Association. When the Mexican War came, he interrupted his frenzy of activity to serve as adjutant of the First Georgia Regiment, 1846–47. He was involved "to a very great extent" in the filibuster schemes of López in 1851, selling bonds and helping secure ordnance and men.[15]

Forsyth returned to Mobile in 1853 and operated a sawmill. Fire ended those plans, so he joined with two partners to purchase the *Register.* Using its pages to promote his own political views and those of Alabama Democrats, Forsyth turned the paper into a powerful political voice in control of "possibly the most incisive writer who has lived in Mobile."[16]

As in Louisville, the Know-Nothing Party was extremely strong in Mobile during the mid-1850s. Violence occurred as Nativists attacked the "Romanish Irish" on the streets. Forsyth's *Register* "stood alone among the city's four dailies in fighting such excesses." Forsyth's position was clear: "If there is anything that we hate with all the intense instincts of the education and sentiments of a freeman, it is religious intolerance."[17] When one of Forsyth's partners, Lewis A. Middleton, drifted into the Know-Nothing camp, Forsyth forced him to withdraw from the ownership of the paper. Knowledge of Forsyth's anti-Know-Nothing position, of course, held great appeal for O'Hara.[18]

Men came and went on Forsyth's staff, Samuel Chester Reid, Jr., being one of the best known. He was one of the correspondents employed by the *Register* and became O'Hara's friend. He was the son of a famous naval hero of the War of 1812, a man who had whipped the British and given the United States the design for its flag.[19] Young Reid was well educated, cosmopolitan in his tastes, and, although born in the North, had developed an affinity for the South. This attitude may have come from clerkship in Quitman's law office, from his duty with the Texas Rangers during the Mexican War, or from the persuasive attraction of the urbane Princetonian John Forsyth. Reid, like O'Hara, had published a book about the Mexican War, *The Scouting Expeditions of McCulloch's Texas Rangers* (1847), and in 1857 would publish an account of his father's most famous sea fight against the British.[20]

Another man drawn to Forsyth and the *Register* was John Bragg, a North Carolina lawyer and politician who migrated to Mobile about the same time. Bragg became highly successful politically in southern Alabama, and Forsyth was his loyal ally. He was an editorial writer who seems to have won Forsyth's trust. Influence and trust from this special relationship would flow to John's younger brother, veteran artillery officer Braxton Bragg, a man who would prove O'Hara's damaging adversary.[21]

Each year Forsyth became more and more involved in politics. In 1856 he went to Cincinnati as a delegate to the Democratic National Convention. He used his influence to have the Alabama delegation support Pierce for fourteen ballots, and though Pierce lost, he acknowledged his gratitude at the end of his term by naming Forsyth minister to Mexico. Forsyth's confidant, "his constant companion and advisor," would be John T. Pickett. Doubtless Pickett influenced Forsyth's choice of O'Hara as editor of the *Daily Register*.[22]

On the eve of his departure Forsyth confessed to his readers his reluctance to leave the South "at a moment when the voice and arm of every true son is needed in the great battle for Constitutional principles and States Rights which now shakes the country." The emergence of the Republican Party and its candidate John C. Frémont alarmed him: "The South ought not to submit. . . . While I would not, for the right arm which guides this pen, raise one finger against the Union, disunion has no terrors for me."[23]

To replace this powerful editorial voice, Forsyth and Alabama Democrats turned to Theodore O'Hara. His record on the defense of Southern rights was proven; he also would welcome the opportunity to join a publication known for its defense of Irish Catholics. Providing editorial punch was easy for O'Hara—others would manage business affairs. So 1857–58 proved an enjoyable year. Indeed, O'Hara's four-year sojourn in Mobile was a most pleasant time. He rented a fine home on North Royal Street and set himself up in style. How long did the money from Kean O'Hara's estate last? A significant sum for the times, it probably had passed through O'Hara's fingers by 1860.

O'Hara entertained frequently and was the toast of the open houses. Madame Levert, a Mobile hostess of note, made certain O'Hara was a regular at her affairs. She would gather to her salon artists, actors, actresses, writers, politicians, and filibusters. Sometimes her all-consuming parties would run from 11:00 A.M. to 11:00 P.M. Mary Walker Fearn and Phoebe Desha Smith competed with Madame Levert, although the parties of the latter were "costly, but not popular." O'Hara enjoyed being in demand socially, and he found the company elegant and stimulating. And Mobile society discovered him to be a man of "genial and generous disposition, and a mind richly stored with knowledge; he was a happy and brilliant conversationalist, who was the charm of many a social gathering."[24]

His heavy drinking and unstable life-style continued, unfortunately, and seems to have grown worse. A young printer at the *Register,* John F. Cothran, reported that O'Hara stayed up late "sometimes, oft times, and generally all the time." O'Hara frequented "Billings' place of conviviality." One night, "when all the convives had gone home," he had Royal Street all to himself, except for a goat who eyed him from the center of the street. O'Hara

> whipped out his pistol and fired upon Guilliemus Capricornus—three separate and specific shots. G. C. capered off, apparently unharmed, but up came the constable or police officer on the run . . . commanding . . . that O'Hara accompany him to the guard-house.
>
> O'Hara stared at the constable for a full minute. . . . Then he bit off the following remarkable string of words, emphasizing each phrase with the hand holding the pistol:
>
> "Mistake of creation, occupant of the lowest office in the gift of the American people, depart! Else will I fill you so full of lead that you will drop to the Seventh Hell and crush through the roof into the Bottomless Pit."
>
> But the officer had already departed, with the same lack of ceremony that had characterized the flight of the goat. O'Hara's sole comment, in reciting the story, was that he had had more to say, and regretted that the performance ended so abruptly.[25]

It is an amusing story, O'Hara staggering about Royal Street encountering goat and constable and invoking Dante. One wonders. There seems a desperation about it all. What did O'Hara really imagine he saw that night in the darkness of Royal Street? Some Celtic chimera? Or Dionysus, perhaps, god of the uninhibited, of excess, of chaos, of self-destruction? Some Dantean fate of his own? O'Hara was by all accounts a crack shot. He would not have missed, unless by intention.

John Forsyth returned in the late fall of 1858 and resumed editing the *Register*. O'Hara remained on the staff, however. Frequently he wrote editorials, since Forsyth spent a great deal of time traveling about the state and the South. More and more O'Hara's columns reflected the Southern rights movement. The *New York Times,* ten years later, would remember how he conducted his editorial work with "great brilliancy and success." O'Hara himself saw his work with the *Register* as a continuation "of fighting the battle of Southern Rights for years with my pen and my voice."[26]

Although his responsibilities lessened considerably after Forsyth's return from Mexico, O'Hara still listed himself as "editor" in the *Mobile City Directory* in 1859. He also involved himself in Spring Hill College, a Jesuit institution west of the city. Two old Kentucky friends, Thomas G. Rapier and Robert M. Sands, important figures at Spring Hill, encouraged O'Hara to share in the life of the college. Rapier, if not Sands, had been a classmate of O'Hara's at St. Joseph's, and all three enjoyed each other's company. Sands, Rapier, and O'Hara retained the "militant but cultured Catholicity" of early Kentucky, and they seemed to share a sense of mission. Teaching at Spring Hill helped fulfill this need. Nevertheless, O'Hara's relationship with the college was informal, irregular at best. Occasional lectures and drop-in visits were the extent of it. O'Hara did come to know many of the students, however, and must have cut an attractive figure on campus. He would turn to these students for help in the fall of 1860.[27]

Politically the *Register* shifted its position as 1860 neared. John Forsyth, encouraged and probably influenced by O'Hara, had withdrawn support from fire-eater William L. Yancey, and, hoping to halt the South's drift toward secession, had become a Stephen A. Douglas man. Forsyth and O'Hara saw Douglas as the only national figure capable of winning who would pledge himself to protect the rights of Southern slave owners.[28]

A political dilemma for the editors of the *Register* developed, however. Douglas and Breckinridge, Buchanan's young and popular vice president and a potential presidential aspirant, once had been friends, but as the Democratic Convention of 1860 approached, they split. Breckinridge had denied his ambitions to O'Hara as late as January 1860: "Thanks for your good wishes about the White House. . . . I do not anticipate being in the way of any body . . . for my old resolution is unchanged, to take no step to promote myself in that direction. . . . I am in a good . . . position now, and am content."[29] Forsyth stayed with Douglas, believing him to be the only hope to defeat Lincoln. Indeed the *Register* became "Douglas' flagship newspaper in the state."[30]

John Forsyth, ca. 1860. Library of Congress.

O'Hara, of course, backed his old friend Breckinridge once the latter announced his candidacy. This would not do, at least to Forsyth's mind. So O'Hara left the *Register,* although the parting appears to have been amicable. Forsyth replaced O'Hara with a twenty-five-year-old Swiss, Henry Hotze, whose "industrious and instructed pen" championed the cause of Douglas and helped him win Mobile in the November 1860 presidential election.[31]

O'Hara used his influence with his friend Breckinridge as the Southern rights candidate, but he found Breckinridge reluctant. Like his native state, Breckinridge sought compromise desperately, but found himself assailed from every side. Some of his critics labeled him an emancipationist. Indeed, "the fewer the number of slaves in a county, the more likely it was to back Breckinridge."[32] Still he headed the Constitutional Democratic Party, an alliance top-heavy with "ultras" (proslavery secessionists). Cries of "disunion" froze the hearts of Breckinridge's Kentucky friends. They knew well Kentucky had more "to lose by civil war than any other border state."[33] This concern became manifest shortly after, when Kentucky would declare itself neutral between the federal government and the rebellious states, though this condition could not last long.[34]

The election of 1860 destroyed American traditional political alliances and splintered the Democratic Party. Kentucky turned her back on her native son, and although Breckinridge carried the slave states, Douglas and John Bell drew off sufficient votes in the border states and in the North to ensure Lincoln's election to the presidency.

O'Hara viewed Lincoln's election as revolution—a direct threat to American constitutional government. He raised the flag of Southern independence in November 1860 and set out to organize a military force, being "one of the very first to take up arms in the cause." Turning to the students at Spring Hill, he asked them to enlist and follow him. Very quickly he recruited a company of mounted infantry, the Mobile Light Dragoons, "the first military company formed in the South, with reference to the probability of war."[35]

Theodore O'Hara saw war ahead. No doubt about that. And he planned to be in the front rank. His motivation would have been quite strong, though filled with ironic contradiction. Nevertheless, his thinking may be seen as highly appropriate to the man and to the cultural and social elements which constituted his heritage. As both a Catholic and a Southerner, he would have had perhaps mixed attitudes toward the institution of slavery, though not enough to have given him much pause. As several historians of the period have concluded, on the two main ideological issues which characterized the South, secession and racism, Catholics were "quite thoroughly acculturated." Several of the bishops, quite prominent ones, were defenders of states' rights and publicly supported the Confederacy.[36] Indeed, O'Hara's father had owned slaves himself, though on a small domestic scale, like many modestly prosperous families in Kentucky. Theoretically, as Monsignor John T. Ellis has pointed out, official church doctrine would not have defined slavery as opposed to divine or natural law, though teaching would have stressed the moral obligations of Catholic slaveholders to treat their subjects fairly and to provide religious instruction.[37]

Some insight into O'Hara's motivation may be provided by English correspondent William H. Russell, who enjoyed the company of O'Hara's close friend John T. Pickett and closely observed the romantic freebooter. Russell could have been describing Theodore O'Hara. "Mr. Colonel Pickett," he reported,

> is a good-looking man, of pleasant manners and well educated. But this gentleman was a professed buccaneer, a friend of Walker, the grey-eyed man of destiny—his comrade in his most dangerous razzie. He was a newspaper writer, a soldier, a filibusterer, and he now threw himself into the cause of the South with vehemence; it was not difficult to imagine he saw in that cause the realization of the dreams of

empire in the south of the Gulf, and of conquest in the islands of the sea, which have such a fascinating influence over
the imagination of a large portion of the American people.[38]

The cavalier attitude, the martial spirit and the love of military titles
among gentlemen of "good breeding"—so often noted in treatments of
the antebellum South—would continue to be major factors in O'Hara's
life. No doubt he believed his political stand consistent with his heritage
of rebellion against tyrannical government, the legacy of Kean O'Hara.
To be a revolutionary identified him.[39] And yet, perhaps the deepest motive of all that impelled him, he could now envision some new opportunities to redeem himself from the public disgrace he had suffered—and
to repair his sense of besmirched honor.

Chapter 9

Search for a Command

In the closing days of 1860, Alabama governor Andrew B. Moore became alarmed for the safety of Mobile and decided to take military action. Moore, ironically, had been a Whig who had won a resounding victory at the ballot box in 1859 over a Southern rights Democrat. But Moore, like the South, had changed. Now he embraced radical plans of action. Employing O'Hara's Light Dragoons and hundreds of kindred spirits in southern Alabama, Moore ordered the seizure of Forts Morgan and Gaines, guarding Mobile Bay. It was accomplished January 5, 1861.

A similar scene occurred at Pensacola, Florida; again O'Hara was centrally engaged. Secessionists had begun gathering in the area, realizing the prime importance of Pensacola. They determined to capture the navy yard and the three forts that defended the entrance to Pensacola Bay—McRee, Barrancas, and Pickens. First they isolated the garrisons by cutting telegraph and overland communications between the forts and the outside world. When Florida seceded on January 10, the U.S. Army officer commanding Fort Barrancas spiked his forty-four cannon and withdrew to Fort Pickens, a few thousand yards offshore on Santa Rosa Island. Fort McRee likewise was abandoned.

O'Hara sailed from Mobile east along the Florida coast, accompanied by the South Alabama Rangers and the Chickasaw Guards, a small unit from Enterprise, Mississippi. As their steamer approached Pensacola harbor and passed Fort Pickens, the Federals "stood to their guns," but O'Hara and his men continued on their way and drew no fire. They landed at the navy yard and marched to the hospital, then separated. The Chickasaw Guards, augmented by many Florida secessionists who did not belong to formal military units, took a position fronting Fort Pickens and erected sand batteries. O'Hara, commanding his Light Dragoons and the South Alabama Rangers, occupied Forts Barrancas and McRee.[1]

Thus the Federal junior officers at Fort Pickens, without orders and guidance, found themselves confronting hostile forces armed with heavy ordnance. In effect, an explosive situation had been created at Pensacola, almost identical to that in Charleston harbor. Fighting might erupt at any minute. Florida Senator Stephen R. Mallory informed Washington that any attempt to reinforce Fort Pickens would result in an attack on the fort. President James Buchanan temporized. He dispatched a relief ship with two hundred troops but had them cautiously anchor within sight of Pickens on January 29. These Federal reinforcements would not land unless secessionists attempted to seize the fort.

The standoff continued through February 1861—both sides ready for a fight, neither ready for war. Southerners came and went informally, but this military confrontation was expensive. A second contingent of Mississippi troops had come down to Pensacola to assist Florida in her struggle for independence, but they quickly exhausted the funds authorized for their subsistence and had to return.

O'Hara settled in as commander of Fort McRee. He worked energetically to put the "dilapidated old fort" in serviceable condition and watched closely the movements of the Federals at Fort Pickens. On March 1 O'Hara, "commanding Fort McRee," wrote Lt. O. H. Berryman, commanding the Federal steamer *Wyandotte*: "Sir: With great respect allow me to suggest to you that in the present very critical attitude of affairs it is not exactly the thing (especially for a Virginian) to be moving up and down, and in a very exceptional manner, with respect to this fortress. I ask you, sir, not again, if you please, to pass this fort (either in or out) as you did this morning and this evening, without an explanation."[2]

As commander of Fort McRee, O'Hara also communicated directly with Confederate secretary of war Leroy Pope Walker about ordnance matters and even the range in yards separating Fort McRee and Fort Pickens. On March 4, 1861, Lincoln's inauguration day, O'Hara took great delight in firing "a broadside of blank cartridges" to alarm the enemy.[3]

However gratifying this activity as commander of the fort may have been, it ended abruptly on March 11, when Gen. Braxton Bragg arrived and took charge of the forces at Pensacola. Bragg remembered O'Hara from old army days in Texas, and one of his first acts, it appears, was to remove him from command and send him packing. The state of O'Hara's Alabama regiment, Bragg wrote Gen. Richard Taylor, was such that "it took a week's big drunk to get . . . [it] organized."[4] Bragg further explained his action in a sullen, vengeful letter to Gen. William W. Mackall two years later: O'Hara, "a drunken loafer from Mobile, . . . was discharged by me when I first assumed command at Pensacola in March '61, as a disgrace to the service."[5]

So despite apparently performing creditably at Pensacola, O'Hara found himself back in Mobile, victim of the vicious backlash of his own reputation. There in Mobile, however, he received from the Confederate War Department his commission as captain, a regular officer, in the Confederate army. He accepted the appointment and began to draw pay, but he had no command.[6]

On April 22, 1861, he received orders from the War Department posting him to recruiting duty in Vicksburg. These orders also sent Capt. Stephen D. Lee on the same duty to Charleston and Lt. Edward Ingraham to Mobile. O'Hara served as an enrolling and recruiting officer in Vicksburg until the middle of June, when he took a train to Richmond in an attempt to secure a line command. Upon arrival in Richmond and taking a room at the Columbia Hotel, he wrote Secretary of War Walker on June 29 requesting that he be assigned command of "certain companies of Alabama Volunteers in this vicinity, now in process of organization as a Regiment":

> As to my capacity for such a command it is not for me to
> speak; I trust I may say, however, that an experience of a
> number of years in the U.S. Army, and in other Military ser-
> vice, justifies me in aspiring to this position.
>   Being an Alabamian also, there would be an appropriate-
> ness in my assignment to the command of these troops, as I
> have reason to believe it would be acceptable to them.[7]

O'Hara's reply came two days later from Confederate adjutant general Samuel Cooper: report for duty in Richmond to Gen. John H. Winder, who had just been assigned inspector general of "the several camps near Richmond," with duties including processing discharge requests, equipping troops for the field, and care of all prisoners of war. This assignment was most unsatisfactory. O'Hara wanted action, a line command. If he served with Winder at all, which is doubtful, it was for less than two weeks.[8]

On July 17, 1861, O'Hara got his wish. The War Department appointed him lieutenant colonel of the Twelfth Alabama Volunteer Infantry Regiment. The colonel was absent, so O'Hara assumed command of the regiment on July 20. Almost immediately he was ordered forward toward Manassas Junction, Virginia, as part of Brig. Gen. Richard S. Ewell's brigade.[9]

Ewell was stationed north of Manassas Junction watching the cross-ings of Bull Run in the event of an enemy advance from Centreville, Virginia. His regiments had fallen back hastily in early July as the result of a Federal advance in force and had taken position on the extreme right of the Confederate army at Union Mills. There they had been pressed hard on July 17. Ewell remained at Union Mills, under orders from Gen. Pierre G. T. Beauregard to hold his command "in readiness to advance at a moment's notice."

As Lieutenant Colonel O'Hara moved his troops north from Rich-mond to join Ewell, the Battle of First Manassas opened. Fighting broke out the morning of July 21, between advancing Federal units and Con-federate troops under Col. Shanks Evans, O'Hara's old Company F friend, southeast of Sudley Springs along the Warrenton Turnpike. To his credit the overmatched Evans gave ground slowly, but the entire left of the army was threatened; and Beauregard, in a series of confusing orders, rushed reinforcements to their aid. Ewell's brigade, however, never ar-rived. They spent the day executing Beauregard's commands, crossing and recrossing Bull Run, marching and countermarching. That night they returned to Union Mills exhausted and utterly frustrated. It was there on the twenty-second that O'Hara and the Twelfth Alabama joined Ewell and his weary brigade.[10]

O'Hara and the Twelfth Alabama remained at Union Mills, Virginia, throughout the summer as part of Ewell's brigade, which consisted of the Fifth Alabama (Col. Robert E. Rodes), Sixth Alabama (Col. J. J. Seibels), Twelfth Mississippi (Col. Richard Griffith), and O'Hara's Twelfth Ala-bama. The colonel of the Twelfth Alabama, Robert Tignall Jones, a West Pointer and a Virginian, did not appear for some time. O'Hara, in the mean-time, seems to have exercised command with initiative and energy. He knew many of his men personally, as three companies had been recruited in Mo-bile. O'Hara reported to Adjutant General Cooper that "going into camp I devoted myself assiduously to the instruction and ministrations of the Regi-ment, so that when the Col arrived I relinquished to him the command of a regiment well advanced in the drill and in the most promising condition."[11]

Indeed, matters looked promising. Colonel Jones told O'Hara that he anticipated accepting command of the Twentieth Alabama, a regiment in the process of being formed, and had so agreed with "certain gentlemen" who were helping to organize the regiment. Jones assured Lieutenant Colonel O'Hara that once the transfer was completed, he would become colonel of the Twelfth himself. And this transfer came about on Septem-ber 30, 1861, when the regiment was mustered into the service of the army of the Confederate States of America. O'Hara was most pleased with his appointment as colonel, commanding the Twelfth Alabama.[12]

As with so many instances in O'Hara's life, however, it would prove a blighted appointment. Colonel Jones left the Twelfth Alabama and went to Richmond. En route, or shortly after his arrival, Jones apparently had a change of heart and decided that he would remain as colonel of the Twelfth Alabama despite orders of the War Department to the contrary. A year later, in a letter to Adjutant General Cooper, O'Hara asserted that Jones "protested against the transfer on the ground that it was made without his assent. The acting Secretary, Mr. Benjamin, decided that he could not lawfully be transferred *without his assent,* and, in there was not *written evidence* of that assent in the Department that Jones must be reinstated. This was accordingly ordered and my commission as Colonel in which capacity I had been in duty some time *was revoked.*"[13]

The new secretary of war, Judah P. Benjamin, took a legalistic stance. He could find no written evidence in the records of the War Department demonstrating that Jones assented to the transfer, although "Benjamin declared that they had every *outside* evidence" that Jones had agreed to the change. Benjamin wired former secretary of war Leroy Pope Walker in Huntsville, Alabama: "Unless some written evidence can be produced showing assent of R. T. Jones to be transferred from the 12th to the 20th Ala regts the promotions in the 12th must be annulled, and Jones reinstated."

According to O'Hara, the required written evidence was forwarded by Walker to the War Department through Col. Isham W. Garrott, and Benjamin wired Walker back: "The papers received from Col. Garrott *fully sustain your action* in the transfer of R. T. Jones from the Twelfth to the 20th Regt. Ala. Volunteers." Despite this information, Benjamin decided to give Jones back his old command and had Cooper issue an order revoking O'Hara's appointment as colonel. Benjamin confided to O'Hara after the fact that "Jones had acted very badly in the matter."[14]

At the time he lost his commission as colonel of the Twelfth Alabama, O'Hara did not know of Benjamin's telegram to Walker. That lack of knowledge would come out about a year later when Gen. Edward Dorr Tracy, who happened to be present with Walker when the controversy arose, related the circumstances to O'Hara. Infuriated by the War Department's blundering and wrongful action, and not wishing to serve under Jones, O'Hara on November 1, 1861, resigned his commission as lieutenant colonel of the Twelfth Alabama to take effect on November 11: "*I,* thus acknowledged to have been wrongfully deprived of my command and my rank, was left to be the sufferer in the case."[15]

O'Hara's plight seems extraordinary. One wonders if there were not a scene within a scene in this drama. Might there have been in Benjamin's mind resentment or malice resulting from his three unsuccessful prosecutions of O'Hara for his filibuster activities? Might there have been an agreement between Benjamin and Jones for the latter to retain command? Might there have been—and this seems more plausible—a determination on the part of Adjutant General Cooper, who knew the O'Hara of Second Cavalry days, to slow his rate of promotion? One could easily argue to the contrary, of course. But the situation remains bizarre. No answer seems satisfactory. One can only imagine the indignation and frustration of O'Hara.

He resigned, O'Hara would contend later, with assurances from Benjamin that he "should be given the Command of a Regt." in the Western Department. So Captain O'Hara (he had reverted to his former rank) left Virginia. Afterward, Gen. Joseph E. Johnston would write, "We were together in the army of Virginia, where this officer commanded an Alabama regiment. My observation in these various circumstances has given me full confidence in Col. O'Hara's capacity, skill & courage."[16] Under new orders issued by the adjutant general on November 13, 1861, Captain O'Hara was to proceed to Bowling Green, Kentucky, and report to Gen. Albert Sidney Johnston for duty. He left Richmond on the thirteenth and arrived at Johnston's headquarters on the twenty-sixth.[17]

Things had come full circle in the five years since Fort Chadbourne. Sidney Johnston, O'Hara's regimental commander in the Second Cavalry, had been in charge of the Western Department of the Confederacy for two months, facing a dangerous if not impossible military situation—defense of a front stretching from the Appalachians to the Mississippi River, with about fifty thousand men. At Bowling Green, fifty-five miles north of Nashville, Johnston anchored his line, with great salients pushed forward at Columbus, Kentucky, under Gen. Leonidas Polk and at Cumberland Gap under Gen. Felix Zollicoffer. Johnston needed more men, more equipment, more arms, desperately.

When O'Hara reported for duty, it was the first time he had seen Johnston since the terrible Fort Chadbourne affair. Despite the severity of Johnston's action, O'Hara did not harbor ill feelings toward him. Indeed, O'Hara loved Johnston and wanted to serve under him. As Albert Brackett observed, "There seems always to have been a feeling of warm friendship between these two men." O'Hara welcomed the opportunity to redeem his reputation in Sidney Johnston's eyes, and he badly wanted the good opinion of his old friend Maj. Gen. William J. Hardee, now a division commander at Bowling Green.

Sidney Johnston, noted for his "overly gentle nature and his childlike faith in human goodness," welcomed O'Hara to the western army. He regretted that he had no regiment available for him to command, but assured him nonetheless that he valued his abilities and would give him

Gen. Joseph E. Johnston, CSA,
1864. Library of Congress.

"the command of the first regiment he should have at his disposal." In
the meantime there was so much organizational and administrative work
to be done and so few men available with a professional military background that he needed help immediately. So Johnston asked O'Hara to
join his staff as acting assistant inspector general.[18]

Throughout the winter of 1861–62, O'Hara performed as Johnston's
staff officer. Little is certain of his specific activities, but it is known that
he spent time shuttling back and forth between Bowling Green and Nashville. In early February 1862, O'Hara was in Nashville, doubtless quartered most agreeably in the Maxwell House, mustering troops and forwarding them as quickly as possible to Bowling Green or to Clarksville,
where a secondary concentration was occurring in response to threatening enemy movements against the river forts Henry and Donelson.[19]

Union forces under Gen. Ulysses S. Grant struck these poorly defended
river forts in February with startling strength and fury, capturing them
together with their priceless supplies and thirteen thousand Confederate
volunteers. With the fall of Fort Donelson on February 16, the way lay
open to Nashville. Sidney Johnston had to abandon Bowling Green to
avoid being cut off north of the Cumberland River. He had ordered a secondary Nashville-Clarksville line established in the fall and expected to

make a stand there, but to his dismay he discovered the fortifications upon which he relied had not been constructed. Furthermore, Nashville's city fathers, fearing a battle at the gates of the city, now insisted that the Confederate forces make no attempt to defend the town.[20]

Chaos reigned in Nashville. Transportation broke down, key officials abandoned their posts and many went over to the enemy, stockpiles of valuable stores were abandoned. Johnston's army fled south to Murfreesboro, where he effected a reorganization, integrating the shattered forces of Zollicoffer and the remnants of the Clarksville-Donelson command.[21] Then Johnston pressed on, eighty miles south to Huntsville, Alabama, thence to Decatur, Alabama, where he and his Army of Central Kentucky crossed the Tennessee River. They headed west toward Corinth, Mississippi, to make a junction with Polk's forces retreating south from Columbus and Bragg's coastal garrisons rushing north from Pensacola and Mobile.

The Confederates determined to combine and to strike Grant, who audaciously had ascended the Tennessee River with thirty-nine thousand men and made a lodgment at Pittsburg Landing on the south bank, almost on the Tennessee-Mississippi border. Grant's reinforcements, under Gen. Don Carlos Buell, were in Nashville, out of immediate supporting distance. Grant must be attacked now. Timing was crucial.

On April 3, 1862, Johnston's combined forces, forty-four thousand strong, began their advance toward Grant's encampment in the vicinity of a little country chapel called Shiloh. Employing an elaborate and confusing battle plan, and hampered by poor roads and heavy rain, the Confederates required three days to move into position. On Sunday, April 6, a magnificent spring day, fighting opened early. Johnston rode to the front himself when he heard the sound of heavy skirmishing. The Confederates, attacking along a broad front, had completely surprised Grant's troops, who reeled back toward the Tennessee River. Johnston moved about the battlefield, acting more like a regimental or brigade commander than army general. Personally making reconnaissances, he moved small units into position and led attacks, staying on the front line with his staff, constantly exposed to enemy rifle fire. Late in the morning, beleaguered Union troops under Gen. Benjamin Prentiss had concentrated in a strong position along an old wagon trail near the center of the line. Repeatedly the Confederates charged the position, which they dubbed the "Hornet's Nest," but could not dislodge Prentiss. The whole Confederate attack had stalled because of his stubborn resistance. Johnston took charge, pulling Breckinridge's reserve corps over from the right and throwing them against the Hornet's Nest.

The struggle was fierce. Johnston's fighting blood was aroused—he slapped his thigh and smiled broadly, indicating that a spent minié ball had "stung him." He kicked his left foot up for volunteer aide Isham G. Harris to see. "Governor," Johnston said, "they came very near putting me hors de combat in that charge." Then he pointed to his boot and Harris saw that a bullet had "struck the edge of the sole of his boot, cutting the sole clear across, and ripping it off to the toe." As the fighting progressed, a Federal battery opened up with enfilade fire, and Johnston sent aide-de-camp Lt. Thomas M. Jack to bring up a battery to suppress it. Next he sent Harris off to bring up Col. W. S. Statham's brigade and throw it against the battery as well. Johnston dispatched O'Hara, who had been galloping on various missions throughout the morning, to bring up even more of Breckinridge's men.

Breckinridge's units attacked, mostly in piecemeal fashion, and met with repulse after repulse. Despite every effort by Breckinridge himself, and especially by his aide-de-camp, Capt. Thomas T. Hawkins, three efforts failed. A final assault, however, this time conducted under the watchful Sidney Johnston, broke the enemy line and sent the Federals reeling back in confusion. Hawkins, unfortunately, was wounded in the face; Johnston was hit also.[22]

In the vicinity of the Peach Orchard, Governor Harris, who had just returned from bringing up portions of Breckinridge's division, found Johnston swaying in his saddle. Alarmed, Harris put his arms around Johnston's shoulders and guided him and his mount away to safety in a ravine about a hundred and fifty yards away. By the time O'Hara returned, he found Johnston on the ground with his head in Harris's lap. Harris was attempting to pour brandy down Johnston's throat, all the while searching through the commanding general's uniform for a serious wound. Harris yelled to O'Hara to get help, and O'Hara rode off toward two cabins in the Sarah Bell clearing. There he found Col. William Preston, Johnston's staff officer and former brother-in-law, observing an artillery duel. He told Preston what had happened and guided him and staff officer Maj. Dudley Hayden back to the ravine. Then O'Hara wheeled his horse and rode off to find a surgeon. Johnston, early that morning, had asked his staff surgeon, Kentuckian David W. Yandell, to tend Confederates wounded in the initial attack.

The officers grouped about Johnston were helpless. "Johnston, do you know me?" Colonel Preston asked. But Johnston was unconscious, and the brandy Major Hayden attempted to pour down his throat ran across his chin. Governor Harris looked up and told them Johnston was dead. It was about 2:30 P.M., some fifteen minutes since they had brought Johnston to the ravine. O'Hara returned just after Johnston died.[23]

The staff wrapped Johnston's body in a blanket and took it back to where he had established his headquarters the night before, leaving it there in care of a friend and quartermaster, W. L. Wickham. Capt. Dudley M. Hayden, Johnston's staff officer and old friend, related, "The curious were told that the corpse was the body of a Colonel Jackson of Texas." Then most of the staff reported to General Beauregard for duty. O'Hara sought out Breckinridge instead. All of Breckinridge's staff were gone except his son Cabell, so he welcomed the sight of his old friend O'Hara and put him to work immediately. When darkness finally fell on April 6, it seemed to the Confederates that the Battle of Shiloh had been won, a bloody but overwhelming victory. Monday's fighting should be mop-up work.

Sunday night Beauregard decided to have Johnston's body taken from the field to Corinth, then shipped to New Orleans. He entrusted this duty to Colonel Preston, O'Hara, and five other members of Johnston's staff. The escort left on their mission at 6:00 A.M., April 7, and as they passed through Corinth with Johnston's body, they learned to their distress that Beauregard had broken off the attack. The Confederates were pulling back. They continued on, nevertheless, boarded a train, and soon arrived in New Orleans, where the governor of Louisiana and his staff and Maj. Gen. Mansfield Lovell and his staff joined the cortege. The body was escorted through streets "thronged with citizens" to City Hall, where it lay in state as the public paid its respects. O'Hara and the staff, accompanied by a host of citizens, then took the body to St. Louis Cemetery, where it was laid in the tomb belonging to Mayor Monroe. It would remain there until transported to Texas in 1867.[24]

A week earlier, as the Confederates were uniting their armies in Corinth, Johnston had spoken to Gen. Braxton Bragg about O'Hara. As he had promised in Bowling Green, Johnston wanted O'Hara to have command of a regiment. He asked Bragg to see to it. Sunday night, April 6, as the fighting wore down, O'Hara and Bragg came together on the field, and Bragg told him "that [he] was a *Colonel*." So, when the sad duty of escorting Johnston's body to New Orleans was done, O'Hara returned to the army at Corinth and reported to Bragg for assignment.

There was no regiment. Bragg appeared confused and explained to O'Hara that "General Johnston had spoken to him about my appointment, had mentioned me by the title of Colonel and left him under the impression that he (Genl Johnston) had himself, given me the command of a regiment." But there was no regiment, no command.[25] O'Hara took his case to Beauregard, explaining the circumstances of the mixup in Richmond and the promises Johnston had made to him. Beauregard listened and assured him that he "would avail himself of the first opportunity to give me the position I expected." But weeks passed, and still there was no regiment.

Breckinridge came to O'Hara's aid in the meanwhile and had him appointed adjutant general on his staff, April 28, 1862, to serve until such time as Breckinridge's regular adjutant general, who had already been assigned, would arrive. So throughout May 1862, O'Hara performed the duties of Breckinridge's adjutant general, although he "was not included among Breckinridge's regularly appointed staff." His friend John T. Pickett wrote from Richmond on May 6: "I learn from Col. Preston Johnston that you have not been given a regiment after all. I feared this as you will remember my asking you if your appointment was cocksure. . . ." As for help with the War Department, Pickett was emphatic. It was "wholly out of the question." "How's Hawkins," Pickett inquired. "Major Hayden's rough notes says he was shot in the chin by a grapeshot!"[26]

Matters were not helped by O'Hara's newspaper crony, Samuel C. Reid. Because of his position as correspondent for the *Register* and because of Bragg's close relationship with John Forsyth, Reid had access to Bragg's headquarters and his papers. Some breach of security occurred, and Reid and Bragg had a terrible row. Bragg ordered Reid from his office "as a nuisance, and my Staff officers and the sentinel at the gate directed to keep him out. He afterwards got in with *Jordan* [Beauregard's Chief of Staff] and used Beauregard's office . . . until I exposed him to B. who ordered him out of the lines of the Army. . . . I have tried to keep clear of such dogs by simplying [*sic*] treating them with . . . contempt." Reid misused his position at Beauregard's headquarters by leaking to the *Memphis Commercial Appeal* news of an expected Confederate movement. On May 24 a furious Beauregard ordered not only Reid but also the press corps to "leave the army on the first train and not to remain within 25 miles of Corinth." There is little doubt that O'Hara's friendship with Reid damaged his relationship with Beauregard and served to confirm Bragg's suspicion of complicity.[27]

A disappointed and disgusted O'Hara acted as a temporary staff officer for Breckinridge for a month, then asked to be relieved. He wrote Beauregard: "It is now within a little of two months since I reported to Brig. Gen. Jordan on my return from New Orleans, and I have yet received no assignment to duty & no orders. I have become convinced that my services are not wanted in this army and therefore ask a leave of absence until they may be thought to be of some value."[28]

On June 6 O'Hara was relieved of duty with Beauregard's army, and on the twenty-fourth was ordered to Richmond "to report for duty to Gen. R. E. Lee." O'Hara arrived in Richmond, took a room in a hotel, and waited for his assignment. And waited.[29] On July 30 O'Hara wrote Adjutant General Cooper, documenting the puzzling treatment he had received:

> Thus at the end of *eighteen months* service—for my services
> commenced in January 1861 in the first warlike movement
> at Pensacola—before the Confederacy was organized—at the

end of eighteen months service I find myself in the same position in which I was at the beginning. While promotion has
been lavished with a liberal hand all around me—while
nearly every officer of the Army who started in the same
rank with me is now occupying some high position in the
Provisional Army—nay, while many of inferior rank have
been made Generals and given every chance to win distinction & honors *I* remain still only a Captain of Infantry without a command or position. Furthermore I . . . [have been]
put back from a higher to a lower rank, and that without
any fault on my part.

I think you must admit, General, that I have good reason
to feel humiliated and degraded by this state of things. I
think I may safely refer to my record in this war to prove
that I have not deserved this fate. I am sure I have not been
behind any one in zeal for the cause in which we are strug-
gling.[30]

R. G. H. Kean, chief of the Bureau of War, endorsed O'Hara's lamenta-
tion on August 8, 1862: "The facts respecting the 12th Alabama appear
by the record of this officer to be as Capt. O'Hara recites them in respect
to the transfer of the Col. Jones, and its subsequent revocation. Capt.
O'Hara's appears to be a case . . . though not one at all calculated to 'de-
grade' him. He has been unlucky—without fault on his part in [being]
without a command."[31]

Unlucky, yes. Yet nothing was done to rectify the situation. Whether
General Lee was consulted about a vacancy in the Army of Northern Virginia is not known, but he probably was. His negative reaction may be
surmised. Yet it stretches one's credulity to imagine that Lee or the Confederate War Department, confronting manpower shortages of every description, might not have found a place for an officer with O'Hara's experience.

More weeks dragged by. On September 22, 1862, Adjutant General
Cooper sent O'Hara back to Bragg somewhere in Kentucky. The invasion of Kentucky by Bragg's Army of Tennessee, however, was well under way by this time, and it is doubtful if O'Hara reached Bragg's army
in central Kentucky before the climactic battle at Perryville occurred on
October 8. In any event, there is no record of his having participated. It
was most unfortunate. Nothing would have pleased O'Hara more than
to have been a member of Bragg's army at that time. Perhaps O'Hara
learned of the planned Kentucky invasion in Richmond and asked to return himself. But once again he was too late.[32]

When he did join Bragg's army, probably in Knoxville or Chattanooga as it retreated south from the repulse in Kentucky, O'Hara did not receive a line command, nor any other assignment. Again Breckinridge came to the rescue. He asked that O'Hara be assigned to his staff as assistant adjutant general. So, on October 23, Captain O'Hara was ordered to report to Breckinridge. In some respects, O'Hara could view it as a glorious assignment. He would be working under Breckinridge, whom he revered.[33] Furthermore, Pickett and Hawkins, Stoddard Johnston, and another friend, John A. Buckner, would be fellow staff officers.[34]

Later, Stoddard Johnston would recall O'Hara's distinctive characteristics and his charm: "In his dress he was extremely neat and in all the details of personal appearance he would have attracted attention in any company as a cultivated, intellectual gentleman of the best breeding, but with all those traits there was a certain aspect of reserve born of his military service, beyond which only his intimates could safely venture. He was a fine conversationalist, widely read, classical in his tastes and allusions, with ready wit and repartee, who could compose a song and sing it, write a sonnet or make a pun with the best."[35]

But O'Hara craved command, a chance for military distinction and recognition of his merits. He knew he was a good soldier. All he needed, he believed, was a chance; but for reasons always beyond his grasp, opportunity eluded him.

Chapter 10

Murfreesboro

After the dulling disappointments of the past two years, staff work under Breckinridge in the late fall of 1862 proved a delight for O'Hara. Murfreesboro was a happy place, full of old companions and new hopes for the future. His fellow Kentuckian, John Hunt Morgan, highlighted the Christmas season by marrying the beautiful Mattie Ready in an elegant ceremony with Bishop Leonidas Polk officiating. The Confederacy turned out in splendor to participate and celebrate. Even Braxton Bragg managed a smile.

Then Morgan was off again—raiding; then Forrest, thus removing much of the cavalry screen between Confederate Murfreesboro and Yankee Nashville. Gen. William S. Rosecrans saw his opportunity and marched columns of blue infantry straight for Murfreesboro. The two armies began to deploy December 28–30, 1862, groping for each other on the west side of coiling Stone's River. Breckinridge's division of four brigades, part of Hardee's corps, remained on the east side of the river. They held an extended position with their right flank resting on Lebanon Pike, thus forming the right of the Confederate line which Bragg had established about a mile and a quarter from Murfreesboro. Originally, Hardee's remaining two divisions also had been on the right, but on the night of December 31, they moved across the river to the extreme left, where they massed and prepared to attack.

As the opposing armies came into contact, O'Hara functioned as Breckinridge's chief of staff.[1] Surviving messages from the eve of the battle reveal O'Hara busy coordinating the division's skirmish lines. He had skirmishers (one company from each regiment) deploy in advance of the main line—the first skirmish line two miles out, the second one mile out. O'Hara specified the commander of each section of the skirmish line and their relief, then cautioned these officers "not to fire on our cavalry who may be in advance." He also ordered them (in Breckinridge's name) to cooperate with each other, using the utmost diligence in observing the enemy, harassing him, and to give ground, if they must, slowly and in good order. All the while they should report to division headquarters frequently. He also attached artillery batteries and ordnance trains organic to the division to the four brigades, subject to recall and deployment at division level.[2]

Hardee struck with a fury at dawn, December 31, 1862, rolling up Rosecrans's right flank. Breckinridge's men heard the roar of battle from across the river and could tell the enemy were being driven north across Wilkinson Pike toward the Nashville Pike, the spine of the Union defense. While Hardee enveloped Rosecrans, Polk and his two divisions smashed against Rosecrans's center. Federal resistance was stubborn in the center, however. Fighting became fierce; casualties soared.

As the morning progressed, Breckinridge expected at any moment to be sent to the left to reinforce Hardee's attack. Yet his division, by itself, held the ground east of Stone's River. This knowledge made him nervous. Frequent cavalry reports came into Breckinridge's headquarters that a heavy enemy column was advancing south down the Lebanon Pike to strike him in the flank. Midmorning, Col. William Clare of Bragg's staff arrived, bringing a verbal order, a "suggestion," that Breckinridge advance against the enemy on the Confederate right (Breckinridge's front) rather than await attack. Breckinridge told Clare of the threat down the Lebanon Pike and sent O'Hara to the commanding general with this message: "The enemy are undoubtedly advancing upon me. The Lebanon road is unprotected, and I have no troops to fill out my line to it."[3] Presently Lt. Col. Stoddard Johnston, now of Bragg's staff, arrived, with intelligence seeming to confirm the enemy's advance on the right yet reiterating the order for Breckinridge to attack "in the direction from which the enemy was supposed to be advancing." Breckinridge moved forward with three of his four brigades but did so reluctantly. He sent O'Hara to Bragg again at 11:30 to explain: "General: I am obeying your order, but my left is now engaged with the enemy, and if I advance my whole line farther forward and still retain communication with my left, it will take me clear away from the Lebanon road, and expose my right and that road to a heavy force of the enemy advancing from Black's."[4]

After moving forward half a mile or so, Breckinridge received another order from Bragg. Support Polk's attack in the center with one brigade, two if possible. Breckinridge immediately detached the brigades of Dan Adams and John Jackson (temporarily assigned to Breckinridge's command) and sent them on their way.[5] A while later Johnston delivered yet another order from the commanding general—bring your entire division, except Roger Hanson's brigade, to Polk's assistance.

Then Bragg changed his mind. Breckinridge's 11:30 dispatch, which O'Hara had brought, alarmed him, and he canceled his order to have Adams and Jackson reinforce Polk. Rather, he considered detaching two brigades from Polk to support Breckinridge.[6] O'Hara rode back and forth to Bragg's headquarters carrying these orders and responses. Frequently he found himself with his old friend Stoddard Johnston, who was serving in the same capacity on Bragg's staff. During that long day of December 31, 1862, their paths crossed frequently.[7]

Bragg unfortunately had chosen to hammer away with Polk's Corps at the Union center, the strongest point of the Union line. He had done so, despite repeated messages from his flanking corps commander Hardee, who requested reinforcement so that the successes of the morning flank attack might be exploited, and despite messages from Breckinridge on the other side of the line that the enemy was advancing upon him in strength. The decision to pull two brigades away from Polk and send them to support Breckinridge reveals the commanding general's uncertainty and anxiety, not to speak of deplorable intelligence work. Bragg had lost sight of his purpose.[8]

About 1:00 P.M. O'Hara reported to Bragg with the following dispatch from Breckinridge: "It is not certain that the enemy are advancing upon me in two lines. General Pegram [commanding Confederate cavalry on Breckinridge's right] promised to report the true condition of things. The two brigades you ordered to me might be held at the ford of the river, subject to further developments."[9]

The cavalry reports had been inaccurate all along, so Bragg reversed himself once again and ordered Breckinridge and his division (less Hanson's brigade) to the west side of Stone's River. Bragg was furious at his inability to employ his reserve and blamed Breckinridge for the delay in getting his division (Bragg's reserve) into action. One can only imagine the difficulties involved in battlefield communications at the time. Staff officers and couriers were not always able to make their way across lines of hostile fire; difficult terrain and the lack of roads, even paths, frustrated their best efforts; the messages themselves were often contradictory or misleading; and then there was the inevitable time lag. Sometimes instructions were ignored. And as Army of Tennessee historian Steven Woodworth has suggested, often senior officers such as Hardee and Polk did not understand their roles because their hostility to Bragg, and their lack of confidence in him, resulted in an almost complete breakdown in communications.[10]

As the brigades of Adams and Jackson crossed Stone's River, Polk took charge of them and committed the units piecemeal, throwing them across a

wide cotton field against Rosecrans's troops protected in a stand of cedars
known as the Round Forest. Yankee artillery fire and a timely counterattack
tore Adams's brigade apart. When Jackson charged, he too was thrown
back with heavy loss. Breckinridge appeared at this point, at the head of
Palmer's column. Adams's defeated men came streaming past. O'Hara and
Breckinridge rode among them, shouted at them, pleaded with them, and
finally succeeded in stopping the rout and reforming them.[11]

Now the brigades of William Preston and Joseph B. Palmer, which
Breckinridge had led across the river, began to deploy. Polk ordered them
to attack over the same ground as Adams and Jackson on a two-brigade
front, but the assault was poorly coordinated, conducted in a half-hearted
manner, and repulsed easily, with relatively light loss. Darkness fell and
put an end to Murfreesboro's bloody madness. Quickly the night grew
cold and hundreds of abandoned wounded, blue and gray, suffered terri-
bly. Weary good Samaritans from both armies ventured back to the dark
and dangerous battlefield on anonymous missions of mercy.[12]

Theodore O'Hara had performed well. Most of his day had been consumed in galloping back and forth between Breckinridge and Bragg, acting as an unwitting third party in that flurry of miscommunication and
misinformation. When Breckinridge's division had gone into action,
O'Hara played an important role in restoring order within a smashed brigade. He exposed himself to enemy fire constantly, winning the thanks
of his chief and the admiration of fellow Confederates.[13]

The Confederates believed they had won a grand victory at Murfreesboro. Indeed, they had driven the enemy from a portion of the field and
bent Rosecrans's line back upon itself; they had inflicted a large number
of casualties and captured a significant amount of weapons and equipment. Bragg, in elation, wired Richmond that a "brilliant victory" had
been won. But at dawn on January 1, Rosecrans's army still remained to
their front, glowering and full of fight.[14]

Almost a division of Federal troops came over Stone's River and took
position on the east side, facing Breckinridge's original line. Early on
January 2, Breckinridge learned of the enemy lodgment and rode forward
to the river accompanied by O'Hara, Maj. James Wilson, and his son
Cabell Breckinridge. They came upon corps commanders Polk and
Hardee and together they rode along the river, examining the ground and
discussing the situation. When Polk and Hardee were called away,
Breckinridge and his staff rode on, five hundred yards forward to the skirmish line. They observed Federals occupying high ground about sixteen
hundred yards in front of Roger Hanson's line. This low ridge was a
dominating terrain feature. Breckinridge pushed forward two Kentucky
regiments to drive in the enemy skirmishers and determine the strength

of the enemy on the slope. By means of this probe, Breckinridge learned he confronted about a division of Federals in a strong position running at a right angle to Hanson's line.[15]

To Bragg this development was critical; possession of the ridge on the east side enabled Rosecrans's guns to enfilade Polk's line. Bragg decided to attack. Shortly after noon Bragg summoned Breckinridge to headquarters and told him that his division would assault the ridge and seize it. Breckinridge argued with Bragg. The enemy was strongly posted on higher ground; he would be moving over open ground commanded by Federal artillery. Bragg, however, was determined. He promised Breckinridge two additional batteries and general support from Polk's artillery. The cavalry brigades of John Wharton and John Pegram would operate on Breckinridge's right and protect his exposed flank.[16]

Breckinridge left Bragg's headquarters furious at the commanding general's decision and made little attempt to conceal his anger. He told his friend and fellow Kentuckian, brigade commander William Preston, that he disapproved of the idea. He also had a premonition of death. When he returned to his own headquarters, Breckinridge was stunned again. There stood Brig. Gen. Gideon J. Pillow. Bragg had sent Pillow over from army headquarters and wanted him to lead one of Breckinridge's brigades in the attack. Breckinridge remembered Pillow from Mexican War days and made no secret of his displeasure. Nevertheless, Breckinridge followed orders and assigned to Pillow his Tennessee brigade, which had been commanded temporarily but capably by Col. Joseph B. Palmer. Many of Palmer's troops had been surrendered at Donelson and imprisoned, and they blamed Pillow for their plight. Now their trusted and highly popular commander was to be removed. They were unhappy, understandably. But the transfer had been ordered by Bragg and was carried out dutifully, but grudgingly. Breckinridge set about retrieving Adams's and Preston's brigades from the west side of the river and positioning them for the attack. It had begun drizzling, and the drizzle began to turn into hard, driving rain.[17]

Breckinridge, in accordance with Bragg's orders, formed his men into two lines—two brigades in front, two close behind. O'Hara led Hanson's Kentucky brigade into position on the left front, then raced back and brought up Adams's Louisiana brigade, now commanded by Randall L. Gibson. As instructed, O'Hara placed Gibson's brigade 150 yards back of Hanson's men—an unusually tight interval.[18]

At 4:00 P.M., a cannon shot signaled the advance and Breckinridge's men stepped off smartly. The rain stopped. The sun shone brightly and the massed division, cheering now, seemed unstoppable. From the cover of protective woods they advanced into a great open cornfield.[19] Before they were halfway across, however, enemy shells began to rip into their

Theodore O'Hara, ca.
1860. Courtesy of the
Filson Club Historical
Society.

ranks from over the river and from their right. Then "the quick eye of
Colonel O'Hara discovered a force extending considerably beyond our
right." O'Hara suggested to Breckinridge that he advance a section of
artillery to engage and "develop" the force on the right. Breckinridge
agreed and dispatched Anderson's Georgia battery to the right.[20] They
silenced the stinging fire from that direction. But where were Wharton
and Pegram? Breckinridge, concerned about his right flank and hoping
for Wharton and Pegram to appear, halted the advance momentarily, but
the enemy's artillery fire from the ridge and from high ground across the
river "had become heavy, accurate and destructive," so the division continued forward, their right flank unprotected.[21]

Despite their losses, the division reached the base of the slope and
charged up, driving the defenders off the ridge back to Stone's River.
Flushed with success, Breckinridge's men roared down the ridge in pursuit; the two lines of the front and rear brigades merged, then jammed
together at the river bank. They made perfect targets for the massed Federal artillery with fifty-eight guns roaring. O'Hara "was to be seen cheer-

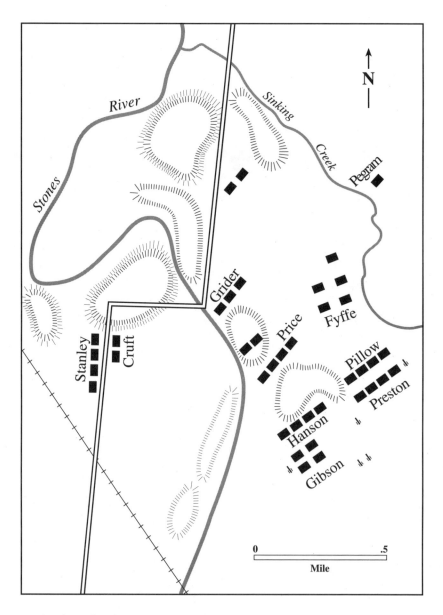

Battle of Murfreesboro, January 2, 1863.

ing and rallying our men," exposing himself to enemy fire recklessly. Breckinridge sent O'Hara racing back across the field to bring up artillery, but he succeeded only in bringing up the division guns. These were grossly insufficient for the task and attracted an enormous volume of fire. Meanwhile, the batteries Bragg had assigned waited in the rear and never came up. Even if their commander Felix Robertson had shown a disposition to support Breckinridge, and had brought his batteries forward to the ridge, it is probable they too would have been sacrificed.[22]

Enemy fire came from every direction. The ridge itself seemed to be exploding. In another alarming development, columns of Federal infantry were seen crossing the river, apparently to mass for a counterattack. Holding the ground which they had won at such a terrible price proved impossible for Breckinridge's men. The division began to waver, retreat, run. O'Hara, Breckinridge, and other officers did their best to halt the rout, but the men could stand no more. They fled back across the field to the shelter of the trees, all the while pounded by relentless Union artillery. The grand assault had failed, disastrously. Breckinridge had led forward forty-five hundred men; he lost thirteen hundred.[23]

When they reached cover from the relentless enemy fire, it was apparent that Breckinridge's men were not only badly disorganized but demoralized. Breckinridge and O'Hara struggled to reform them. As soon as there was a semblance of order, Breckinridge sent O'Hara to Bragg to report the results. Bragg already knew. He dismissed O'Hara, telling him that he had sent Patton Anderson's brigade across to the east side of the river to block the pursuing Federals and buy time for Breckinridge to regroup. Breckinridge must hold.

O'Hara rode back to the Confederate right in the dark. Upon his return he discovered Anderson had just arrived. After positioning this brigade on the left of Breckinridge's division and reporting to his commander, O'Hara went to sleep. Fortunately, the Union troops did not press their advantage.

The next day, January 3, the division remained in position while a disheartened Bragg began pulling other sections of his army out of line. Breckinridge's turn came at midnight. He fell back, taking a temporary defensive position covering the retreat of the rest of Hardee's Corps south through Murfreesboro on the Manchester Road.[24]

Who would bear responsibility for the defeat? The *Augusta Chronicle* and the *Chattanooga Rebel* pointed fingers at Bragg. When the *Charleston Mercury* and the *Richmond Examiner* observed laconically there had been no "exercise of military genius" by the commanding general, Bragg saw the hand of his enemy: correspondent Samuel C. Reid. He also suspected Breckinridge was stirring up trouble. Then Bragg was staggered when the friendly *Mobile Register* published an account of the battle provided by

Reid which had been censored by John Forsyth. The editor of the *Register* called Reid's report "graphic and interesting. . . . However, it has one blemish. The chief actor [Bragg] in the brilliant and bloody scene does not appear. It is the play of Hamlet with the part of Hamlet left out."[25]

Bragg, in a note dripping with self-pity, wrote Breckinridge that he found himself "abused in private and public." This "deluge of abuse . . . will destroy my usefulness and demoralize the army." Then he confided, in a scarcely disguised threat, that "many of the accusations and insinuations" have come from "staff officers of my Generals."[26]

There seems little doubt that Bragg referred to O'Hara, and there is little doubt that O'Hara was in league with Samuel Reid, leaking information to the correspondent and passing along opinions and observations of well-placed general and staff officers. In his letters to Breckinridge in January 1863, O'Hara refers to Hardee and Hardee's staff frequently, quoting them and using their statements and opinions to support his assertions: "Hardee has sent copies of *the correspondence* to the President—he told me so in confidence. I am delighted that he did so. B. B. reminds me of the poetic simile of 'the scorpion begirt by fire.' If he bites himself he is sure to die of his own loathsome venom."[27]

Breckinridge had performed poorly at Murfreesboro, and Bragg, with some correctness, blamed him for the defeat. But Bragg himself had performed badly. Hardee was disgusted with the commanding general; Polk was openly antagonistic to Bragg and still simmered over being made the scapegoat for the botched Kentucky Campaign that fall; the Kentuckians—chiefly Breckinridge, Preston and Buckner—became in effect an anti-Bragg cabal.

Indeed, Breckinridge's headquarters tent in Tullahoma became a center for intrigue. Breckinridge himself went on to Knoxville, leaving Theodore O'Hara, acting chief of staff, in charge. The importance of this appointment seemed to sharpen O'Hara's awareness of the treachery he witnessed, and he faithfully reported to his chief Breckinridge on January 19, "Old Bragg is moving Heaven and Earth to prepare to wage against *you a war to the knife.*" And again on the twenty-third, "B. B. is evidently preparing & marshalling all his resources of shallow cunning and foolish chicanery, energized by a rankling hate, to make war upon you & wreak to the utmost his ignoble spite against you."

As to his work as chief of staff, O'Hara took justifiable pride in the efficiency with which he performed those duties, reporting: "Well every thing is going well in the Division. I am working like a beaver & have got things working evenly like clock-work. I get along very well with Preston. I have convinced him I understand the business & commit no mistakes & he relies upon my skill & intelligence in affairs military & so everything goes."[28]

But his buoyancy was short-lived, and he urged Breckinridge to return

Maj. Gen. John C. Breckinridge, CSA, 1864. National Archives.

quickly: "You have got to prepare yourself to confront him [Bragg] boldly on the issue [Bragg's official report], and to bring to bear against him your superior character, capacity & prestige. It would be better if you could anticipate his onslaught upon you by convincing him of the danger he is incurring—by cowing him—which I think you could do." Underscoring his anxiety not to be misunderstood, O'Hara added, "Do not think it the result of precipitate conclusion, or overzealous suspicion on my part. I *know* what I say—and furthermore if you do not come back here to watch the movements of the enemy & *give back bone to your* Co. (Conspirators, I had like to say) Bragg will gain an important advantage over you . . . 'give you Hell' in his report."[29]

O'Hara was correct. Bragg was gathering evidence about Breckinridge's role in the battle. O'Hara countered by gathering statements from fellow staff officers and forwarded them to Breckinridge. He lined up the brigade commanders involved in the January 2 assault and secured promises of statements supporting Breckinridge. One who refused to go along, Col. Robert P. Trabue (who took command of Hanson's brigade when the latter was mortally wounded), O'Hara denounced: *"Trabue has actually gone to Bragg & clingingly, basely, dirtily backed out from his expression of opinion."* The resulting reports, charges, and countercharges by both sides brought into the open the great dissension that existed within the highest command of the Army of Tennessee. Kentuckian J. Stoddard Johnston, torn between personal loyalty and professional duty, resigned from Bragg's staff because of the latter's animosity toward Breckinridge. Despite Bragg's entreaties to return, Johnston refused and took a position on the staff of fellow Kentuckian Simon B. Buckner. Breckinridge's days with the army were numbered; so were O'Hara's.[30]

Bragg began with Samuel Reid. He decided to arrest him (for publishing a circular Bragg had written to his corps commanders). O'Hara, through his informants in Bragg's headquarters (probably Stoddard Johnston), got word and alerted Reid in time to make his escape on horseback from Tullahoma. After fleeing Bragg and Middle Tennessee, Reid would work in Chattanooga and East Tennessee for a while and later that spring (1863), because of orders from Forsyth to leave the Army of Tennessee and go to Charleston, thus having to curtail his anti-Bragg campaign, Reid would switch from the *Register* to the competing *Mobile Tribune*. And, as if to deliberately bait Bragg, Reid returned to Middle Tennessee. Bragg watched Reid as he would a snake and in June 1863 arrested him and put him in jail in Shelbyville, Tennessee.[31]

Knowing his remaining time with the Army of Tennessee was short, O'Hara once again sought a permanent post, line command preferably. To Gen. Joseph Johnston, who had been in Tullahoma since late January trying to patch up differences between Bragg and his senior commanders, O'Hara offered to raise a Kentucky regiment and Johnston promised him to send him authority to do so, "subject to ratification at Richmond." Johnston left Tullahoma early in February, and nothing was heard by O'Hara until March 7. On that day O'Hara received "authority to raise a Regiment of lancers or Cavalry in Kentucky" and was "hereby relieved from duty with the Army of Tennessee," with permission to leave the department. Nothing seems to have come of this opportunity, however. Instead, O'Hara seems to have pursued another futile campaign of correspondence to gain "reparation for me for a gross wrong and injustice which I had suffered from this administration of ours [revocation of his commission as colonel of the Twelfth Alabama]."[32]

On March 19 Joseph E. Johnston returned to the Army of Tennessee in Tullahoma to take command from Bragg. He never did, of course, but his arrival was a cause of rejoicing. Hardee, a close friend of Johnston's, arranged a review of his corps in his honor. About ten thousand troops participated and citizens came in large numbers to observe. Breckinridge's and Cleburne's divisions had drilled and passed in review, Hardee's corps "introduced the charge of a brigade in line of battle, by regiments, with a shout, at double quick time." Johnston, to Bragg's chagrin, chose to compliment the maneuvers of the Kentucky brigade particularly.

After the review, the troops enjoyed horse racing, and then Breckinridge

had his division formed in a great hollow square with the Twentieth Tennessee regiment in the center. All was quiet as Theodore O'Hara marched
to the front of that regiment. Projecting his voice effectively, he told the
assembled troops that Mrs. Mary C. B. Breckinridge, their commander's
wife, had made a battle flag from her wedding dress. She had asked her
husband to give the banner to his most gallant regiment. After the Twentieth Tennessee of Preston's brigade had been selected, O'Hara made the
presentation for General and Mrs. Breckinridge, explaining the choice of
the Tennesseans:

> The answer I think is too obvious to need expression. . . . In
> view of this record of its heroic service and patriotic devo-
> tion it has been decided . . . to confer upon the Twentieth
> Tennessee Regiment this beautiful banner wrought by the
> fair hands of the most distinguished women of Kentucky. I
> feel that I may safely undertake to declare it is the opinion of
> those ladies that to no more deserving and loyal custody
> could this emblem of our cause be confided, and let me, fel-
> low soldiers, assure you that the men of Kentucky share their
> opinion and endorse their award. They feel also that is to no
> alien hands that this trust is confided. . . . In this confidence,
> I as their representative, commit this banner to your keeping.
> I believe that history has already determined the common
> political fate of Kentucky and Tennessee, and that this
> simple ceremony here to-day is but the symbol of the affilia-
> tion of two millions of people, with the fortune and destiny
> of the Southern Confederacy.

It was a wonderful speech, everyone agreed, expressive of the sentiments
of the Breckinridges and of Kentucky Confederates. Those who were
present would remember O'Hara's eloquence.[33]

Braxton Bragg survived the criticism arising from the failure of the
Kentucky campaign, the defeat at Murfreesboro, and the open lack of
confidence displayed by his senior commanders. By May he was once
again in firm control of the Army of Tennessee, and one of his first acts
was to rid the army of Breckinridge. On the twenty-third, Breckinridge
and his division (pared to three brigades) left the Army of Tennessee for
Mississippi. O'Hara went with them. On the twenty-seventh they passed
through Montgomery, Alabama, by train. There Englishman Col. Arthur
Fremantle observed them. They "all seemed in the highest spirits, cheering and yelling like demons."[34] O'Hara remained at Breckinridge's headquarters, although he held no official position. He appears to have been
present with the division and engaged in the fighting at Jackson, Missis-

sippi, in July 1863. O'Hara apparently served in an informal and incon-
sequential capacity, as he is not mentioned in reports or dispatches covering engagements in Mississippi. Breckinridge explained: "Colonel
O'Hara has not been reporting to me since he was relieved from duty
with the Army of Tennessee in March last by Genl Johnston's orders. He
has been with me for some time past as a guest & volunteer."[35]

On August 28, 1863, Breckinridge and his division left Mississippi and
returned to Bragg's Army of Tennessee, retreating south from Tullahoma.
The battle of Chickamauga following soon after was to prove deadly for
the entire division, especially the Kentuckians, the "Orphans." A story
about Chickamauga persists that, at the height of the fighting, staff officer
O'Hara offered himself in Cabell Breckinridge's place, when the general
determined to send his son on a dangerous mission. Breckinridge, "with
great emotion," decided he must not spare his son and dispatched him
with a message over perilous ground. Cabell succeeded in reaching his
objective and delivering his message, but Cabell's escape from death or
being wounded "seemed miraculous."[36]

Unfortunately, this story, related by a member of the Orphan brigade,
appears to be apocryphal. Stoddard Johnston, who was at Chickamauga,
and who later became Breckinridge's chief of staff, states that O'Hara did
not return to Tennessee with the division in August: "I did not see him
again during the war." O'Hara also does not appear in Breckinridge's
Chickamauga report, and Breckinridge was always careful to credit staff
officers.[37]

Chapter 11

Languishing in Inactivity

It appears that O'Hara left Gen. Joseph E. Johnston's Western Department in early August 1863, about the time Breckinridge and his division departed Mississippi to rejoin Bragg's Army of Tennessee in Chattanooga. Goaded by the continued pattern of unrealized expectations, O'Hara instead went to Columbus, Georgia, where he took lodging in either a local hotel or in the home of kinsman John J. Grant and his wife, Tomzon. In all probability, O'Hara's sister, Mary Helen O'Hara Price, also was living nearby. There in Columbus, O'Hara awaited orders from the War Department—which never came. He continued, however, to receive pay as captain in the Confederate army, a very strange circumstance indeed.[1]

He went to Mobile in December 1863 to consult with his benefactor John Forsyth. How might he get back into the war? Forsyth had an idea, so he wrote the new Alabama governor, Thomas H. Watts, on O'Hara's behalf. Watts intended to organize a home defense force consisting of state regiments, and Forsyth urged Watts to make use of O'Hara. Let O'Hara command them, he recommended. Forsyth, in his argument, recapped O'Hara's service in the old army and his notable performances at Shiloh and Murfreesboro:

> Regularly reporting to the War Department for duty & despairing of the active service he so much desires, I have ventured to suggest to him that you [Watts] might make his military talent & experience useful in the organization of the new State forces called by the President. . . .

> For no fault of his & against his ardent desires, he has
> been languishing in inactivity. It is a pity that abilities &
> courage like his should be wasted at a time when our cause
> & country stand in such need of defenders. He has talents,
> enterprise & daring to fit him for responsible command.[2]

Two weeks later, from his headquarters in Dalton, Georgia, General
Johnston also wrote Watts in support of the appointment of O'Hara "for
high position in the body of troops you are organizing. . . . I have failed
in an attempt to procure for him a high command in the army to which I
belong. Had I the power to make him a brigadier general he would not
now be without a command."[3] John C. Breckinridge followed Johnston's
appeal with even stronger support in mid-February 1864: "At the beginning of the present contest [O'Hara] employed his powerful pen for the
Southern cause and then laid it aside for Sword. He has served with me
in several battles and I know him to be a thorough soldier—cool, very
brave, and with the quickest eye I have seen on the field. In addition to
this, he is a thorough gentleman and a faithful friend. I think him admi-
rably fitted for the command he desires. Please consider that I give him
the strongest endorsement I can express."[4]

O'Hara traveled from Mobile to Montgomery for a series of conferences
with Governor Watts. According to O'Hara, Watts was receptive, indeed
enthusiastic, about Forsyth's idea and armed with the assurances of
Johnston and Breckinridge, gave O'Hara "the absolute promise of the command of the State Troops which he was organizing in the winter of 1864,
but an act of Congress intervened merging that force in the Confederate
Army and thus preventing the Governor from conferring the command."[5]

Thus, despite the golden opportunity Watts offered him and the impressive support mustered, O'Hara had come full circle once again. In the
eyes of the Confederate government he was still a captain of infantry, not
a one-time colonel aspiring to be a brigadier. The War Department continued to refuse to reinstate him as colonel; indeed, they ignored him in a
studied manner. Believing in his heart that he had been wrongfully and
willfully deprived of his commission and thus thwarted in his efforts to
serve his country, O'Hara pointed his finger at Jefferson Davis.

In a fury, he wrote Alabama's most influential political leader, C. C.
Clay, "You must pardon this ebullition of indignation into which I find
myself betrayed, but I cannot think of the outrageous wrong that has
been done me with any patience, and if God lets me live and a life devoted to that sole object may promise a chance of vengeance I'll have satisfaction for it. I shall live to that purpose alone."[6]

O'Hara went further. He enlisted the Kentucky and Alabama congressional delegations, and using Clay as his spokesman, attempted to reopen

the revocation of his commission as colonel of the Twelfth Alabama. The appeal floundered, however. The war situation had deteriorated badly for the Confederacy; there was hardly time to open investigations into past personal injustices. Furthermore, it helped little that Clay had misplaced important documents (a letter from Edward Dorr Tracy about the Benjamin-Jones-Walker mixup) the War Department required. Clay, although blaming himself, procrastinated, postponing his response to O'Hara.[7]

In desperation O'Hara wrote former secretary of war Judah Benjamin, openly and angrily blaming Davis: "Our President will rather persist in an act of injustice, however plainly denounced, than practically acknowledge by repairing it that he has done a wrong act; and that you cannot do more to embitter *& set him* against you than by showing him wherein he has wronged you."[8]

One wonders if the hand of Brig. Gen. Gideon J. Pillow is to be seen in this indiscreet protest of his former staff officer O'Hara against Davis and the injustices Davis perpetrated through the Confederate War Department. They were both embittered Confederate castoffs; their passionate, slashing, partisan letters sound alike; Pillow was close to Watts and had the ear of Joseph Johnson; and Pillow was in Montgomery during the winter of 1863–64, desperately seeking a new command and full of vengefulness. It is reasonable to assume Pillow and O'Hara spent time together.[9]

The resentful, deeply discouraged O'Hara appears to have given up, remaining in Columbus, dutifully reporting his whereabouts to the War Department once a month and requesting assignment. On June 11 the War Department ordered him to report to General Johnston in Atlanta, but nothing appears to have come of this assignment. Perhaps he remained with Johnston and the Army of Tennessee during its battles of the late summer and went with them in their desperate invasion of Tennessee in the fall of 1864. But this is extremely doubtful, for he does not appear in the official documents of the Army of Tennessee nor in the personal correspondence of its higher-ranking officers during this period.

O'Hara was gone from Columbus, however, and did not return until December 1864. As far as Confederate records are concerned, O'Hara vanished from June 1864 until early 1865. There are tantalizing shreds of evidence (undated) connecting him with an attempt to organize a cavalry company, Company F, Fifteenth Confederate Cavalry in Alabama, but these references are flimsy and defy further investigation.[10] Perhaps he could have been with his old friend Thomas T. Hawkins, who had absented himself from Breckinridge's staff and is reported "absent sick" much of 1863–64. In November 1864 Hawkins was at Bladen Springs, Alabama. O'Hara could well have been with him.[11]

O'Hara reappeared in Columbus in January 1865. As he reported in a letter to his friend Mrs. Dick Wintersmith, he had returned "some fortnights ago." O'Hara always seemed to enjoy Columbus, especially so during these hopeless days. Good society always seemed to revive his spirits, and he found himself in the winter of 1864–65 in the company of "fine ladies" and a "great many nice people" who had fled to Columbus as refugees. "I have been having a very gay time since I came—parties, &c."[12]

He owed money to Dick Wintersmith, and that obligation embarrassed and troubled him; and he grieved for the plight of the Confederate revolution. He would be going to Richmond in a few days "to report for duty . . . and probably have a fuss with Jeff Davis . . . before I get away." He regretted having to leave Columbus, "but the condition of our cause which is in 'a weaving way' just *now* requires that every man should rush to the rescue, else ruin will engulf it ere long. I am afraid, as it is, that Jeff Davis, Bragg & co have carried us so far on the road to the Devil that nothing can reclaim us from ruin." It is clear that he separated his loyalty to "the cause" from his contempt for some of its leaders, especially Davis. He confided, however, that he had "laid an anchor to windward," making arrangements with fellow Confederates to flee to Sonora, Mexico.[13]

An unforeseen opportunity awaited in Richmond. About a week after O'Hara wrote Mrs. Wintersmith, and as he prepared to leave Columbus, Jefferson Davis summoned John C. Breckinridge to Richmond and offered him the post of secretary of war. Breckinridge accepted the cabinet position and took office February 7. By then O'Hara was already in Richmond and had reported by letter to the adjutant general. That day, in all probability, he went to call on his old friend to congratulate him. When they met, it is reasonable to assume that Breckinridge counseled his protégé that he could reopen the appeal for reinstatement as colonel, and perhaps make a case for himself to be promoted to brigadier. In the meantime Breckinridge had Adjutant General Cooper on February 18 prepare orders for O'Hara to report to Beauregard, who was gathering troops to resist Sherman's advance northward through the Carolinas.[14]

So O'Hara set to work. He prepared a "Memorandum for Information of the Secretary of War," outlining his discussions with Governor Watts about becoming commander of the Alabama forces and mentioning that "there are several Alabama brigades, in the Army of Virginia, and in Beauregard's Army, now commanded by Colonels, the brigades either being without Generals, or their brigadiers commanding vacant divisions."[15]

O'Hara also prepared a lengthy review of his Confederate service in a letter to Breckinridge on February 20, carefully documenting the Twelfth Alabama debacle, and ended it with this bitter lament, emphasizing his sullied honor and the need for redress:

Although I can defy any one to point to an act of mine since

this war began that should bring down punishment or degra-
dation upon me, I remain now, what I was at the commence-
ment of the war—a *Captain of Infantry* in the C. S. Army! I
came out of the Mexican War, sixteen years ago a Brevet
Major . . . I have seen almost every man who was my junior
in rank and age in the service at the beginning of the war go
up and forward and leave me out of sight in the career of
professional advancement. I cannot regard all this otherwise
than as a reflection upon my character and indeed as an absolute disgrace. I have borne the deep and poignant humilia-
tion in patience and silence as long as I can. I have resolved
to make a last appeal to the justice and magnanimity of my
government for redress. Such is the intent of this communication, and I respectfully await to learn whether or not I am
to continue to suffer the mortifying & degrading ostracism I
have endured for four years from all the chances of honorable distinction in this war.[16]

O'Hara's friends, Humphrey Marshall and James W. Moore, and other
members of the Kentucky and Alabama congressional delegations supported his application for appointment to brigadier.[17] It was too late,
however. The Confederacy was collapsing.

When the end came, O'Hara was with Breckinridge.[18] The secretary
of war was a hunted man and, following the surrender of Johnston's
army near Durham, North Carolina, fled south. On May 6, about seven
miles outside Washington, Georgia, Breckinridge dismissed his escort,
which included about fifty Kentucky volunteers. One of the young Kentuckians present recorded the event. Breckinridge

shook hands with the few soldiers around him and rode into
the Georgia forest to make good his escape to the coast and to
Cuba.[19] Of those Major O'Hara was the last to bid us farewell,
and we sat on our horses for a few moments after the others
had ridden off. It was perfect day; the full apple orchard just
over the fence from the road was in full bloom; in the yard
near by were hundreds of roses, the scene was a pastoral, fruit-
ful, peaceful scene. . . . We recall being amused with the antics
of a dog that a private soldier was worrying. . . .

O'Hara held our hand in his and said, "Perhaps in prison
or in Kentucky the next time—but if not we staid to the
end." He was a gifted man—a true genius; he was an elegant
scholar; but above all he was a heroic spirit; neither defeat—
and this was often his fate—nor failure—and this he suffered

often, nor poverty—and this he felt—could bend or daunt
his lofty and resolute soul. He was a chivalric knightly
gentleman and at King Arthur's Round Table would have sat
among equals.[20]

A lofty tribute, indeed, but the cause, like Arthur's, had been lost.

It is not known how far O'Hara accompanied Breckinridge on his escape through southern Georgia into Florida. Probably he parted from his chief in Sanderson, Georgia, at the time young Clifton Breckinridge and Capt. James B. Clay, Jr., left. Certainly O'Hara was not with Breckinridge beyond Madison, Florida.[21]

As Breckinridge made his way down the Florida coast in a small boat, O'Hara returned to Columbus, Georgia. After securing his parole, he may have attempted to teach, perhaps for a few months, perhaps a year. In the winter of 1865 or early 1866, it seems, he decided to join his relative, Capt. John J. Grant, in the cotton commission-warehousing business. While in Columbus, O'Hara led "a steady and faithful Catholic life," attending mass at Sts. Philip and James Churches regularly. As always he continued to be "much sought after socially, as he had the charm of manner and pleasing personality which made him a welcome guest."[22]

Fate continued to torment him, however. Fire destroyed the cotton warehouse, and O'Hara appears to have given up in despair.[23] He abandoned the cotton business and Columbus itself, retiring forty miles southwest to a plantation probably owned by the Grants near Guerryton, in Barbour County, Alabama. There he remained, passing his time reading and visiting neighbors. It is doubtful that he wrote poetry or attempted any historical articles or memoirs. A family story persists about his marksmanship, however. Still a crack shot at the age of forty-seven, he would take his rifle out on the back porch of the house and carefully fire at some "recalcitrant goats."[24] Always the goats.

For pleasure he would borrow a horse from his friend Dr. Hamilton M. Weedon of Eufaula and ride about the countryside. He and Weedon often would sit and talk into the night. He was fortunate to have had Weedon with him during these last days. The young cosmopolitan doctor was a Floridian who had received his medical training in New York and practiced there. During the war he had become brigade surgeon for Gen. William Preston and later division surgeon for Breckinridge. He and O'Hara shared many memories and friends. Another man who did much to make O'Hara feel at home in Guerryton was forty-year-old Col. Hiram Hawkins of the Fifth Kentucky, a fellow Catholic and an original member of the Orphan Brigade who had served faithfully through the hardest fighting of the war. Close by also lived Shanks Evans, whose frequent intoxication had ruined his promising career as a Confederate general officer. Following the war Evans settled in Midway, Alabama, close to Guerryton, and there assumed the role of high school principal. Doubtless he frequently found himself in the company of his old friend from Company F.[25]

O'Hara was seriously ill by the late spring of 1867. Most accounts state that he suffered from "bilious fever," a generic nineteenth-century term for a condition that could have been typhoid, or, more likely, cirrhosis of the liver.[26] Other accounts attribute his death to tuberculosis. If he had contracted tuberculosis, however, there should have been references to the disease earlier in his correspondence, or by his family or contemporaries.[27]

O'Hara's condition worsened in the late spring of 1867, and he died at the Grant plantation near Guerryton on Friday afternoon, June 7, 1867, after receiving the holy sacrament "from the hands of a pious clergyman." His body was taken to Columbus and buried in Linwood Cemetery.[28]

Late that summer, when Gen. William Preston learned of O'Hara's death, he wrote John C. Breckinridge, "Poor O'Hara is dead, as you doubtless have heard."[29] The Commonwealth of Kentucky was saddened also, for O'Hara was known widely and beloved in many circles. The State Cemetery in Frankfort, which represented for Kentuckians the glories and passions of their past, seemed incomplete without their Irish bard.

In a gesture of reconciliation, O'Hara's friends appealed to the Kentucky legislature in 1874 to have his body returned and buried in the State Cemetery. At the same time they wished to have reinterred the bodies of O'Hara's friend, Union general Cary H. Fry, major of the Second Kentucky Infantry in the Mexican War, and Adjutant George F. Caldwell, another Kentucky veteran of the Mexican War.[30]

The public received the idea enthusiastically. Why not honor this Confederate? Had not the city of Boston, in 1867, paid "The Bivouac of the Dead" the "singular compliment" of inscribing its lines upon a monument to the Union dead?[31] Upon hearing of the plan, Confederate captain J. S. Van de Graaf was prompted to write:

Bring Back the Hero's Dust
Son of the "dark and bloody ground"
    Thou must not slumber there;
Tho' sister states thy praises sound
    Along the southern air.
Kentucky's soil should be thy grave—
    Thy native soil thy tomb. . . .[32]

Stoddard Johnston, who had returned home from the war to become editor of O'Hara's old paper, the *Frankfort Yeoman*,[33] drafted a resolution for the Kentucky legislature and had O'Hara's friend, Unionist Harry

Innis Todd, introduce it: "And as their mother Kentucky claims the ashes of her brave, it is due these sons who have added such lustre to her name that their ashes should be brought to that Mother's bosom and laid beside their compatriots, McKee, Marshall, Clay, Willis, Vaughan and the host of heroes whose monument already marks the spot where they should rest."[34]

Todd's motion was approved as a joint resolution on April 24, 1873. The enabling bill was passed on February 2, 1874, and signed by Governor Preston H. Leslie on the twelfth.[35] Leslie commissioned Stoddard Johnston to make the necessary arrangements for the reinterment and designated another old friend of O'Hara's, Gen. Thomas Hart Taylor, of the First Kentucky, to bring the remains from Georgia.[36]

On the morning of July 3, 1874, Taylor had the grave opened in Linwood Cemetery, Columbus, Georgia. O'Hara's remains were removed from their wooden coffin and placed in a new metallic burial case and taken to the railroad express office. There, that afternoon, the Columbus Guards and the City Light Guard combined into a battalion-sized escort of honor. The metal casket was placed upon an express wagon, appropriately draped, and the procession marched slowly to the depot. As a dirge the guards' band playing the death march from Handel's opera "Saul." The body was placed aboard the express car of a Southern Railroad train and the journey north began. At train stop after stop, in Georgia, Tennessee, and Kentucky, there would be speeches by local officials and sometimes music, as tributes were paid to O'Hara en route. Once the body arrived in Frankfort, it was taken to the State Cemetery and deposited in the state vault.[37]

Early on September 15, 1874, several thousand people began to gather near the state house in Frankfort. Businesses closed as time came for the procession to form. General Taylor, as marshal, ordered the groups. First, the hearses; second, about thirty Mexican War veterans carrying faded and frayed Mexican War banners of three Kentucky regiments; then the families, including O'Hara's sisters, Mrs. Susanna Hardie and Mary Helen Price, and his brothers, James P. and Charles; then friends and citizens. The procession wound up the hill through the State Cemetery to the Mexican War monument. The "very sky above seemed to mourn with the relatives . . . dark clouds gathered and hovered." Low thunder could be heard "mingled with the sad roll of muffled drum." The three bodies were buried, O'Hara's being the last. As his remains were lowered in the ground, a detachment of the State Guard fired "farewell volleys of musketry." Then the grave was heaped with beautiful flowers. O'Hara was buried just to the east of the great military monument, between it and the grave of Vice President Richard M. Johnson. O'Hara's grave would be marked with a rectangular marble slab displaying a wreath and crossed swords, identical to those of the other Mexican War heroes, and engraved simply

THEODORE O'HARA
Major and A. D. C.
Died June 6, 1867

Later the Kentucky Historical Society would erect at his grave a memorial of Italian marble, on which is engraved "in bas-relief an exquisite harp."[38] The harp, if one looks closely, has a broken string, symbolic of the now silent singer.

Stoddard Johnston had had a pavilion constructed for the occasion, decorated with cedar and vines. After the soldiers' remains had been buried the crowd gathered there. Hardly had the speakers taken their seats on the platform, however, before "a terrible rain fell and compelled the audience to leave the cemetery." That evening many reassembled in a building in Frankfort, and there the funeral orations were delivered. O'Hara's eulogy was given by Gen. William Preston, and followed by a reading of "Bivouac of the Dead." Despite the objections of Mary Helen O'Hara Price, Governor Leslie had chosen poet, lawyer, and newspaper editor Henry T. Stanton to read the poem.[39] Actually, Leslie's choice of Stanton seems to have been inspired. He had been a passionate Confederate writer in prewar days who turned soldier, serving on Breckinridge's staff with O'Hara, and one who had remained with Gen. Joseph Johnston until the end at Durham Station.

Stanton solemnly introduced O'Hara's masterpiece with the remark that "the heart of the poet burst with the heroism of the soldier, and in giving utterance to his song, he became at once the builder of his own monument and the author of his own epitaph."[40]

Chapter 12

The Public Poet, the Private Man

It is deeply ironic that Union quartermaster general Montgomery C. Meigs selected "The Bivouac of the Dead" as the poem to grace the cemeteries honoring the Union dead even as Theodore O'Hara was fighting for the cause of the Confederacy. We may be sure that O'Hara himself never knew of this selection—and thus his own oblique path to glory. It seems certain as well that none of the O'Hara clan had ever been informed about this curious translation of Theodore's work until sometime after the plaques appeared in those federal cemeteries during the mid-1880s, when questions began to be directed to officials about the identity of the anonymous author whose name was not acknowledged on the plaques.[1]

Two major lines of inquiry, one by George Ranck, Kentucky historian and editor, the other by Major Edgar Hume, a highly decorated U.S. Army medical officer, both resulted in modest but enlightening studies of the life of Theodore O'Hara. Both of these pioneering biographers, in providing some pieces of information, transmitted errors and gross misinterpretations which found their way into subsequent newspaper and journal articles. A large proportion of those items about O'Hara, his days and his works, seem to have been cut from the same cloth—and doubtless were.

The American tradition of visiting military cemeteries, especially on official holidays, would have periodically renewed those six quatrains of the elegy in the public mind; and curiosity about the author would from time to time beget another biographical sketch. The O'Hara files at the Kentucky Historical Society in Frankfort contain a variety of letters seeking

information about the poet and his family background. The information
the society could provide, however, was minimal; but a certain pattern
of information about his life, however erroneous, did emerge.

It would seem, then, that a substantial measure of fame had finally and
irrevocably rested on a man for whom temporal success had been so elusive. Yet, sad to state, even the relatively modest niche he once held has
eroded. In at least two of those national cemeteries, the plaques with
O'Hara's poetry have been removed and have by official accounts "disappeared." In Arlington, some visitors from Kentucky in the early 1930s
noted that those stirring lines, once so prominently placed, seemed to
have vanished. Where were they? The answer was simple: The National
Commission of Fine Arts, involved in refashioning the grounds, decided
that aesthetically the plaques were "not in harmony with the character
of the cemeteries and detracted from rather than enhanced their beauty
and appearance" and recommended to have them removed[2]—as if the
jurisdiction were that of the commission and not the War Department,
and specifically the quartermaster general and his superior, the secretary
of war.

The indignant outcry at this news, especially in Kentucky, resulted in
a series of negotiations between the commission, the American Legion,
and the congressman from the Frankfort district, the Honorable Virgil
M. Chapman.[3] On January 3, 1935, Chapman introduced in the House
of Representatives H.J. 20, a joint resolution which was referred to the
Committee on Military Affairs, to wit:

> To provide for the erection of a tablet in the Arlington
> Memorial Amphitheater.
>   *Resolved by the Senate and House of Representatives of
> the United States of America in Congress assembled,* That
> the Secretary of War is authorized and directed to place
> upon the wall of the Memorial Amphitheater building in
> Arlington National Cemetery the following stanzas of the
> poem by Theodore O'Hara entitled "Bivouac of the Dead":
> [This statement was followed by the entire revised version of
> the elegy.][4]

It therefore appeared that the presence of the poem in Arlington would
soon take on a newer, more aesthetically pleasing form, at the focal point
of the cemetery, adjacent to the Tomb of the Unknown Soldier.

On February 12 of that same year an Associated Press release in the
New York Times stated that Representative Chapman announced that "a
compromise was effected whereby the complete poem would be placed
on the amphitheater walls. Efforts to have the tablets replaced . . . will

be dropped."[5] This time, also, it seemed certain that the poet's name would appear with his lines; but such was not to be. It appeared that the misfortunes which beset the poet followed him beyond the grave. For reasons now unknown, plans for this project were never completed—if indeed they were ever ordered. A recent search for the old plaques at Arlington ended in vain, with no information whatever among the attendants about whether the compromise project ever got off the planning table.

A letter to the Commission of Fine Arts yielded this response from the secretary: "I am afraid we have little light to shed on the matter. When the plaques were removed by the National Park Service in 1934, the Commission of Fine Arts was asked to consider other suitable locations where they might be reinstalled. They suggested the Trophy Room at the Memorial Amphitheater, but this was never done, and there is nothing in our files to indicate the ultimate fate of the plaques. . . . If they were indeed placed throughout Arlington Cemetery, the fact remains they are not there now. . . . So the matter would appear to remain a mystery."[6]

A mystery indeed—how approximately eighteen or twenty metal plaques measuring one foot six inches by three feet would have vanished, even in a place as large as Arlington and with as disciplined a staff as one would find anywhere. And there were no answers forthcoming about why this federal agency took the arbitrary action of choosing not to follow its commitment, especially after the public announcement, which later appeared in Kentucky newspapers, as well as the *New York Times,* that the poem would be given a permanent place of honor.[7] This letter from the secretary addresses the issue of the vanished plaques, but it ignores the question of the marble tablets that never materialized. A subsequent letter from the commission indicated that "literally hundred of House Resolutions that get introduced in each session of Congress . . . go nowhere and are never heard of again."[8] Doubtless true, but we must find it surprising that one so clearly publicized could get lost—and that no Kentucky congressman or other official monitored the progress of the endeavor—or subsequently took up the issue.

A similar disappearance occurred at the large Chattanooga National Military Cemetery. In 1962 a prominent local educator noted that the "Bivouac" plaques—seven of them—had been removed from that location; and along with many other citizens he called for their restoration, not for official but for sentimental reasons. The official public explanation, reported in the *Chattanooga Times,* was that extensive work and expansion in the cemetery had resulted in taking the tablets down, because of the added work in keeping them in satisfactory condition.[9] The plaques were repaired and later restored, and the furor died away. Some

time after—no one in authority can now say when—they were again removed and are presumed irrevocably lost. Again, it is unusual that such
heavy and one would presume cumbersome slabs of metal could have
been misplaced, especially given their appeal to the general public and
their historical importance.[10]

"The Bivouac of the Dead" itself remained current for a time. In the

McClellan Gate, Arlington Cemetery, with "Bivouac of the Dead"
inscription. T. C. Ware Collection.

latter part of the nineteenth century the poem was included in a well-known collection, Bryant's *Library of Poetry and Song.* It appeared both in the *Little Classic* series, edited by Rossiter Johnson, and in the Harper's collection *Our Children's Songs,* as well as in a number of other anthologies. George Ranck's hardbound edition of the work, in 1898, made it available in its fully revised form to turn-of-the-century audiences. The poem appeared regularly in newspapers, yet no evidence exists of any royalties ever being paid.

The reception of the poem may be further traced through Edith Granger's reference work, *An Index to Poetry and Recitations,* published at intervals since the early decades of this century. The 1920 edition of this index listed twenty-five anthologies and collections which included the work, nineteen of these in its full length. In 1940 there were still twenty-five total listings; in 1953 and again in 1963, twenty-four. By 1973, however, the number had fallen to sixteen; and in the seventh edition, which included anthologies from 1970 to 1981, there were no listings at all, although this omission may have been inadvertent.[11]

As a declamatory utterance, stressing "Glory," "Honor," "Nation," and "Valor," the "Bivouac" is clearly not the kind of sentiment which would have been popular during the Vietnam War era. As a poem it is not likely these days to be read in literature classes at the college level, but as part of the legacy of American history, it can and should endure—along with the story of the man who wrote it.

And what of the man who wrote it, the private man, whose life, so filled with promise, ended early, and with so little material achievement. Did Theodore O'Hara live behind a mask, after all? His contemporaries saw the romance, the idealism, the dash of the man, the delicate, refined, and modest poet-revolutionary afire with the love of humanity and the willingness to sacrifice himself for others—for "the Cause," for honor, for ideals, for whatever he regarded as just or noble. They saw the soldier, sitting upright in his saddle, fist hard against his hip in studied gesture, utterly defiant, indifferent to the missiles of death. They saw, perhaps, the genial guest, sitting to the right of his hostess, gay and attentive, listening with great courtesy, then complying with the wishes of the company and telling a story of his own, an enchanting tale, bringing to the dinner table elements of the past, dressed in unfaded colors. They heard and read the poet, the orator, the editor, one who reached into their shared trunk of language, shaking words and phrases free of dust, reordering them with grace and vitality like a magician.

But much of this was indeed witchery, of sorts. Another Theodore O'Hara lived often through the dark night of the soul and into the early hours the morning, unable to sleep, unable to free himself from whatever demons that sought to divert and humiliate him, demons determined to break to pieces commitments he wished with all his heart to honor. When the pace of life slowed, he grew uneasy, despondent, and distressed. The only way he could silence his inner torment, it seems, was to drive them into the corners of his mind with whiskey. Not wine, nor rum: those would have been unmanly, unpatriotic, un-Democratic.

Why finally did Theodore O'Hara make a ruin of his life? Perhaps he was not the responsible party. Perhaps he was a latent alcoholic all along, cursed with a disorder over which he would never gain control, fashioned that way by a father who let the curse fall on him at the age of four, allowing a glass of whiskey to be placed in his hand, and lifting him high on a table, like a household pet, to bring laughter to cousins and strangers in an Irish public house. Was O'Hara then an alcohol abuser from childhood? Perhaps. One may clearly see the instability and the inconstancy of his ambitions, of his careers, from the earliest documented moments: teaching, the law, poetry, soldiering, journalism, juxtaposed in time like jars of candy with a child's hand dipping into one, then the other. Never owning a home, moving frequently from town to town, he wandered as though there were some geographic alexin he sought. One may note the implications within the words of those who knew him— the understated concerns of his friends, the overstated compliments, embellishments, and apologies of his admirers, his defenders, his family.

He was not a solitary drinker, it appears, at least if he could escape that burden. It is difficult to picture Theodore O'Hara alone and brooding, except in the State Cemetery—or while writing poetry. We see him in the company of others, a convivial drinker, with a Shanks Evans or a John C. Breckinridge by his side, and then the last to leave the party, the last customer to leave the saloon. Occasionally, like Ulysses S. Grant, O'Hara would disappear for a time, and be thought to be on an extended binge.

The history of authorship in the United States is heavily weighted with accounts of those whose careers were seriously and permanently impaired because of addiction to alcohol. One is reminded of Jack London, who began drinking at the age of five; of Stephen Crane, who horrified onlookers as he sought death on the battlefield in Cuba; or of the "positively reckless" Sinclair Lewis or the impeccably dressed Theodore Dreiser. But the author whose background most resembles O'Hara is Eugene O'Neill: Irish, Roman Catholic, with an illustrious father the son seemed unable to satisfy or surpass. And this Oedipal struggle was made more turbulent by O'Neill's frequent descents into alcoholic morass.

Did O'Hara feel chronically anxious about his lack of achievement? Hardly, it would seem, although one might argue that his treatment at the hands of the authorities in Richmond destroyed his self-possession. Did a lack of official recognition and loneliness eat away his confidence, his sense of purpose? It seems unlikely. Testimony of too many contemporaries contradicts this notion. Did his religious faith fail him? This speculation seems faulty as well. His Roman Catholic beliefs and practices, as far as one may tell through the darkened glass of a century and a

Theodore O'Hara's grave. T. C. Ware Collection.

half, seem to have been integral to his life and very important at his death. Did he measure himself constantly against the Homeric image of his father Kean, the teacher before whom presidents bowed, an intellect supreme, a man who turned primitive forests into gold? Was Theodore taught inadequacy, fastened with corroding guilt, from the time he was a toddler? Perhaps, though we are assured that he was his father's favorite pupil.

The Furies denied O'Hara the scenario that would have been most apt: throwing his body in front of the bullet at Shiloh intended for General Sidney Johnston. Few, however, are granted lives and deaths of tragic grandeur. O'Hara died quietly and in a place remote from the major chapters of his adventures. But now he lies in Frankfort near the grave of Daniel Boone and among those he celebrated in verse. And though it took some time for his fellow Kentuckians to grace his tomb in an appropriate fashion, the lines carved on his stone are sixteen of those he himself wrote.

> The muffled drum's sad roll has beat
> The soldier's last tattoo;
> No more on life's parade shall meet
> That brave and fallen few.
> On Fame's eternal camping-ground
> Their silent tents are spread,
> And Glory guards with solemn round
> The bivouac of the dead.
>
> Rest on, embalmed and sainted dead!
> Dear as the blood ye gave!
> No impious footstep here shall tread
> The herbage of your grave;
> Nor shall your glory be forgot
> While Fame her record keeps,
> Or Honor points the hallowed spot
> Where Valor proudly sleeps.

Nothing could be more fitting.

Appendix: And After

Bragg, Braxton, would end the war creating confusion at Bentonville, then become chief engineer of Alabama after the war and fall dead on the street while enjoying a stroll with a friend.

Breckinridge, John Cabell, would wander abroad for four years following the war, then return to Kentucky in 1869, where he would maintain a low profile for the rest of his life, although regarded as "perhaps the most popular man in the state."

Cooper, Samuel, the highest ranking Confederate general officer throughout most of the war, would surrender the War Department archives when resistance became hopeless and live quietly at his home near Alexandria, Virginia, until his death in 1876.

Crittenden, John Jordan, would work hard to prevent war between the North and South but yield finally to his Unionist impulses, returning to the U.S. Senate and serving there until his death in 1863.

Evans, Nathan George ("Shanks"), would win the thanks of the Confederate Congress and a gold medal for his performance at Balls Bluff in 1861. As a brigade commander he would serve with mixed results until excessive drinking resulted in formal charges brought against him and loss of command. He would end his life as O'Hara's neighbor, dying soon after his friend.

FORSYTH, JOHN, would continue as a powerful voice in southern Alabama, serving as mayor of Mobile and continuing to edit the *Register*, using its columns to oppose vigorously Reconstruction legislation.

HARDEE, WILLIAM JOSEPH, would rise to lieutenant general and beloved corps commander but end his life in the unfamiliar pursuits of farming and railroad management.

HAWKINS, THOMAS THEODORE, would spend the balance of his life as an invalid as the result of war wounds. He would die in 1879 and be buried in the State Cemetery close beside his faithful friend Theodore O'Hara.

JOHNSTON, JOSIAH STODDARD, would return to the *Kentucky Yeoman* after the war and edit it for years. He also would serve as adjutant general and secretary of state of Kentucky, 1875–79. From 1903 to 1908 he would be associate editor of the *Courier-Journal* of Louisville. Before his death in 1913, he would have completed a number of articles and books about the history of Kentucky and its leading citizens.

JONES, ROBERT TIGNALL, would lead the ill-fated Twelfth Alabama into action at Fair Oaks, Virginia, on May 31, 1862, and be killed at the head of his regiment.

LEWIS, ARMSTRONG IRVINE, would die of fever in Mobile within a year after the *Pampero* debacle.

NOBLE, JOHN C., would join the staff of fellow Kentuckian Abraham Buford as a quartermaster. Following the war, "ardent Democrat" Noble would edit the *Paducah Herald*.

O'SULLIVAN, JOHN, fiery editor for the Democracy, would win Pierce's favor and become minister resident in Portugal. A Southern sympathizer, he would live in Lisbon, London, and Paris until 1871, then die in obscurity in New York City in 1895.

OWSLEY, WILLIAM, would tire of public affairs and the law and retire to his farm near Danville, Kentucky, where he would die in 1862.

PICKETT, JOHN THOMAS, would return to Mexico in 1865–66 and serve as Santa Anna's chief of staff. Following the latter's arrest, Pickett would attempt to resurrect the dreams of his father, involving himself with the Louisiana Tehuantepec Company. After its failure he would settle in

Washington, D.C., and practice law until his death in 1884. His life would be rendered more comfortable by selling the correspondence of the Confederate State Department to the Library of Congress for seventy-five thousand dollars.

PILLOW, GIDEON JOHNSON, would return to farming and the practice of law after the war, but fall prey to Pennsylvania predators, who hounded him for his Civil War misdeeds and eventually bankrupted him.

POPE, HENRY CLAY, would not long enjoy the sweets of civilian life. An angry combatant killed him in a duel June 13, 1849.

PRESTON, WILLIAM, would fight on with Breckinridge, rise to the rank of brigadier general, be appointed Confederate minister to Mexico in 1864, and flee abroad in 1865. Soon he would return and resume his law practice in Lexington and prosper. As a delegate to the 1880 National Democratic Convention, he would nominate for president Union general Winfield S. Hancock.

QUITMAN, JOHN ANTHONY, would be elected easily to Congress in 1854 and again in 1856, but he would become ill suddenly in 1858 and die at his "Monmouth Plantation" near Natchez.

REID, SAMUEL CHESTER, JR., would continue to move about the South looking for action and tirelessly reporting the war for several newspapers. His accounts of John Hunt Morgan would be published after the war and become a significant source for the study of Morgan's last campaign. He would die in 1897, soon after the republication of his book about *General Armstrong*.

SANDERS, GEORGE NICHOLAS, would serve the Confederacy faithfully and colorfully in Europe and Canada, and for his efforts have a twenty-five-thousand-dollar bounty placed on his head. He would remain a revolutionary to the day he died, encouraging political radicals throughout Europe.

STAPP, WALTER W., O'Hara's partner at the *Times*, would be rewarded by Buchanan and become consul in Pernambuco (northeastern Brazil).

TAYLOR, MARION C., the reliable chronicler of the Cárdenas expedition, would become colonel of the Fifteenth Kentucky Volunteers, U.S.A., and fight against his old commander O'Hara.

TAYLOR, THOMAS HART, the Kentucky commander of the post at Mobile late in the war, would go into business there after the war but leave in 1870 and return to Kentucky, becoming chief of police in Louisville.

TITUS, HENRY THEODORE, inveterate revolutionary and troublemaker, would become a blockade runner during the Civil War and afterward settle in isolated Sand Point, Florida, which he would transform by industry and imaginative marketing into Titusville, "one of the finest combinations of saloons and hotels on the east coast of Florida." At the close of the twentieth century it stands as "the gateway to the John F. Kennedy Space Center." (Ianthe Bond Hebel, "Colonel H. T. Titus, Founder of Titusville, Florida, 1865," Florida State Univ. Archives; Antonio R. de la Cova, "Ambrosio José Gonzales: A Cuban Confederate Colonel" [Ph.D. diss., West Virginia Univ., 1994]).

TRACY, EDWARD DORR, O'Hara's friend in Huntsville who enjoyed the confidence of Leroy Pope Walker, would rise to brigadier general rapidly but would be killed at Port Gibson on May 1, 1863, before he could testify to the justice of O'Hara's claim about being wrongfully deprived of appointment as colonel of the Twelfth Alabama.

VAN DORN, EARL, would rise quickly to Confederate major general and win important victories, but misfortune stalked him. He would be murdered in 1863.

WATTS, THOMAS HILL, would see his personal property destroyed or confiscated in the closing days of the war and find himself imprisoned in 1865. With great resilience, however, he would resume the practice of law after the war and die a prosperous and influential man in 1892.

WEEDON, HAMILTON M., would give up the practice of medicine, enter the drug business with a brother-in-law, and live prosperously and happily in Eufaula thereafter.

WHEAT, CHATHAM ROBERDEAU, would fight with Garibaldi in 1860 and return home and organize "Wheat's Tigers" in New Orleans. Fighting in the Army of Northern Virginia, he and his command would become legendary, but he would be wounded fatally at Gaines' Mill in 1862.

WINTERSMITH, RICHARD CURD, would return to Kentucky after the war, enjoy his reputation as raconteur and wit, and eventually be appointed consul to Colon, Panama, by President Grover Cleveland.

Notes

1. An Irish Odyssey

1. Giovanni Costigan, *History of Modern Ireland, with a Sketch of Earlier Times* (New York, 1969), 113.
2. Handwritten note, ca. 1933, by Mary O'Hara Branham, in possession of Thomas C. Ware, Chattanooga, Tennessee.
3. Terence O'Rorke, *History of Sligo; Town and County*, 2 vols. (Sligo, Ireland, 1889), 2:58–64.
4. Kean's brother James had a son named James who was five years Theodore's junior. A lawyer and judge in Grant County, Kentucky, James O'Hara was imprisoned in 1862 for his southern sympathies. Upon his release he was compelled to remain north of the Ohio River. Even after the war, when he returned to Kentucky, Judge O'Hara "was required to make a daily report of his whereabouts and was not released from this troublesome task until September 10, 1866." Clement A. Evans, *Confederate Military History* (expanded ed.), 12 vols. (Atlanta, 1899), 11:488–89.
5. Edgar E. Hume, *Colonel Theodore O'Hara, Author of The Bivouac of the Dead,* in *Southern Sketches* 6, ed. J. D. Eggleston (Charlottesville, Va., 1936), 4.
6. Marianne Elliott, *Partners in Revolution: The United Irishmen and France* (New Haven, Conn., 1982), 235–36.
7. Nettie H. Glenn, *Early Frankfort, Kentucky, 1786–1861* (Frankfort, 1986), 165 n. 11.
8. George W. Ranck, *The Bivouac of the Dead and Its Author,* 2d ed. (New York, 1898; reprint, 1909), 4.
9. Lawrence Elliott, *The Long Hunter: A New Life of Daniel Boone* (New York, 1976), 41–44.
10. George W. Ranck, *O'Hara and His Elegies* (Baltimore, 1875), 20; Hume, *O'Hara,* 4.
11. Carl B. Wittke, *The Irish in America* (Baton Rouge, La., 1956), 6–7.
12. Edith Abbott, *Immigration, Select Documents and Case Records* (New York, 1969), 10.
13. Mary O'Hara Branham handwritten note, ca. 1933, in possession of Thomas C. Ware; Ann B. Bevins and Rev. James R. O'Rourke, *"That Troublesome Parish": St. Francis/St. Pius Church of White Sulphur, Kentucky, Mother Church of the Diocese of Covington* (Georgetown, Ky., 1985), 10.
14. Mary O'Hara Branham note.
15. Lewis Collins, *History of Kentucky*, 2 vols. (Louisville, 1874), 1:410.
16. Hume, *O'Hara,* 4.
17. Erma Jett Darnell, *Filling the Chinks* (Frankfort, Ky., 1966), 73.
18. Hume, *O'Hara,* 5; An intriguing question has lingered about the source of education for Kean, his father, and his brothers. At the time, the only secular establishment of higher education in Ireland was Trinity College in Dublin, to which professed Catholics were by law denied access. But the history of their native region clearly indicated the zeal and the academic preparation of the priests assigned to the pastoral duties in Collooney, where their education would have taken place. O'Rorke, *History of Sligo,* 480–85.
19. Hume, *O'Hara,* 4.

20. Ibid., 5.
21. Benjamin J. Webb, *The Centenary of Catholicity in Kentucky* (Louisville, 1884), 162, 453–54.
22. "EDUCATION: The undersigned will open a school in a convenient room on Broadway, nearly opposite the State House, on the first Monday in January next. In his upper class will be taught the languages and Mathematics at $25 per session of twenty five weeks. In his second class, Reading, Writing, English Grammar and Geography, at $15 with a proportionable share of wood, from each pupil. Hours of Tuition from sunrise till two o'clock. He respectfully solicits patronage; and promises the utmost diligence" (Hume, *O'Hara*, 6).
23. A contemporary of Kean's was Dr. Anthony McGinty of Paris (Bourbon County), Kentucky. "He was a bookish man," one of his students remembered, "a graduate of Dublin University, I believe, and also of the Medical Department of Glasgow University. As one of the 'men of '98,' he had caved in the head of a British constable . . . and escaped to Baltimore. . . . 'Come to my office or library rather,' he invited the young man, 'and let me teach you. I will make you know your Latin and your Greek.'"

    Young Sam Williams studied with McGinty, only to be interrupted occasionally by the appearance of the doctor's brother, Peter, "an unfrocked Catholic priest, who devoted the entire remainder of his days to severe penance, imposed by himself for some violation of his religious vows, committed in the heat of an Irish revolt." The eccentric Peter would enter the library, give "a distinctly scanned declamation of some Virgilian page from memory, and [withdraw] as unceremoniously as he had entered." Samuel Williams, *Kentucky Memories of Uncle Sam Williams*, ed. Nathaniel C. Hughes, Jr. (Chattanooga, 1978), 97–98.
24. Hume, *O'Hara*, 6.
25. Ibid., 1:410.
26. Collins, *History of Kentucky*, 1:410.
27. Mary O'Hara Branham note.
28. Townsend, "Kean O'Hara and His Son Theodore: A Proposed Adventure," undated clipping in the O'Hara Papers of Thomas C. Ware. Quite likely this effort occurred in the early 1930s, a period in which Townsend, a historian of Kentucky authors, was broadcasting radio presentations entitled "Great Kentucky Authors" on Louisville station WHAS.
29. Bertram Wyatt-Brown, *Southern Honor: Ethics and Behavior in the Old South* (New York, 1982), 12.

2. The Formative Years

1. Collins, *History of Kentucky*, 1:410.
2. Albert G. Brackett, "Colonel Theodore O'Hara," *Louisville Courier Journal*, Aug. 1891, as reprinted in *SHSP*, 19:275. One may, however, compare the account in Ranck, *Bivouac of the Dead*, 26.
3. Albert G. Brackett, "Colonel O'Hara's Career Made Famous by a Poem,"

Vedette, Dec. 1892, 3–4. In this sketch, Brackett stresses O'Hara's penchant for telling amusing anecdotes about his Irish relatives and their interest in him.

4. Ervin Craighead, *From Mobile's Past: Sketches of Memorable People and Events* (Mobile, Ala., 1925), 181.

5. "Alfred Beckley's Recollections of Kentucky," *Register of Kentucky History* 60:312–13.

6. Hume, *O'Hara,* 8.

7. Brackett, "Colonel Theodore O'Hara," *SHSP,* 19:275; C. Hugh Holman, "A Cycle of Change in Southern Literature," in *The South in Continuity and Change,* ed. John C. McKinney and Edgar T. Thompson (Durham, N.C., 1965), 390–91.

8. William Edmondstone Aytoun, *Lays of the Scottish Cavaliers* (Edinburgh, 1872). This work was extraordinarily popular during the middle decades of the nineteenth century on both sides of the Atlantic. This 1872 publication was the twenty-second edition. It seems ironic that Aytoun, a professor of belles lettres at Edinburgh University, was responsible for furthering a certain genre of stilted and declamatory heroic verse. He was also coauthor of *The Bon Gaultier Ballads* (1845), a collection of parodies of that kind of verse as written by T. B. Macaulay, Tennyson, and other Victorian poets. Both Brackett and Ranck make reference to O'Hara's love for this work.

9. Wyatt-Brown, *Southern Honor,* 93.

10. George Ranck, for example, cites an admirer of Theodore who was present when he made his graduation address: "It was the most perfect thing of its kind I ever heard, for elegance of style, depth of thought, truthfulness of sentiment, and beauty of composition." Ranck, *Bivouac of the Dead,* 27.

11. Academic Ledger, St. Joseph's College, now in the Getz Museum, on the grounds of St. Joseph's parish church, Bardstown, Kentucky.

12. See Hume, *O'Hara,* 8; Ranck, *Bivouac of the Dead,* 27; Josiah Stoddard Johnston, "Sketch of Theodore O'Hara," *RKHS* 11, no. 33 (Sept. 1913):67.

13. "Antebellum College Life and the Relations Between Fathers and Sons," in *The Web of Southern Social Relations: Women, Family, & Education,* ed. Walter J. Fraser, Jr., R. Frank Saunders, Jr., and Jon L. Wakelyn (Athens, Ga., 1985), 109.

14. Franklin County, Kentucky, Will Book 2, 694.

15. Brackett, "Colonel O'Hara's Career," 2.

16. Delicate in color, almost a purplish pink.

17. Johnston, "Sketch of Theodore O'Hara," 71. General Brackett also indicated that "it was necessary to know O'Hara sometime before his good qualities were appreciated, and it is safe to say that he had many of them." Brackett, "Colonel O'Hara's Career," 3.

18. John Wilson Townsend, script for a radio talk, on WHAS, Louisville, Kentucky, June 1, 1932, 1, in possession of Thomas C. Ware.

19. Jennie Chinn Morton, "Biographical Sketch of the Life and Writing of Theodore O'Hara, Author of 'The Bivouac of the Dead,'" *RKHS,* 1:49.

20. Especially notable in this well-known group were the works of Edward Young ("The Complaint, or Night Thoughts"), Robert Blair ("The Grave"), and of course Thomas Gray ("Elegy Written in a Country Churchyard").

21. Phillipe Aries, *The Hour of Our Death,* trans. Helen Weaver (New York, 1981), 410.
22. Hume, *O'Hara,* 9.
23. Wilson, "Theodore O'Hara," *Century Magazine* 18:106.
24. This letter was first cited in an article by Daniel E. O'Sullivan, "Theodore O'Hara," *Southern Bivouac* 11:493.
25. O'Sullivan, "Theodore O'Hara," 490.
26. Memorandum dated Jan. 31, 1933, Theodore O'Hara Papers, FC.
27. O'Sullivan, "Theodore O'Hara," 493.
28. Ibid., 490.
29. Theodore O'Hara, *Obituary Addresses Delivered Upon the Occasion of the Re-Interment of the Remains of Gen. Charles Scott, Maj. William T. Barry, and Capt. Bland Ballard and Wife, in the Cemetery of Frankfort, November 8, 1854* (Frankfort, Ky., 1855), 24–25.
30. Paul Farley, "Uncle Sam's Official Poet," *Columbia,* New Haven, Conn., Apr. 1930, 13.
31. TOH to C. C. Clay, Jan. 3, 1864, Clement C. Clay Papers, DU.
32. Dickson D. Bruce, Jr., *Violence and Culture in the Antebellum South* (Austin, 1979), 41–43, 195.
33. TOH to J. T. Pickett, Dec. 8, 1851, John T. Pickett Papers, LOC. This extensive collection is of "great historic value," containing "the whole diplomatic correspondence of the Confederacy." See Burton J. Hendrick, *Statesmen of the Lost Cause: Jefferson Davis and His Cabinet* (New York, 1939), 138.

3. The Muffled Drum Resound!

1. Franklin County, Kentucky, Will Book 2, 235; TOH to John C. Breckinridge, Jan. 19, 23, 1863, T. O'Hara MSR, RG 109; John C. Breckinridge to Robert J. Breckinridge, Feb. 17, Apr. 20, June 16, 1840, in William C. Davis, *Breckinridge: Statesman, Soldier, Symbol* (Baton Rouge, La., 1974), 16–17; W. C. Mallalieu, "William Owsley," in *Dictionary of American Biography* 7:123; Johnston, "Sketch of Theodore O'Hara," 67; J. M. Armstrong, ed., *Biographical Encyclopaedia of Kentucky of the Dead and Living Men of the Nineteenth Century* (Cincinnati, 1878), 445; Hume, *O'Hara,* 8; Morton, "Theodore O'Hara," 49; L. Frank Johnson, *History of Franklin County, Ky.* (Frankfort, 1912), 186.
2. No copies of the *Democratic Rally* survive. Knowledge of its existence is owed to a column in the *Louisville Daily Dime* of May 24, 1844. O'Hara's friend and biographer, Stoddard Johnston, maintains that O'Hara was associated with yet another Frankfort newspaper during the early 1840s, the *Frankfort Daily Sun. Kentucky Yeoman,* Aug. 3, 26, 1843; Willard R. Jillson, *The Newspapers and Periodicals of Frankfort, Kentucky, 1795–1945* (Frankfort, 1945), 6, 16–18; Richardson Hardy, *The History and Adventures of the Cuban Expeditions from the First Movements Down to the Dispersion of the Army at Key West, and the Arrest of General López. Also: An Account of the Ten Deserters at Isla de Mugeres* (Cincinnati, 1850), 20–21; Collins, *History of Kentucky,* 1:410–11; LOC data base search, Feb. 9, 1992; Morton, "Theodore O'Hara," 50; Johnston, "Sketch of Theodore O'Hara," 65; Armstrong, *Biographical*

Encyclopaedia, 445; Stanley J. Kunitz and Howard Haycraft, eds., *American Authors, 1600–1900, a Biographical Dictionary of American Literature* (New York, 1938), 580; J. Stoddard Johnston, *Memorial History of Louisville from Its First Settlement to the Year 1896,* 2 vols. (Chicago, 1896), 68; Johnson, *History of Franklin County,* 1:194.

3. William R. Erwin, Jr., to N. C. Hughes, Jr., Apr. 29, 1992; George W. Ranck, "The Poet O'Hara," *Southern Journal of Education* (n.d.):24–28, in O'Hara File, Biographical Section, KHS Library, 24; Chief Clerk, U.S. Treasury Dept. to Maj. Edgar E. Hume, May 9, 1935, in Hume, *O'Hara,* 12–13.

4. A young friend of O'Hara's in the U.S. Treasury was Tennessean Washington C. Whitthorne, sixth auditor. For a lively, detailed account of life during the capitol during Polk's administration, see W. C. Whitthorne Diary, 1845–46, Tennessee State Library and Archives, Nashville, Tenn.

5. One source maintains that O'Hara read "The Old Pioneer" at Boone's reinterment, but this is doubtful. "It is almost sure," however, that O'Hara traveled back from Washington to witness the ceremony. Hume, *O'Hara,* 9–12; W. F. Sherman to N. C. Hughes, June 10, 1992, citing information from Settled Miscellaneous Treasury Accounts, 1790–1894, Treasury Dept., NARS; Ranck, *Bivouac of the Dead,* 17–20, 28–29; William Tanner to Gen. James Taylor, Sept. 8, 1845, James Taylor and Family Collection, KHS; *Danville (Ky.) Advocate-Messenger,* Sept. 23, 1905; Ella H. Ellwanger, "A Soldier of Fortune Who Won Fame Through a Single Poem," unpublished study in KHS.

6. It is interesting to speculate that O'Hara first met Rob Wheat at this time. C. Roberdeau Wheat was a second lieutenant in the Regiment of Tennessee Mounted Volunteers commanded by Col. Jonas E. Thomas, in the brigade of Gideon J. Pillow.

7. Hume believes O'Hara "was with General Pillow in 1846 during his brief and inactive service on the Mexican border." This is not correct. O'Hara did not join Pillow's staff until 1847. More likely, O'Hara acted in a quartermaster role with one of the brigades of regulars or in general logistical support, stationed at one of the primary supply dumps.

8. TOH to John M. McCalla, Nov. 16, 1846, J. M. McCalla Papers, DU; K. Jack Bauer, *The Mexican War, 1846–1848* (New York, 1974), 85–102, 201–2; K. Jack Bauer, *Zachary Taylor: Soldier, Planter, Statesman of the Old Southwest* (Baton Rouge, La., 1985), 191.

9. TOH to Kean O'Hara, Dec. 30, 1846, Theodore O'Hara Papers, FC.

10. TOH to Kean O'Hara, Dec. 30, 1846, Theodore O'Hara Papers, FC; Robert E. May, *John A. Quitman: Old South Crusader* (Baton Rouge, La., 1985), 165–70; reports and dispatches from William B. Campbell's First Tennessee Regiment Dec., 15–29, 1846, Campbell Family Papers, DU; Bauer, *Mexican War,* 204–5.

11. TOH to Kean O'Hara, Mar. 2, 1847, Theodore O'Hara Papers, FC; Marie O'Hara Branham memorandum, in possession of T. C. Ware; TOH to John M. McCalla, Mar. 3, 1847, McCalla Papers, DU.

12. O'Hara reported regretfully that he had been unable to fulfill his promise to Louisa McCalla—to find her a "golden image." So far, "the virgins and saints" available in Mexico had been done up in "miserable metal." TOH to John M. McCalla, Mar. 3, 1847, McCalla Papers, DU.

13. TOH to J. M. McCalla, Mar. 3, 1847, McCalla Papers, DU.
14. TOH to John M. McCalla, Mar. 28, 1847, McCalla Papers, DU; Bauer, *Mexican War*, 241–45; May, *Quitman*, 173.
15. Bauer, *Mexican War*, 248–53; TOH to John M. McCalla, Mar. 28, 1847, McCalla Papers, DU.
16. In his study of Jefferson Davis and his Mississippi regiment, Joseph Chance places O'Hara on May 17, 1847, at Monterrey, where he witnesses a dress parade of the garrison. The "ceremony caught the imagination of a young man in the audience, Theodore O'Hara of the Kentucky Cavalry, prompting him to write 'The Bivouac of the Dead.'" This is highly improbable. Joseph E. Chance, *Jefferson Davis's Mexican War Regiment* (Jackson, Miss., 1991), 126–27.
17. Directive of W. L. Marcy, Secretary of War, May 29, 1847, Adjutant General's File, Mexican War Index 2, RG 94, NARS; Bauer, *Mexican War*, 268–71.
18. J. F. Irons to TOH, June 27, 1847, Dreer Collection, HSP; Nathaniel C. Hughes, Jr., *The Life and Wars of Gideon J. Pillow* (Chapel Hill, 1993), 355 n. 60.
19. Two sources maintain O'Hara was wounded at Churubusco, another states that he was hit in the assault on Chapultepec. This appears to be fanciful biography, however, totally unsubstantiated by the battle reports of his superiors. Furthermore, O'Hara's name does not appear in the officer casualty lists so carefully compiled at army headquarters. S. L. Butler, Military Reference Branch, NARS, to N. C. Hughes, July 7, 1992.
20. *Kentucky Yeoman*, Aug. 31, 1848; George F. Price, *Across the Continent with the Fifth Cavalry* (New York, 1883), 321–23; Brackett, "Colonel Theodore O'Hara," 280; Francis B. Heitman, *Historical Register and Dictionary of the United States Army, 1789–1903*, 2 vols. (Washington, D.C., 1903), 1:759; Mexican War Index 3, Adjutant General's Office, RG 94, NARS; Gideon J. Pillow to Mary E. Pillow, Aug. 27, 1847, G. J. Pillow Letters, Beinecke Library, Yale Univ.; Hume, *O'Hara*, 14–15; Hughes, *Gideon J. Pillow*, 93–96.
21. Another source, however, places him at division headquarters in Mixcoac and thus in a supporting position during the attack. Johnston, "Sketch of Theodore O'Hara," 68; L. Frank Johnson, *History of the Franklin County Bar* (Frankfort, Ky., 1932), 91; U.S. War Dept., *Official List of Officers with the Army under Command of Major-General Winfield Scott* (Mexico City, 1848), 4; Richard P. Weinert, "'The Hard Fortune of Theodore O'Hara,'" *Alabama Historical Quarterly* 28:33.
22. TOH to John A. Quitman, Oct. 9, 1847, J. A. Quitman Collection, HLH.
23. O'Hara's handsome membership badge was sent by the Club in 1885 to his legacy, Judge James O'Hara, eldest son of his older brother Charles. Theodore O'Hara File, Aztec Club Archives, U.S. Army Military History Institute, Carlisle Barracks, Pennsylvania.
24. William W. Mackall, *A Son's Recollections of His Father* (New York, 1930), 23, 120; Hume, *O'Hara*, 16.
25. J. E. Johnston to Thomas H. Watts, Jan. 7, 1864, O'Hara MSR, RG 109.
26. At the time O'Hara was in Mexico City (late 1847–48) Hawkins was serving in the 16th Infantry.
27. G. J. Pillow to J. K. Polk, Dec. 12, 1847, J. K. Polk Papers, LOC; TOH to

General R. Jones, Dec. 13, 1847; H. C. Pope to W. Scott, Dec. 6, 1847; H. C. Pope to J. K. Walker, Dec. 1847; TOH to R. Jones, Dec. 13, 1847, Adjutant General's File, Mexican War Index 1, RG 94, NARS.

28. Davis, *Breckinridge*, 36–38; Hughes, *Gideon J. Pillow*, 117.

4. Cuba Libre

1. [Scott, John A.], *Encarnaciòn Prisoners*, ed. Theodore O'Hara (Louisville, 1848), 6–26.
2. Scott, *Encarnaciòn Prisoners*; Brackett, "Colonel O'Hara's Career"; Bauer, *Mexican War*, 206–7.
3. Hardy, *Cuban Expeditions*, 21; O'Sullivan, "Theodore O'Hara," 494; Townsend, "Kean O'Hara and His Son Theodore"; Wilson, "Theodore O'Hara," 206; John W. Townsend, *Kentucky in American Letters, 1784–1912*, 2 vols. (Cedar Rapids, Iowa, 1913), 2:219; George H. Genzmer, "Theodore O'Hara," *DAB*, 22 vols. (New York, 1928–58), 14:4; Craighead, *From Mobile's Past*, 181; Johnston, "Sketch of Theodore O'Hara," 68; Sidney Herbert, "Colonel Theodore O'Hara, Author of 'Bivouac of the Dead,'" *RKHS* 15:63; Ranck, "Poet O'Hara."
4. O'Hara abandoned the paper and took himself back to Washington during the winter of 1849–50. The last issue of the *Campaign Yeoman* appeared on April 22, 1850.
5. Perhaps it was just as well, as the *Champion of Reform* suspended publication on April 27, 1850. William Tanner was the printer for both the *Champion of Reform* and the *Campaign Yeoman*. Hardy, *Cuban Expeditions*, 21; Jillson, *Newspapers and Periodicals of Frankfort*, 16, 20–21.
6. James C. Pickett had served as secretary of legation in Columbia, minister to Ecuador, and chargé d'affaires in Peru.
7. For accounts of the turbulent life of John T. Pickett, see Thomas Schoonover, "John T. Pickett," in *Encyclopedia of the Confederacy*, ed. Richard N. Current et al., 4 vols. (New York, 1993), 3:1209–10; John E. Finding, *Dictionary of American Diplomatic History* (Westport, Conn., 1989), 417; and Dewitt C. Nogues, *Desha Genealogy: A Survey* (Austin, Tex., 1983), 15, 71.
8. Hendrick, *Statesmen of the Lost Cause*, 118.
9. Terrible disillusionment for the enthusiastic southerners came in 1852, not only from the failure of the Cuban expeditions but also from Kossuth being "appropriated" by the abolitionists. Kossuth, however, soon found himself abandoned by America, not only by once-avid southerners, but by his Free-Soil allies as well. Hardy, *Cuban Expeditions*, 21; Basil Rauch, *American Interest in Cuba: 1848–1855* (New York, 1948), 216–17; Anderson C. Quisenberry, *López's Expeditions to Cuba, 1850–1851* (Louisville, 1906), 37–40; Armstrong, *Biographical Encyclopaedia*, 593.
10. Samuel F. Bemis, *Diplomatic History of the United States* (New York, 1950); Robert G. Caldwell, *The López Expeditions to Cuba, 1848–1851* (Princeton, 1915), 3, 28.
11. Followers of Don Carlos (1788–1855), brother of Ferdinand VII, initiated a civil war in Spain to oust the descendants of Ferdinand from power.

Carlists would continue to foment civil unrest in Spain until Franco settled the issue of succession in 1969.

12. Antonio R. de la Cova, "Ambrosio José Gonzales: A Cuban Confederate Colonel" (Ph.D. diss., West Virginia Univ., 1994), 31–32.

13. Herminio Portell Vilá, *Narciso López y su Epoca 1848–1850,* 3 vols. (Havana, 1938–58), 1:14–59.

14. For a full discussion of Polk and his actions and attitudes toward the annexation or purchase of Cuba, see de la Cova, "Gonzales," 35–37.

15. This flag of López, with its single white star on a red triangular field against five alternating blue-and-white stripes, became Cuba's national flag in 1902 and ironically remains, almost a hundred years later, as "a visual suggestion of Cuba's aspiration to join the Union." Hugh Thomas, *Cuba: The Pursuit of Freedom* (New York, 1971), 217; Hume, *O'Hara,* 26. See also Antonio R. de la Cova, "Filibusters and Freemasons: The Sworn Obligation," *Journal of the Early Republic* 17 (Spring 1997):105–6.

16. O'Hara's involvement at this point cannot be substantiated. Although he appears to have been active in newspaper work in Kentucky, he is known to have been at the Irving House in New York City during the crucial days in July 1849, probably participating with John T. Pickett in planning the Round Island expedition. *New York Herald,* July 16, 1849.

17. For a transcript of Taylor's proclamation, see the *Washington Union,* Aug. 15, 1849.

18. *New York Herald,* Dec. 6, 1849. Caldwell, *López Expeditions* 1:43–48, 57; "General López, the Cuban Patriot," *United States Magazine and Democratic Review* 25 (Feb. 1850):107–12; Charles H. Brown, *Agents of Manifest Destiny: The Lives and Times of the Filibusters* (Chapel Hill, 1980), 52; Edgar E. Hume, "Colonel Theodore O'Hara and Cuban Independence," *Bulletin of the Pan American Union* 71 (May 1937):363–64; *Nation* 102 (June 29, 1916):710–11; Thomas, *Cuba,* 212–15; Bemis, *Diplomatic History of the United States,* 313–15; Hume, *O'Hara,* 26; U. R. Brooks, *Stories of the Confederacy* (Columbia, S.C., 1912), 286; Chester S. Urban, "New Orleans and the Cuban Question during the López Expeditions of 1849–1851," *Louisiana Historical Quarterly* 22 (Oct. 1939):1115; Louis Schlesinger, "Personal Narrative of Louis Schlesinger, of Adventures in Cuba and Centra," *United States Magazine and Democratic Review* 31 (Sept.–Dec. 1852):211; de la Cova, "Gonzales," 68–69.

19. Tennessean and longtime political ally of Gideon Pillow.

20. Portell Vilá, *Narciso López,* 1:118.

21. There are striking similarities between Gonzales and O'Hara noted by Gonzales biographer Antonio R. de la Cova. The former's "father was also a school teacher, a strict disciplinarian who educated his son. Gonzales was also an impeccable dresser, had excellent manners (according to Mary Boykin Chesnut's diary), and was the life of the social functions he attended. Like O'Hara, he was also a teacher, studied law, wrote for newspapers, was musically inclined (sang opera and played the piano), was a voracious reader, and except for his married life from 1856–1869, lived in city hotels and boarding houses most of his life. 'Gonzie,' like O'Hara, was also five foot eight and had hazel eyes. O'Hara's early friendship with Breckinridge was similar to Gonzie's

boyhood friendship with P. G. T. Beauregard." A. de la Cova to N. C. Hughes, Feb. 12, 1995; de la Cova, "Gonzales," 2.

22. According to Herminio Vilá, quoting Gonzales, Breckinridge [N. C.], Jack Allen, "and other scions of the best stock of the State" were with O'Hara. Portell Vilá, *Narciso López*, 2:219, 417.

23. In the summer of 1848, when López arrived in New York, he had made similar offers to Mexican War veterans Worth, Davis, and Lee, but they declined. Caldwell, *López Expeditions*, 48; Brooks, *Stories of the Confederacy*, 285–87; A. de la Cova to N. C. Hughes, Feb. 12, 1995.

24. Hardy, *Cuban Expeditions*, 8, 21; Brooks, *Stories of the Confederacy*, 286; Caldwell, *López Expeditions*, 58; Brown, *Agents of Manifest Destiny*, 53–54; Edgar E. Hume, "O'Hara and Cuban Liberation," *Bulletin of the Pan American Union* 71:364; de la Cova, "Gonzales," 80–81.

25. De la Cova, "Gonzales," 95; Brown, *Agents of Manifest Destiny*, 54–55.

26. Calderon de la Barca to Vincente Antonio de Larrañaga, Feb. 25, 1850, Papers of Spanish Ministry of Foreign Affairs, Charleston Consulate, DU.

27. Brown's *Agents of Manifest Destiny* states that Sigur recruited men in the columns of the *New Orleans Delta*. Filibuster historian Antonio R. de la Cova, however, disputes this. Having searched the *Delta* for 1850–51, he did not find "a single recruiting notice." De la Cova to N. C. Hughes, Feb. 12, 1995.

28. The efforts of López, however, were being obstructed, indeed undermined, by a treacherous rival, Cristobal Madán, president of the clandestine Cuban Council of Organization and Government: "Madán's Council steadfastly refused to turn over the armament salvaged from the Round House affair that was still in New Orleans." De la Cova, "Gonzales," 64–90, 97–98.

29. Hume, "O'Hara and Cuban Liberation," 364; Thomas, *Cuba*, 215–16; Brown, *Agents of Manifest Destiny*, 52, 55–56; Brooks, *Stories of the Confederacy*, 286; Holman Hamilton, *Zachary Taylor*, 2 vols. (Indianapolis, 1941–51), 2:150–56; Urban, "New Orleans and the Cuban Question," 1115; Philip S. Foner, *A History of Cuba and Its Relations with the United States*, 2 vols. (New York, 1963), 2:49.

30. Hardy, *Cuban Expeditions*, 5.

31. A number of Confederates were engaged at one time or another in filibustering. Congressman Thomas A. Harris of Missouri and Col. John C. Reid of Alabama are two lesser known figures discovered by historian Bruce Allardice. Bruce S. Allardice, *More Generals in Gray* (Baton Rouge, La., 1995), 121–22, 194–96.

32. Hardy, *Cuban Expeditions*, 3–7; Brown, *Agents of Manifest Destiny*, 54–55; TOH to William Nelson, Mar. 18, 1854, Quitman Papers, Mississippi Dept. of Archives and History; Edward S. Wallace, *Destiny and Glory* (New York, 1957), 59, 61.

33. Hardy, *Cuban Expeditions*, 8; Chaffin, *Fatal Glory*, 99–100.

34. Caldwell, *López Expeditions*, 58; Hume, "O'Hara and Cuban Liberation," 365; Brown, *Agents of Manifest Destiny*, 56; Wallace, *Destiny and Glory*, 60–61; Foner, *History of Cuba*, 2:50; Hardy, *Cuban Expeditions*, 8–9; Quisenberry, *López's Expedition*, 40, 46; sketch of O'Hara, June 10, 1901, in O'Hara File, KHS Library.

35. Quisenberry, *López's Expedition*, 40; Hume, "O'Hara and Cuban Liberation," 364; Hardy, *Cuban Expeditions*, 20–22, 76.

36. A contingent of the regiment were quartered in New Orleans, however. These were Jack Allen's men who had come down river aboard the *Saladin* a day later than the *Martha Washington. New Orleans Daily Picayune*, Apr. 13, 1850; Hardy, *Cuban Expeditions*, 9–12; Caldwell, *López Expeditions*, 59; Anderson C. Quisenberry, "Col. M. C. Taylor's Diary in López's Cárdenas Expedition, 1850," *RKHS* 19 (Sept. 1921):80–81.

37. "Captain Rufus Benson attested on the cargo manifest as bound for Chagres with 'Coal Ballast, Passengers, their provisions & Baggage.'" De la Cova, "Gonzales," 99.

38. Hardy, *Cuban Expeditions*, 18–20; Caldwell, *López Expeditions*, 59; Quisenberry, "Taylor's Diary," 80–82.

39. See O'Hara's official report, *New Orleans Daily Picayune*, June 28, 1850.

40. Hardy, *Cuban Expeditions*, 22–25, 64–65; Brown, *Agents of Manifest Destiny*, 57; Caldwell, *López Expeditions*, 60; Charles L. Dufour, *Gentle Tiger: The Gallant Life of Roberdeau Wheat* (Baton Rouge, La., 1957), 43; Quisenberry, "Taylor's Diary," 48. See O'Hara's official report, *New Orleans Daily Picayune*, June 28, 1850.

41. See O'Hara's official report, *New Orleans Daily Picayune*, June 28, 1850.

42. Hardy, *Cuban Expeditions*, 18–29; Quisenberry, *López's Expedition*, 48; Caldwell, *López Expeditions*, 60–61; Quisenberry, "Taylor's Diary," 83–84.

43. O. D. D. O. [J. C. Davis], *The History of the Late Expedition to Cuba* (New Orleans, 1850), 31–32; Hardy, *Cuban Expeditions*, 33–34.

44. Hardy, *Cuban Expeditions*, 30–34; Caldwell, *López Expeditions*, 63–65; Quisenberry, "Taylor's Diary," 84; Quisenberry, *López's Expedition*, 48–49; Dufour, *Gentle Tiger*, 43–44, 46; Brown, *Agents of Manifest Destiny*, 60.

45. Except for the *crawfishers*. Some thirty-nine of them, either Louisiana deserters or "men (not Kentuckians) who had come in the vessel with my party . . . and whose intention was to desert us [in Chagres], and thus pilfer a free passage so far on the way to California," were left behind on the beach. As the *Creole* pulled away, they raised a black flag defiantly. Some officers wished to fire upon them, but López stopped them.
Their fate would be sad enough. The *Georgiana* and the *Susan Loud* (the boat which brought Wheat's regiment to its rendezvous with the *Creole*) were captured by the Spanish, the men imprisoned, and one poor Kentuckian who had been married only a few days earlier and "pined for his bride" was shot. The incident quickly escalated into a confrontation between the United States and Spain. Presently the men were freed, the captain general of Cuba replaced, and the defenses of the island greatly strengthened. Quisenberry, *López's Expedition*, 49–51; Hardy, *Cuban Expeditions*, 92–94; Caldwell, *López Expeditions*, 64–65; "Barque Georgiana, and Brig Susan Loud," 32d Cong., 1st sess., H. Exec. Doc. 83; Brown, *Agents of Manifest Destiny*, 67.

46. Having to keep the bow of the *Creole* in the "eye of the wind," they were forced "4 points out of our way." It proved fortunate, however, for the course correction caused them to miss the "Spanish steamers that had been sent from

Havana to the Island of Mugeres to apprehend us, and which captured the *Georgiana* and *Susan Loud* the next day." O. D. D. O., *Expedition to Cuba,* 51; Hardy, *Cuban Expeditions,* 35–36, 65; Quisenberry, *López's Expedition,* 51; Dufour, *Gentle Tiger,* 46; Caldwell, *López Expeditions,* 66.

47. De la Cova, "Gonzales," 109.

48. O'Hara's report, *New Orleans Daily Picayune,* June 28, 1850; Quisenberry, *López's Expedition,* 51–52; Hume, "O'Hara and Cuban Liberation," 365; Caldwell, *López Expeditions,* 66; Hardy, *Cuban Expeditions,* 66.

49. The Yager, U.S. rifle model 1841, was more commonly called the Mississippi rifle. Made widely popular by Jefferson Davis and his regiment at Buena Vista, this .54-caliber weapon was naturally the choice of Bunch's Mississippians.

50. O. D. D. O., *Expedition to Cuba,* 64; Quisenberry, *López's Expedition,* 52; Quisenberry, "Taylor's Diary," 84.

51. Missourian Fayssoux, a veteran of the navy of the Texas Republic, would later gain a measure of fame as the commander of William Walker's one vessel in Nicaragua. Fayssoux's grandfather, incidentally, commanded a division under General Washington when he crossed the Delaware River. O. D. D. O., *Expedition to Cuba,* 65; A. J. Gonzales, "The Cuban Crusade: A Full History of Georgian and López Expeditions," *New Orleans Times Democrat,* Mar. 30, 1884; Evans, *Confederate Military History,* 8:409–10.

52. Hardy, *Cuban Expeditions,* 38–39, 66; Caldwell, *López Expeditions,* 66–67; Quisenberry, "Taylor's Diary," 84; Dufour, *Gentle Tiger,* 47–48; Brown, *Agents of Manifest Destiny,* 62; Quisenberry, *López's Expedition,* 53; Hamilton, *Zachary Taylor,* 2:369; Brooks, *Stories of the Confederacy,* 287; Wallace, *Destiny and Glory,* 71.

53. Pickett did not specify how many locomotives in his report. One source contends he seized three, another only one. Hardy, *Cuban Expeditions,* 39, 68; Quisenberry, *López's Expedition,* 54; Hume, "O'Hara and Cuban Independence," 365; de la Cova, "Gonzales," 111, 114.

54. O'Hara's report, *New Orleans Daily Picayune,* June 28, 1850. Actually the barracks "were not in the plaza but in another part of town," so O'Hara was mistaken about the intent of the guide. De la Cova, "Gonzales," 114.

55. O. D. D. O., *Expedition to Cuba,* 66.

56. De la Cova, "Gonzales," 114–17.

57. O'Hara's report, *New Orleans Daily Picayune,* June 28, 1850; Hardy, *Cuban Expeditions,* 39–42, 67, 71; Caldwell, *López Expeditions,* 67–69; Portell Vilá, *Narciso López,* 2:314–17, 378–83; de la Cova, "Gonzales," 115–17; Collins, *History of Kentucky,* 1:411; Hume, "O'Hara and Cuban Liberation," 365; Johnston, "Sketch of Theodore O'Hara," 68; Wallace, *Destiny and Glory,* 71–72; Dufour, *Gentle Tiger,* 48–49; Quisenberry, *López's Expedition,* 55–57.

58. O. D. D. O., *Expedition to Cuba,* 73–75; Caldwell, *López Expeditions,* 70.

59. Six Americans were left behind and four of these would be executed six days later. Hardy, *Cuban Expeditions,* 70–71, 73–75, 77–78; Quisenberry, "Taylor's Diary," 28–29; de la Cova, "Gonzales," 117, 120.

60. O. D. D. O., *Expedition to Cuba,* 76–77; Hardy, *Cuban Expeditions,* 42–46; Caldwell, *López Expeditions,* 69–72; Quisenberry, *López's Expedition,*

56–57; Foner, *History of Cuba,* 2:51; Quisenberry, "Taylor's Diary," 86; Dufour, *Gentle Tiger,* 50.

61. Hardy, *Cuban Expeditions,* 46–47, 69–70; Caldwell, *López Expeditions,* 70–73; Brown, *Agents of Manifest Destiny,* 64–65; Dufour, *Gentle Tiger,* 50; Hamilton, *Zachary Taylor,* 2:369; Quisenberry, *López's Expedition,* 57.

62. O. D. D. O., *Expedition to Cuba,* 80–81; Caldwell, *López Expeditions,* 73–74; Hardy, *Cuban Expeditions,* 47–48; Brown, *Agents of Manifest Destiny,* 66; Hume, "O'Hara and Cuban Liberation," 366.

63. Foner, *History of Cuba,* 2:53; Brown, *Agents of Manifest Destiny,* 67; "Barque Georgiana, and Brig Susan Loud," 32d Cong., 1st sess., H. Exec. Doc. 83, 45; Hardy, *Cuban Expeditions,* 48–52, 70; Caldwell, *López Expeditions,* 74–75.

5. While Fame Her Record Keeps

1. Elliot, *Long Hunter,* 171–72.
2. The arguments about whether the state of Kentucky did or did not "get Boone" has created a great deal of acrimony and mischief over the years, the most recent biographer, John Mack Faragher, has noted. His own account sums up the main currents of this controversy, indicating that the principal motive keeping the issue alive has not been state pride but money: that is, tourist dollars. Whether a mistake could have occurred in the removal of disintegrating coffins and skeletal remains seems not so much a central concern as the fact that the record "clearly indicates that the Boone family actively participated in pointing out the graves." John Mack Faragher, *Daniel Boone: The Life and Legend of an American Pioneer* (New York, 1992), 360.
3. Hume, *O'Hara,* 9–12.
4. Monroe F. Cockrell, "'The Bivouac of the Dead' and 'The Old Pioneer,' by Theodore O'Hara: A Venture into the Shadows of Yesterday," KHS Library.
5. Morton, "Theodore O'Hara," 59.
6. O'Hara actually returned to Louisville on Sunday, July 7, in the company of Hawkins and Dr. T. J. Kennedy. Cincinnati *Enquirer,* July 10, 1850.
7. Bruce, *Violence and Culture,* 181.
8. Hume, *O'Hara,* 18. Comparable apocryphal stories exist about many famous speeches.
9. Ranck, *O'Hara and His Elegies,* 30.
10. Hume, *O'Hara,* 19.
11. Theodore O'Hara File, FC.
12. Theodore O'Hara File, FC. This item appeared first in the *New York Times,* Aug. 11, 1900.
13. Item in the O'Hara family file, KHS.
14. Information brochure, "McClellan Gate," received from Kathryn Sheakle, Arlington National Cemetery.
15. War Dept., Quartermaster General's Office, June 10, 1881, NARS. One of the implications of this latter comment suggests that some "wooden tab-

lets" containing lines from the poem already existed in these cemeteries, but nothing has been found to verify this point.

16. Rock Island Arsenal, Illinois, letter of June 19, 1883, NARS.

17. Letter to NARS, under the subject "National Cemeteries."

18. Letter from the War Dept., Quartermaster General's Office, Sept. 18, 1902, NARS, under the subject "National Cemeteries."

6. The Fine Gentleman and Gallant

1. Taylor would die suddenly on July 9, 1850, but his successor, Millard Fillmore, surprised many by revealing an equal determination to bring the filibusters to justice.

2. Bauer, *Zachary Taylor,* 280. See also de la Cova, "Gonzales," 140–54.

3. Franklin County, Kentucky, Will Book 2, 235–37.

4. *Kentucky Yeoman,* Mar. 29, 1851, quoting *New Orleans Daily Delta,* Mar. 14, 1851.

5. Caldwell, *López Expeditions,* 78–79; L. M. Perez, "The López Expeditions to Cuba, 1850–1851. Betrayal of the Cleopatra, 1851," *Publications of the Southern Historical Association,* 10:356–60; Bemis, *Diplomatic History of the United States,* 315–16; Robert Douthat Meade, *Judah P. Benjamin, Confederate Statesman* (New York, 1943), 66–67; Frederic Rosengarten, *Freebooters Must Die* (Wayne, Pa., 1976), 62–67; Hume, "O'Hara and Cuban Liberation," 366.

6. Probably the armament "stored in the sawmill of Cárdenas veteran Henry T. Titus on the bank of the St. John's River in Jacksonville." De la Cova, "Gonzales," 195.

7. The secret hiding place for the major portion of the ordnance for the *Cleopatra* expedition was just to the north, across the state line, at Woodbine Plantation on the St. Mary's River. This hidden location had been used seventy-five years earlier by the galleys of American patriot Joseph John Hardy, who struck out against British warships and privateers and thereby earned for himself "criminal status." *New York Tribune,* May 2, 1851; De la Cova, "Gonzales," 175; Nathaniel C. Hughes, Jr., *General William J. Hardee, Old Reliable* (Baton Rouge, La., 1965), 4–5.

8. O'Hara was registered at the Jacksonville Hotel (Col. S. Buffington, proprietor) on April 25, the day before the *Cleopatra* expedition was scheduled to depart. With him was his friend and fellow Cárdenas veteran, Col. Henry Theodore Titus. *Florida Republican,* May 1, 1851.

9. De la Cova, "Gonzales," 169–82.

10. Ianthe Bond Hebel, "Colonel H. T. Titus, Founder of Titusville, Florida, 1865," Florida State Archives, Tallahassee; *New Orleans Evening Picayune,* Apr. 16, 19, 1851; de la Cova, "Gonzales," 173.

11. De la Cova, "Gonzales," 189–90.

12. De la Cova, "Gonzales," 193–94.

13. This landing, the Bahía Honda expedition, resulted in fifty filibusters who accompanied Narciso López, including Col. William L. Crittenden, being captured and executed.

14. De la Cova, "Gonzales," 204–5.
15. De la Cova, "Gonzales," 208; *Jacksonville News,* Aug. 30, 1851.
16. Portell Vilá, in his definitive biography of López, 3:656, maintains that O'Hara was excluded from the *Pampero* expedition by López and "did not hide his resentment." This seems to be directly contradicted, however, by the Jacksonville and Tallahassee newspaper accounts. *Jacksonville News,* Sept. 6, 1851; *Florida Sentinel,* Sept. 9, 1851.
17. Caldwell, *López Expeditions,* 78–79; Brooks, *Stories of the Confederacy,* 289; Perez, "The López Expeditions to Cuba," 356–60; Bemis, *Diplomatic History of the United States,* 315–16; Meade, *Judah P. Benjamin,* 66–67; Rosengarten, *Freebooters Must Die,* 62–67; Hume, "O'Hara and Cuban Liberation," 366; Hardy, *Cuban Expeditions,* 56–63; Collins, *History of Kentucky,* 1:411; Hamilton, *Zachary Taylor,* 1:369.
18. For a full account of the disastrous Pampero affair, see Antonio R. de la Cova, "Cuban Filibustering in Jacksonville in 1851," *Northeast Florida History* 3 (1996): 25–33.
19. *Florida Republican,* Sept. 18, 1851. Following the Bahía Honda disaster and the death of López, the Cuba Libre movement in the United States went underground. Lack of secrecy and lack of resources seemed to have compromised every effort, so the filibusters set about quietly organizing a wider base of support. They established cells, or "chapters," of those "desirous of Extending the Area of Liberty" in major southern cities and in New York. This network became known as the Order of the Lone Star, which had a membership estimated at five to fifteen thousand. Headquarters of the order were in New Orleans, with the constitution printed on the presses of Sigur's *Delta.* The extent of O'Hara's participation in Order of the Lone Star, however, is unknown, although there is little doubt that he was involved. May, *Quitman,* 271; Rauch, *American Interest in Cuba,* 228.
20. Titus and his "border ruffians" would depart Kansas in December 1856 and reappear in the forces of William Walker. Hebel, "Colonel H. T. Titus"; William Oscar Scroggs, *Filibusters and Financiers; the Story of William Walker and His Associates* (New York, 1916), 237; de la Cova, "Gonzales," 186 n. 80.
21. *Florida Republican,* Oct. 9, 1851.
22. O'Sullivan, indeed, had coined the phrase "Manifest Destiny." James M. McPherson, *Battle Cry of Freedom: The Civil War Era* (New York, 1988), 48; Frederick Merk, *Manifest Destiny and Mission in American History: A Reinterpretation* (New York, 1963), 52.
23. While preparing his biography of Gonzales, Antonio de la Cova discovered that Gonzales, López, Quitman, Hawkins and Cuban Henry T. Titus were Freemasons. This led him to prepare a study, "Filibusters and Freemasons: The Secret Agenda." A. de la Cova to N. C. Hughes, Jan. 23, 1995; Rauch, *American Interest in Cuba,* 229.
24. *Jacksonville News,* Dec. 6, 1851, quoting the *Kentucky Yeoman,* n.d. The editor of the *News* ended his notice of O'Hara's journey with the following tribute: "We wish Col. O'Hara all the celebrity and substantial rewards his chivalrous character and efforts in the Cuban cause so richly merit."
25. Quisenberry, *López's Expedition,* 118.

26. TOH to John T. Pickett, Dec. 8, 1851, Pickett Papers, LOC. The section of this letter relating to O'Hara and his father is quoted in chapter 2.

27. TOH to John T. Pickett, Dec. 8, 1851, Pickett Papers, LOC.

28. Major proved a first-rate editor, and by the outbreak of the Civil War the *Yeoman* was "generally acknowledged to be one of the best political papers in Kentucky." Major would be joined in 1867 by Stoddard Johnston and in 1870 by Maj. Henry T. Stanton, a local poet beloved by Kentuckians and regarded by them as second only to O'Hara. Major developed angry personal and political enemies. One, Nat Ewing of Washington, Texas, wrote J. J. Crittenden that Major was "a Rascal of the Blackest die." Major, according to Ewing, had stolen a horse from him at age fifteen, then ran away to North Carolina where he seduced a young lady, spent her money and ran off to Illinois. Jillson, *Newspapers and Periodicals of Frankfort,* 16; Nat Ewing to J. J. Crittenden, Aug. 22, 1850, N. Ewing Letter, KHS.

29. *Proceedings of the National Democratic Convention, 1852* (Washington, D.C., 1852), 24; TOH to John T. Pickett, Dec. 8, 1851, Pickett Papers, LOC; *Kentucky Yeoman,* Nov. 20, 1851.

30. Rauch, *American Interest in Cuba,* 216–17; TOH to John T. Pickett, Dec. 8, 1851, Pickett Papers, LOC; Merle E. Curti, "George N. Sanders," *DAB,* 8:334; James W. Patton, "John L. O'Sullivan," *DAB,* 7:89; Robert W. Johannsen, *Stephen A. Douglas* (New York, 1973), 345–49.

31. TOH to Orlando Brown, Dec. 1851, Orlando Brown Papers, FC; Franklin County, Kentucky, Order Book, 1852, 350–52; Johnston, *Memorial History of Louisville,* 2:70; *Louisville Times,* Mar. 1, 1852.

32. *Louisville Times,* Mar. 1, 1852; Johnston, *Memorial History of Louisville,* 2:70; Collins, *History of Kentucky,* 1:180; Genzmer, "O'Hara," 5; Kunitz and Haycraft, *American Authors,* 580; Martin E. Schmidt, "Early Printers of Louisville," *Filson Club History Quarterly* 40:325.

33. Kunitz and Haycraft, *American Authors,* 580; Hume, *O'Hara,* 29; Johnston, "Sketch of Theodore O'Hara," 67–68, 6–14; Annie Mae Hollingsworth, "Theodore O'Hara, Immortal Poet of One Song," *Alabama Historical Review* 7:419; Hendrick, *Statesmen of the Lost Cause,* 118; *Louisville Times,* Mar. 20, June 11, Sept. 2, 1852; Franklin County, Kentucky, Will Book 3, 162; Johnson, *History of Franklin County,* 194.

34. John Tracy Ellis, *American Catholicism,* 2d ed., rev., ed. Daniel J. Boorstin, The Chicago History of American Civilization (Chicago: 1969), 85.

35. *Louisville Times,* Mar. 4, 20, 1853; Mildred L. Rutherford, *The South in History and Literature, a Handbook of Southern Authors from the Settlement of Jamestown, 1607, to Living Writers* (Athens, Ga., 1906), 207; Hume, *O'Hara,* 30–32; Johnston, *Memorial History of Louisville,* 1:99.

36. Albert Brackett relates a story about O'Hara and Cass. O'Hara "had among his friends a gentleman from Michigan, and once, when in this playful mood, said: 'I am fond of Michigan, it is the home of two of my best friends—General Cass, who is the greatest statesman in the world, and Mr. W——, who is the poorest.' Mr. W. saw the point at once, and joined in the merriment it occasioned." Brackett, "Colonel Theodore O'Hara," 277.

37. This passage, from Virgil's *Eclogue* 4, may be translated thus: "A second Tiphys shall be, and a second *Argo* to sail with chosen heroes; There will be

the old wars over again, and again a great Achilles will be sent to Troy."
Louisville Times, Mar. 4, 1853.

38. TOH to Franklin Pierce, Apr. 12, 1853, McCalla Papers, DU; William F. Sherman to N. C. Hughes, June 10, 1992.

39. Lt. Cummings has not been identified although he was probably either Arthur C. Cummings, a Virginian and a Mexican War hero, or Francis Markoe Cummings, a New Yorker and former officer in the 1st Infantry. *Jacksonville Florida Republican,* Apr. 28, 1853.

40. The *Times* would perish in 1855, victim of the Know-Nothings' victory in 1854, when they gained control of the city council. The frightening anti-immigrant riot in Louisville would come on August 6, 1855. One biographer has O'Hara running against Know-Nothing candidate Charles S. Morehead for governor in late 1854, but this is incorrect. Beverly L. Clarke opposed Morehead. Johnston, *Memorial History of Louisville,* 1:99; Kunitz and Haycraft, *American Authors,* 580; Genzmer, "O'Hara," 5; *Louisville Times,* Oct. 25, 1853.

41. De la Cova, "Gonzales," 226; J. T. Pickett to J. A. Quitman, Aug. 18, 1853, Quitman Papers, Mississippi Dept. of Archives.

42. May, *Quitman,* 271–75; TOH to William Nelson, Mar. 18, 1854, Quitman Papers, Mississippi Dept. of Archives and History.

43. Pierce's favorable stance regarding the filibusters appears to have changed as early as January 1854. De la Cova, "Gonzales," 233.

44. May, *Quitman,* 281–90; Chester S. Urban, "The Abortive Quitman Filibustering Expedition to Cuba, 1853–1855," *Journal of Mississippi History* 18 (1956):183–84.

45. O'Hara, *Obituary Addresses*; Johnson, *History of Franklin County,* 139.

46. Hume, *O'Hara,* 33–35; Johnston, "Sketch of Theodore O'Hara," 69; Ranck, *Bivouac of the Dead,* 34; Brackett, "Colonel Theodore O'Hara," 279–80; Genzmer, "O'Hara," 5; Townsend, *Kentucky in American Letters,* 2:219; John L. Idol, Jr., "Theodore O'Hara," in *Southern Writers, a Biographical Dictionary,* by Robert Bain, Joseph M. Flora, and Louis D. Rubin, Jr. (Baton Rouge, La., 1979), 333; Morton, "Theodore O'Hara," 60–62; Brackett, "Colonel O'Hara's Career," 2.

47. TOH to J. A. Quitman, Dec. 22, 1854, Jan. 8, 1855, Quitman Papers, MDAH; May, *Quitman,* 288–95; Rauch, *American Interest in Cuba,* 298–99.

48. TOH to AG, Jan. 1, 1855, in AG Letters Received, RG 107, NARS; TOH to J. Davis, Jan. 29, Feb. 1, 1855, J. S. Chrisman to J. Davis, Feb.? 1855, in Lynda L. Crist and May Seaton Dix, eds., *The Papers of Jefferson Davis,* 9 vols. (Baton Rouge, La., 1971–97), 5:402, 412.

7. Hard Fortune

1. Price, *Fifth Cavalry,* 11; Carl Coke Rister, *Robert E. Lee in Texas* (Norman, Okla., 1946), 34; Nathaniel C. Hughes, Jr., "William J. Hardee, USA" (Master's thesis, Univ. of North Carolina, 1956), 173.

2. Statement of the Regular Army Service of Theodore O'Hara, by Maj. Gen. James F. McKinley, Adjutant General, Apr. 16, 1935, GHB-442, NARS; Price, *Fifth Cavalry,* 322; Hume, *O'Hara,* 35.

3. William H. Emory served a short time as junior major but was transferred. Davis offered the post to Braxton Bragg, and when he declined, the post went to Thomas.

4. Severyn H. Middagh, comp., "The History of the Fifth U.S. Cavalry from March 3, 1855 to December 31, 1905," in Oversize Document Collection, Adjutant General's Office, RG 94, NARS; Hume, *O'Hara*, 36; M. L. Crimmins, "First Sergeant John W. Spangler, Company H, Second United States Cavalry," *West Texas Historical Association Year Book*, 26:69–70.

5. O'Hara was solicitous about the welfare of the men he had recruited and wrote the adjutant general from Frankfort concerning medical needs and supplies. TOH to AG, May 17, Aug. 11, 1855, in AG Letters Received, RG 107, NARS.

6. W. J. Hardee to AG, Sept. 11, 1855, in AG Letters Received, RG 1077, NARS; Regimental Order No. 10, July 27, 1855, RG 94, NARS; Hume, *O'Hara*, 36–37; Douglas Southall Freeman, *R. E. Lee: A Biography*, 4 vols. (New York, 1934–35), 1:361; Statement of the Regular Army Service of Theodore O'Hara, by Maj. Gen. James F. McKinley, Adjutant General, Apr. 16, 1935, GHB-442, NARS; Price, *Fifth Cavalry*, 29–32; Robert G. Hartje, *Van Dorn: The Life and Times of a Confederate General* (Nashville, 1967), 50.

7. W. J. Hardee to AG, Sept. 16, 1855, in AG Letters Received, RG 107, NARS; Richard W. Johnson, *A Soldier's Reminiscences in Peace and War* (Philadelphia, 1886), 98.

8. General Orders No. 13, Aug. 15, 1855, in War Dept. General Orders, 1838–1861, RG 107, NARS; Crimmins, "First Sergeant John W. Spangler," 69; Hughes, "Hardee," 174–77.

9. See TOH to AG, Oct. 20, 1855, in AG Letters Received, RG 107, NARS.

10. A. S. Johnston to Adjutant General, Nov. 14, 1855, in AG Letters Received, RG 94, NARS; Freeman, *R. E. Lee*, 1:362; Hume, *O'Hara*, 37; Price, *Fifth Cavalry*, 32; Middagh, "Fifth U.S. Cavalry," 28.

11. Brackett, "Colonel O'Hara's Career," 3.

12. Brackett, "Colonel Theodore O'Hara," 276.

13. Price, *Fifth Cavalry*, 32–33; Crimmins, "First Sergeant John W. Spangler," 70.

14. William Edmondstoune Aytoun—Scottish poet, 1813–1865.

15. Brackett, "Colonel Theodore O'Hara," 275–79.

16. Antonio de la Cova, who studied López closely while preparing his biography of Gonzales, summed up the Liberator thusly: "López was impulsive and never learned from his mistakes." Brackett, "Colonel O'Hara's Career," 3; De la Cova, "Gonzales," 381.

17. *National Intelligencer*, Mar. 15, 1856; E. K. Smith to Mrs. Frances K. Smith, Nov. 30, 1855, in Kirby Smith Papers, SHC.

18. *National Intelligencer*, Mar. 15, 1856; Johnson, *Soldier's Reminiscences*, 104; Price, *Fifth Cavalry*, 33–34; Crimmins, "First Sergeant John W. Spangler," 70.

19. Price, *Fifth Cavalry*, 41–42; Robert W. Frazer, *Forts of the West* (Norman, Okla., 1963), 147; Hughes, "Hardee," 187–88; Rister, *Lee in Texas*, 35.

20. Capt. Charles Radziminski to Col. William M. Emory, May 18, 1856, in private collection of Thomas R. Hay, Locust Valley, New York; Emily Van Dorn Miller, *A Soldier's Honor: With Reminiscences of Major-General Earl*

Van Dorn (New York, 1902), 339; Weinert, "Hard Fortune of Theodore O'Hara," 36.

21. Price, *Fifth Cavalry,* 37, 41–43, 322; Johnson, *Soldier's Reminiscences,* 104–6; Hartje, *Van Dorn,* 53; Brackett, "Colonel Theodore O'Hara," 277.

22. Brackett, "Colonel Theodore O'Hara," 279; Brackett, "Colonel O'Hara's Career," 3–4.

23. Ranck, *Bivouac of the Dead,* 36.

24. Statement of the Regular Army Service of Theodore O'Hara, by Maj. Gen. James F. McKinley, Adjutant General, Apr. 16, 1935, GHB-442, NARS; Heitman, *Historical Register,* 1:969; Hume, *O'Hara,* 37; Brackett, "Colonel Theodore O'Hara," 277.

25. Freeman, *R. E. Lee,* 1:360; R. C. Crane, "Robert E. Lee's Expedition in the Upper Brazos and Colorado Country," *West Texas Historical Association Year Book* 13 (Oct. 1937):54; Rister, *Lee in Texas,* 19; Hartje, *Van Dorn,* 53.

26. This splendid soldier had led the brilliantly successful flank attack against Valencia's strong position at Contreras. Perhaps Louisiana's most promising military leader, Smith would die in 1858.

27. Price, *Fifth Cavalry,* 45; Statement of the Regular Army Service of Theodore O'Hara, by Maj. Gen. James F. McKinley, Adjutant General, Apr. 16, 1935, GHB-442, NARS; Freeman, *R. E. Lee,* 1:365–66; Hume, *O'Hara,* 36; M. L. Crimmins, "Major Van Dorn in Texas," *West Texas Historical Association Year Book,* 16:123; Rister, *Lee in Texas,* 40–43; Hartje, *Van Dorn,* 55–56; Crane, "Robert E. Lee's Expedition," 54.

28. Charges and Specifications against Capt. Theodore O'Hara, 2nd Cavalry, June 19, 1856, Letters Received, Adjutant General's Office, RG 94, NARS; D. C. Buell to TOH, Aug. 13, 1856, D. C. Buell to R. E. Lee, Aug. 13, 1856, Letters Sent, Dept. of Texas and the 8th Military Dept., 1854–1858, RG 393, NARS.

29. Freeman, *R. E. Lee,* 1:366; Crane, "Robert E. Lee's Expedition," 56; Rister, *Lee in Texas,* 44–45; Hartje, *Van Dorn,* 56.

30. Price, *Fifth Cavalry,* 322; Hartje, *Van Dorn,* 56–57; Rister, *Lee in Texas,* 46–52; Crimmins, "Major Van Dorn," 16:123; Freeman, *R. E. Lee,* 1:366–67; Crane, "Robert E. Lee's Expedition," 59; M. L. Crimmins, "Camp Cooper and Fort Griffin, Texas," *West Texas Historical Association Year Book,* 17:34.

31. Price, *Fifth Cavalry,* 49, 322; J. K. F. Mansfield, "Colonel J. K. F. Mansfield's Report of the Inspection of the Department of Texas in 1856," *Southwestern Historical Quarterly* 41:142; Rister, *Lee in Texas,* 53, 56.

32. D. C. Buell to TOH, Aug. 13, 1856, Letters Sent, Dept. of Texas and the 8th Military Dept., 1854–1858, RG 393, NARS.

33. TOH to Col. Samuel Cooper, Aug. 18, 1856; TOH to Maj. D. C. Buell, Aug. 18, 1856, Letters Received, Adjutant General's Office, RG 94, NARS; Ranck, *Bivouac of the Dead,* 35–36.

34. Price, *Fifth Cavalry,* 322; Johnson, *Soldier's Reminiscences,* 108; Hume, *O'Hara,* 36; Weinert, "Hard Fortune of Theodore O'Hara," 38; Brackett, "Colonel Theodore O'Hara," 277–78.

35. Conversation with T. C. Ware, Nov. 7, 1995.

8. Mobile

1. Maj. R. H. Chilton to Col. B. F. Larned, Dec. 13, 1856, Quartermaster General Consolidated Correspondence File, RG 92, NARS.
2. See William V. Wells, *Walker's Expedition to Nicaragua*; Charles W. Doubleday, *Reminiscences of the "Filibuster" War in Nicaragua*; and Scroggs, *Filibusters and Financiers*.
3. Genzmer, "O'Hara," 5; Hume, *O'Hara*, 37.
4. *New York Times*, June 16, 1867; L. Frank Johnston, *History of the Franklin County Bar* (Frankfort, 1932), 91; Armstrong, *Biographical Encyclopaedia*, 445; Ranck, *Bivouac of the Dead*, 33–34; Wilson, "Theodore O'Hara," 106; Collins, *History of Kentucky*, 1:411; "Theodore O'Hara," unidentified clipping in Theodore O'Hara Papers, June 10, 1901, UKL.
5. Fred B. Shepard, Colin J. McRea, and William F. Cleveland to Isaac Toucey, Jan. 30, 1858, Miscellaneous Letters Received by the Secretary of the Navy, RG 45, NARS; Hebel, "Colonel H. T. Titus." Titus ultimately proved a liability to Walker and as a military leader was considered incompetent. Finally, he turned against Walker and assisted in the latter's downfall and destruction. Scroggs, *Filibusters and Financiers*, 281, 295; Dufour, *Gentle Tiger*, 95–97.
6. For a recent, thoughtful discussion of Manifest Destiny and militant expansionist sentiment and activities from 1844–60, see McPherson, *Battle Cry of Freedom*, 48–52, 104–16.
7. Scroggs, *Filibusters and Financiers*, 378–79; William Oscar Scroggs, "William Walker," *DAB*, 10:364.
8. Fred B. Shepard, Colin J. McRea, and William F. Cleveland to Secretary of Navy Isaac Toucey, Jan. 30, 1858, Miscellaneous Letters Received by the Secretary of the Navy, RG 45, NARS; WW to CIF, 11, 17, 23, Dec. 29, 1858.
9. TOH to C. I. Fayssoux, Oct. 5, 1859, C. I. Fayssoux Papers, Howard-Tilton Memorial Library, Tulane Univ.
10. For a brief, understandable account of Walker and his adventures, and how they fit into the southern desire for "an empire for slavery," see McPherson, *Battle Cry of Freedom*, 111–16.
11. *Louisville Courier-Journal*, Sept. 16, 1874; Collins, *History of Kentucky*, 1:410–11; O'Sullivan, "Theodore O'Hara," 491; Morton, "Theodore O'Hara," 51; James G. Wilson and John Fiske, eds., *Appleton's Cyclopedia of American Biography*, 6 vols. (New York, 1900), 4:566; Hume *O'Hara*, 24–25; Clem J. O'Conner, "On Many a Tombstone," *Louisville Courier Journal*, n.d., in Theodore O'Hara Papers, UKL; Robert P. Letcher to Logan Hunton, Feb. 16, 22, 1852, L. Hunton Letters, FC; Meade, *Judah P. Benjamin*, 66, 73–75, 113; Eli N. Evans, *Judah P. Benjamin, the Jewish Confederate* (New York, 1988), 44–47, 93; Ralph Poore, "History of the Mobile *Press Register*," in possession of Ralph Poore, Mobile, Ala., 65; Armstrong, *Biographical Encyclopaedia*, 445; J. G. Barnard, *The Isthmus of Tehuantepec* (New York, 1852), 1–25, 119–24; Judah P. Benjamin, *Memoir Explanatory of the Transcimos and Tehuantepec Route between Europe and Asia* (Washington, D.C., 1851), 4–32.

12. *Daily American Star,* Dec. 5, 1847.
13. Franklin County, Kentucky, Deed Book 6.
14. O'Hara was lobbying for his friend Pickett to become minister to Guatemala. He is "eminently qualified," O'Hara wrote, by his experience in Central America and "his intimate acquaintance with the character of the Hispanic-American people and his thorough knowledge of the language of the country." TOH to J. A. Quitman, Nov. 25, 1857, Quitman Papers, MDAH.
15. De la Cova, "Gonzales," 169.
16. Peter J. Hamilton, *Mobile of the Five Flags* (Mobile, Ala., 1913), 205; J. Cutler Andrews, *The South Reports the Civil War* (Princeton, 1970), 39; Rhoda C. Ellison, *History and Bibliography of Alabama Newspapers in the Nineteenth Century* (University, Ala., 1954), 120–21; Thomas McA. Owen, *History of Alabama and Dictionary of Alabama Biography,* 4 vols. (Chicago, 1921), 3:598; Luther N. Steward, Jr., "John Forsyth," *Alabama Review* 14:98–110; Poore, "History of the *Mobile Press Register,*" 63–66.
17. Minnie C. Boyd, *Alabama in the Fifties* (New York, 1931), 168.
18. Poore, "History of the *Mobile Press Register,*" 63–68; Alan S. Thompson, "Southern Rights and Nativism as Issues in Mobile Politics, 1850–1861," *Alabama Review* 35:138–39.
19. 35th Cong., 1st sess., Feb. 5, 1859, H.R. 160.
20. Andrews, *South Reports the Civil War,* 119; Allan Westcott, "Samuel Chester Reid," *DAB,* 8:480–81; Samuel C. Reid, Jr., *The Case of the Private Armed Brig of War Gen. Armstrong* (New York, 1857).
21. R. Poore to N. C. Hughes, Jr., May 5, 1992.
22. Hendrick, *Statesmen of the Lost Cause,* 117–19.
23. Poore, "History of the *Mobile Press Register,*" 63–70.
24. *Mobile City Directory,* Mobile, Ala., 1859; Harriet E. Amos, *Cotton City: Urban Development in Antebellum Mobile* (Tuscaloosa, 1985), 67; *National Cyclopaedia of American Biography,* 63 vols. (New York, 1893–1919), 362.
25. Craighead, *From Mobile's Past,* 180–81.
26. *New York Times,* June 16, 1867; Michael Kenny, *Catholic Culture in Alabama: Centenary Story of Spring Hill College, 1830–1930* (New York, 1931), 118; TOH to C. C. Clay, Jan. 5, 1864, Clay Papers, DU.
27. Kenny, *Catholic Culture in Alabama,* 118–19.
28. Poore, "History of the *Mobile Press Register,*" 73; Steward, "John Forsyth," 116–17; Albert Burton Moore, *History of Alabama* (Tuscaloosa, 1951), 205.
29. J. C. Breckinridge to TOH, Jan. 19, 1860, Frederick Dearborn Collection, HLH.
30. Poore, "History of the *Mobile Press Register,*" 77; Moore, *History of Alabama,* 267.
31. Andrews, *South Reports the Civil War,* 39.
32. James C. Klotter, *The Breckinridges of Kentucky, 1760–1981* (Lexington, Ky., 1986), 117.
33. J. C. Breckinridge to TOH, Jan. 19, 1860, Dearborn Collection, HLH; Davis, *Breckinridge,* 218–47.

34. Steven E. Woodworth, *Jefferson Davis and His Generals: The Failure of Confederate Command in the West*, Modern War Studies, ed. Theodore A Wilson (Lawrence, Kans., 1990), 35.

35. TOH to C. C. Clay, Clay Papers, DU; Kenny, *Catholic Culture in Alabama*, 119; Craighead, *From Mobile's Past*, 183; Ranck, *Bivouac of the Dead*, 37; TOH to J. C. Breckinridge, Feb. 20, 1865, O'Hara MSR, RG 109.

36. Joseph H. Fichter and George L. Maddox, "Religion in the South, Old and New," in *The South in Continuity and Change*, ed. John C. McKinney and Edgar T. Thompson (Durham, N.C., 1965), 371.

37. Ellis, *American Catholicism*, 89.

38. William H. Russell, *My Diary, North and South*, 2 vols. (London, 1863), 1:95.

39. Bruce, *Violence and Culture*, 162–63.

9. Search for a Command

1. TOH MSR, RG 109; Genzmer, "O'Hara," 5; Evans, *Confederate Military History*, 11:21–23, 12:39; Baxter McFarland, "A Forgotten Expedition to Pensacola in January, 1861," *Publications of the Mississippi Historical Society* 9:18–21.

2. Ranck, *Bivouac of the Dead*, 37; Hume, *O'Hara*, 38; TOH to S. Cooper, July 30, 1862, TOH MSR, RG 109; U.S. Navy Dept., *Official Records of the Union and Confederate Navies in the War of the Rebellion*, 31 vols. (Washington, D.C., 1894–1919), 4:216.

3. *OR,* vol. 52, pt. 2:22–24; GO No. 13, Pensacola Command, Apr. 3, 1861, Nat Ewing Letter, KHS; Evans, *Confederate Military History*, 7:731.

4. T. Michael Parrish, *Richard Taylor: Soldier Prince of Dixie* (Chapel Hill, 1992), 127. For an account of a young printer in O'Hara's regiment, John Young Gilmore, see Evans, *Confederate Military History* 13:426.

5. It is of interest to note that Bragg's acting assistant adjutant general at this time was Capt. Robert C. Wood, Jr., one of the official witnesses of the incidents at Fort Chadbourne in 1856. *OR,* vol. 52, pt. 2:22–24; GO No. 13, Pensacola Command, Apr. 3, 1861, Nat Ewing Letter, KHS; Evans, *Confederate Military History,* 11:22; B. Bragg to W. W. Mackall, Feb. 14, 1863, Mackall Papers, SHC.

6. TOH MSR, RG 109; Confederate States of America, *Journal of the Congress of the Confederate States of America, 1861–1865*, 58th Cong., 2d sess., Senate Doc. No. 234, 1:154–55.

7. TOH to L. P. Walker, June 29, 1861, TOH MSR, RG 109.

8. Receipts, June 1–July 31, 1861, AG Special Order dated Apr. 22, 1861, TOH MSR, RG 109; TOH to S. Cooper, July 30, 1862, TOH MSR, RG 109; Hume, *O'Hara*, 38–39; *OR*, ser. 4, vol. 1:220; Special Order No. 85, AGO, RG 109, NARS; *OR*, ser. 2, vol. 3:683, 687, 689.

9. TOH Confederate Service Summary, TOH MSR, RG 109; TOH to S. Cooper, July 30, 1862, TOH MSR, RG 109; Herbert, "Colonel Theodore O'Hara," 64.

10. O'Hara's old paper, the *Mobile Daily Advertiser and Register,* could hardly restrain itself, declaring First Manassas to be as decisive as the defeat of the Spanish Armada. *Mobile Daily Advertiser and Register,* July 24, 1861; *OR,* vol.

2:536; Evans, *Confederate Military History,* 12:94; Percy G. Hamlin, *Old Bald Head (General R. S. Ewell)* (Strasburg, Va., 1940), 101; Robert E. Park, "The Twelfth Alabama Infantry, Confederate States Army," *SHSP,* 33:195–97; William C. Davis, *Battle at Bull Run* (Baton Rouge, La., 1977), 104–5, 109–10.

11. *OR,* vol. 2:1000; Hume, *O'Hara,* 40, 43; Hamilton, *Mobile,* 313; Park, "12th Alabama," *SHSP,* 33:195–97, 213.

12. Samuel Cooper's office officially listed O'Hara as commander of the Twelfth Alabama on 30 September 1861. *OR,* ser. 4, vol. 1:626.

13. TOH to S. Cooper, July 30, 1862, TOH MSR, RG 109.

14. Ibid.; TOH to C. C. Clay, Jan. 5, 1864, Clay Papers, DU; TOH to J. C. Breckinridge, Feb. 20, 1865, TOH MSR, RG 109.

15. Influential C. C. Clay substantiated O'Hara's claim about Tracy's testimony in a letter to the secretary of war in 1864. C. C. Clay to J. A. Seddon, Apr. 1864; TOH to J. C. Breckinridge, Feb. 20, 1865, TOH MSR, RG 109.

16. TOH to P. G. T. Beauregard, June 3, 1862, TOH MSR; Special Order No. 474, First Corps, Army of the Potomac, Nov. 1, 1861, Special Order No. 216, AGO, TOH MSR; J. E. Johnston to Gov. T. H. Watts, Jan. 7, 1864, TOH MSR, RG 109.

17. AGO Special Order No. 220, Nov. 13, 1861, TOH MSR, RG 109.

18. Thomas L. Connelly, *Army of the Heartland: The Army of Tennessee, 1861–1862* (Baton Rouge, La., 1967), 62; TOH to S. Cooper, July 30, 1862, TOH MSR, RG 109; Brackett, "Colonel Theodore O'Hara," 280; TOH to P. G. T. Beauregard, June 3, 1862, TOH MSR, RG 109.

19. Receipts, Feb. 7, 1862, TOH, MSR, RG 109; Compiled Service Record, 54th Tennessee Volunteer Infantry, RG 109, NARS.

20. Stanley F. Horn, *The Army of Tennessee* (Norman, Okla., 1941), 83–102; Connelly, *Army of the Heartland,* 130–33.

21. Ed Porter Thompson in his *History of the Orphan Brigade* (Louisville, 1898), 81, maintains that O'Hara joined Breckinridge's staff in Murfreesboro as the army retreated through that town, but O'Hara stated that he had remained on Johnston's staff throughout, from late November 1861 until Shiloh.

22. Evans, *Confederate Military History,* 11:69–70.

23. *OR,* vol. 10, pt. 1:403–4; Wiley Sword, *Shiloh: Bloody April* (Dayton, Ohio, 1983), 270; William Preston Johnston, *The Life of Gen. Albert Sidney Johnston* (New York, 1878), 613–15; J. Forsyth to T. H. Watts, Dec. 17, 1863, TOH MSR, RG 109; Charles Roland, *Albert Sidney Johnston, Soldier of Three Republics* (Austin, 1964), 336–38.

24. Roland, *Johnston,* 338–39, 353; *OR,* vol. 10, pt. 1:405; Thompson, *Orphan Brigade,* 367; Price, *Fifth Cavalry,* 323; Johnston, *Johnston,* 688; TOH to T. Jordan, June 3, 1862, TOH to J. C. Breckinridge, Jan. 23, 1863, TOH MSR, RG 109.

25. TOH to P. G. T. Beauregard, June 3, 1862, TOH MSR, RG 109.

26. TOH Confederate Service Summary, TOH MSR, RG 109; J. T. Pickett to TOH, May 6, 1862, Pickett Papers, LOC; Thompson, *Orphan Brigade,* 109.

27. B. Bragg to W. W. Mackall, Feb. 14, 1863, Mackall Papers, SHC; Andrews, *South Reports the Civil War,* 146–47, 156–57.
28. Beauregard, Gonzales's friend from boyhood, came to oppose all filibusters, regarding Walker and López as "Military carpetbaggers." Perhaps his contempt for the Cuban liberators (which seems to have developed after the mid-1850s) extended to O'Hara as well and helped frustrate the latter's hopes for a promising position. TOH Apr. 30, June 30, 1862, TOH to P. G. T. Beauregard, June 3, 1862, TOH MSR, RG 109; De la Cova, "Gonzales," 348.
29. O'Hara's friend Pickett might have been with him. Pickett, who had met with disaster as the Confederate minister to Mexico in 1861, also resigned from Breckinridge's staff citing poor health. Special Order No. 74, Western Dept., TOH MSR, RG 109; Special Order No. 145, June 24, 1862, TOH MSR, RG 109; TOH to T. Jordan, June 30, 1862, TOH MSR; J. C. Breckinridge to J. T. Pickett, July 18, 1862, Pickett MSR.
30. TOH to S. Cooper, July 30, 1862, TOH MSR, RG 109.
31. TOH to S. Cooper, July 30, 1862, TOH MSR, RG 109.
32. Bragg had asked John Forsyth to accompany the army so that operations could be reported accurately. Forsyth acted as correspondent for four southern newspapers and sent back accounts with a spin favorable to Bragg, despite the widespread disappointment over the failure of the campaign. Special Order No. 221, AGO, Sept. 22, 1862, NARS; Andrews, *South Reports the Civil War,* 241, 246–49.
33. Pickett had resigned from Breckinridge's staff on July 15, declaring his "strength unequal to the military service: believing too that I can otherwise contribute more to the general good, & having withall cogent private reasons." J. C. Breckinridge to J. T. Pickett, July 18, 1862, Pickett Papers, LOC.
34. John A. Buckner, "Greatest Martial Eulogy," undated clipping in possession of Thomas C. Ware; Special Order No. 17, Dept. No. 17, NS, TOH MSR, RG 109. Buckner (1832–ca. 1904), the son of Henry M. Buckner, had attended Centre College, then trained to be a physician, but instead became a cotton planter in East Carroll Parish, Louisiana.
35. Johnston, "Sketch of Theodore O'Hara," 71.

10. Murfreesboro

1. Col. John A. Buckner had succeeded John T. Pickett as assistant adjutant general on Breckinridge's staff in July 1862. Buckner was absent on leave but would return when heavy fighting began. Johnston, "Sketch of Theodore O'Hara," 69; *OR,* vol. 20, pt. 1:787.
2. Special Order No. 60, Breckinridge's Division, Dec. 25, 1862, Theodore O'Hara Papers, UVA; Special Order No. 59, Breckinridge's Division, Dec. 29, 1862, HSP.
3. *OR,* vol. 20, pt. 1:783, 789.
4. Responsibility for covering the Confederate right, including the Lebanon Road, belonged to the cavalry brigade of John Pegram. Pegram spotted the

infantry of Gen. Horatio Van Cleve's division, Crittenden's Corps, crossing Stone's River, and reported it, but when Hardee's attack opened on the Union right, Rosecrans halted Van Cleve and ordered him back across the river. Van Cleve's withdrawal to the west bank, Pegram either failed to notice or failed to report. Breckinridge charitably characterized Pegram's reconnaissance work as "careless." *OR,* vol. 20, pt. 1:789.

5. No one agrees on how much reinforcement Bragg requested. Bragg indicated he asked for two brigades; Breckinridge maintained in his report that Bragg requested one, two if they could be spared. O'Hara, in his memorandum, supports Breckinridge and agrees two were ordered while John A. Buckner indicates only one was requested, but that Breckinridge generously dispatched two. Nevertheless by 11:30 A.M., Breckinridge had ordered the brigades of Adams and Jackson to cross and aid Polk. Thomas Lawrence Connelly, *Autumn of Glory* (Baton Rouge, La., 1971), 60.

6. TOH to J. C. Breckinridge, Jan. 16, 1863, Breckinridge Papers, NYHS.

7. Johnston, "Sketch of Theodore O'Hara," 71–72; Peter Cozzens, *No Better Place to Die* (Chicago, 1990), 159–60; Thompson, *Orphan Brigade,* 185–86; J. A. Buckner to J. C. Breckinridge, May 20, 1863; W. Clare to B. Bragg, June 2, 1863; TOH to J. C. Breckinridge, Jan. 16, 1863, Breckinridge Papers, NYHS; Connelly, *Autumn of Glory,* 59–60; *OR,* vol. 20, pt. 1:783; Bragg's Murfreesboro Report, in B. Bragg Papers, William P. Palmer Collection, Western Reserve Historical Society, Cleveland, Ohio.

8. Hughes, *General William J. Hardee,* 142–43; Cozzens, *No Better Place to Die,* 159–61; Connelly, *Autumn of Glory,* 58.

9. *OR,* vol. 20, pt. 1:789–90.

10. Woodworth, *Jefferson Davis and His Generals,* 225.

11. Cozzens, *No Better Place to Die,* 162–64; Thompson, *Orphan Brigade,* 185–86; *OR,* vol. 20, pt. 1:783.

12. *OR,* vol. 20, pt. 1:783–84, 796; Cozzens, *No Better Place to Die,* 163–66; TOH to J. C. Breckinridge, Jan. 16, 1863, Breckinridge Papers, NYHS; Connelly, *Autumn of Glory,* 60–61, 65–66.

13. *OR,* vol. 20, pt. 1:786–87; J. S. Johnston Diary and Reminiscences, J. S. Johnston Papers, FC; *Richmond Examiner,* Feb. 23, 1863; William C. Davis, *The Orphan Brigade: The Kentucky Confederates Who Couldn't Go Home* (Garden City, N.Y., 1980), 164.

14. Connelly, *Autumn of Glory,* 61.

15. Rosecrans had crossed most of Van Cleve's division—three brigades on line, directly supported by another infantry brigade and two batteries. Davis, *Breckinridge,* 338–40; *OR,* vol. 20, pt. 1:778.

16. R. E. Graves to J. C. Breckinridge, Jan. 25, 1863, Breckinridge Papers, NYHS; Davis, *Breckinridge,* 340–41; Connelly, *Autumn of Glory,* 63–64.

17. James L. McDonough, *Stone's River—Bloody Winter in Tennessee* (Knoxville, 1980), 77; Robert O. Neff, "The Best and the Bravest," *Confederate Chronicles of Tennessee* 2 (1987):97; Connelly, *Autumn of Glory,* 62–64; Cozzens, *No Better Place to Die,* 181–83; Davis, *Breckinridge,* 340; *OR,* vol. 20, pt. 1:785.

18. TOH to J. C. Breckinridge, Jan. 16, 1863, Breckinridge Papers, NYHS; *OR,* vol. 20, pt. 1:787, 796; Davis, *Breckinridge,* 342.

19. *OR,* vol. 20, pt.1:786, 778; William D. Pickett, "A Reminiscence of Murfreesboro," *Nashville American,* Nov. 10, 1907; W. J. McMurray, *History of the 20th Tennessee Regiment Volunteer Infantry, C.S.A.* (Nashville, 1904), 237; Davis, *Breckinridge,* 344–45.
20. Anderson's battery was also known as Capt. S. A. Moses's battery, one of the original six companies of the Fourteenth Georgia Artillery Battalion.
21. Davis, *Breckinridge,* 346–47; *OR,* vol. 20, pt. 1:785–88, 668, 793, 812–13; H. B. Clay, "On the Right at Murfreesboro," *CV,* 21:588; Connelly, *Autumn of Glory,* 65.
22. R. E. Graves to J. C. Breckinridge, Jan. 25, 1863, Breckinridge Papers, NYHS; Connelly, *Autumn of Glory,* 65; *Richmond Examiner,* Feb. 23, 1863.
23. J. A. Buckner to J. C. Breckinridge, May 20, 1863; TOH to J. C. Breckinridge, Jan. 16, 1863, Breckinridge Papers, NYHS; Clay, "On the Right at Murfreesboro," *CV,* 21:588; Davis, *Breckinridge,* 346–47; *OR,* vol. 20, pt. 1:785–87, 668, 765–66, 793, 808, 812–13; Connelly, *Autumn of Glory,* 65; *Richmond Examiner,* Feb. 23, 1863.
24. TOH to J. C. Breckinridge, Jan. 16, 1863, TOH MSR, RG 109; John A. Buckner to J. C. Breckinridge, May 20, 1863, Breckinridge Papers, NYHS; Connelly, *Autumn of Glory,* 65.
25. Bragg blamed his friend Forsyth too. Six months later he wrote W. W. Mackall, "Four times my friend Forsyth has been informed of infamous falsehoods published in his paper over the signature of this fellow [Reid]. He has expressed his regret each time, but I see no amendment. Being considered as my special friend, his paper has thus done me more injustice and more real harm than all those in the country" (B. Bragg to W. W. Mackall, Feb. 14, 1863, Mackall Papers, SHC). Connelly, *Autumn of Glory,* 73–74; Poore, "History of the Mobile Press *Register*"; Andrews, *South Reports the Civil War,* 257–59, 357.
26. B. Bragg to J. C. Breckinridge, Jan. 11, 1863, Breckinridge Papers, NYHS.
27. TOH to J. C. Breckinridge, Jan. 23, 1863, TOH MSR, RG 109; TOH to J. C. Breckinridge, 16, Jan. 19, 1863, Breckinridge Papers, NYHS.
28. TOH to J. C. Breckinridge, Jan. 23, 1863, TOH MSR, RG 109.
29. Davis, *Orphan Brigade,* 164; TOH to J. C. Breckinridge, Jan. 23, 1863, TOH MSR, RG 109.
30. Davis, *Orphan Brigade,* 164; Klotter, *Breckinridges of Kentucky,* 125; Connelly *Autumn of Glory,* 72–76; J. S. Johnston Diary and Reminiscences, Johnston Papers, FC; TOH to J. C. Breckinridge, Jan. 24, 1863, TOH MSR, RG 109.
31. Jan. 21, 1863, entry, S. C. Reid Diary, quoted in Andrews, *South Reports the Civil War,* 337, 341; Poore, "History of the *Mobile Press Register.*"
32. Circular of the Army of Tennessee, Mar. 7, 1863, Thompson Papers, FC; Special Order No. 33, Dept. No. 2, Mar. 7, 1863, TOH MSR, RG 109; TOH to C. C. Clay, Jan. 5, 1864, Clay Papers, DU; TOH to B. S. Ewell, Feb. 24, 1863, quoted in Hume, *O'Hara,* 46; Connelly, *Autumn of Glory,* 83–85.
33. Mary C. Breckinridge to J. C. Breckinridge, Feb. 15, 1863, Breckinridge MSR, RG 109; McMurray, *History of the 20th Tennessee Regiment,* 250–52; Evans, *Confederate Military History,* 9:169–70; Mar. 19 entry,

Johnston Diary, Johnston Papers, FC; Davis, *Breckinridge*, 364; Johnston, "Sketch of Theodore O'Hara," 69.

34. Arthur J. L. Fremantle, *The Fremantle Diary*, 2d ed., ed. Walter Lord (Boston, 1954), 107.
35. May 23, 1863 entry, J. S. Johnston Diary, J. S. Johnston Papers, FC; Ranck, *Bivouac of the Dead*, 39; TOH to B. S. Ewell, July 26, 1863, J. C. Breckinridge to B. S. Ewell, TOH MSR, RG 109; Johnston, "Sketch of Theodore O'Hara," 69–70.
36. Klotter, *Breckinridges of Kentucky*, 122; Davis, *Orphan Brigade*, 187; Thompson, *Orphan Brigade*, 506.
37. Johnston, "Sketch of Theodore O'Hara," 69–70. Cabell would not fare so well in the subsequent battle at Missionary Ridge. He would be captured and his father narrowly escaped capture himself. Peter Cozzens, *Shipwreck of Their Hopes: The Battles for Chattanooga* (Urbana, Ill., 1994), 315.

11. Languishing in Inactivity

1. Hume, *O'Hara*, 46; TOH to S. Cooper, Nov. 24, 1863, Feb. 21, 1864, TOH MSR, RG 109.
2. J. Forsyth to T. H. Watts, Dec. 17, 1863, TOH MSR, RG 109.
3. J. Johnston to T. H. Watts, Jan. 7, 1864, TOH MSR, RG 109.
4. J. C. Breckinridge to T. H. Watts, Feb. 15, 1864, TOH MSR, RG 109.
5. Memorandum for information of Secretary of War, Feb. 1865, TOH MSR, RG 109.
6. TOH to C. C. Clay, Jan. 5, 1864, Clay Papers, DU.
7. C. C. Clay to J. A. Seddon, undated, TOH MSR, RG 109.
8. TOH to J. P. Benjamin, Jan. 30, 1864, quoted in E. Merton Coulter, *The Confederate States of America, 1861–1865*, vol. 7, *A History of the South*, ed. Wendell Holmes Stephenson and E. Merton Coulter (Baton Rouge, La., 1950), 108.
9. Hughes, *Gideon J. Pillow*, 277–80.
10. The Fifteenth CSA Cavalry, "somewhat of an independent organization," is a mysterious command to track. Some authorities believe it may have been the Fifteenth Florida or the First Alabama-Mississippi-Tennessee or perhaps the Clarke Rangers. Certainly it contained Florida cavalry units as well as several, perhaps as many as five, independent Alabama cavalry companies. Weinert, "Hard Fortune of Theodore O'Hara," 42; TOH to S. Cooper, Feb. 21, May 8, 1864; Receipts, Jan. 1–June 30, 1864; *OR*, vol. 38, pt. 4:769; Alabama Dept. of Archives and History memorandum for Maj. E. E. Hume, Apr. 5, 1935, TOH MSR, RG 109; Joseph H. Crute, Jr., *Units of the Confederate Army* (Midlothian, Va., 1987), 71.
11. See MSR of Thomas T. Hawkins for 1863–64 correspondence between him and Breckinridge's headquarters and the Confederate Adjutant General's Office, RG 109.
12. Wintersmith of Elizabethtown, Hardin County, Kentucky, had served as commissary of subsistence on Simon B. Buckner's staff early in the war and been captured at Fort Donelson. Later he joined O'Hara on Breckinridge's

staff, then became a major upon rejoining the staff of Buckner. TOH to Mrs. R. C. Wintersmith, Jan. 15, 1865, Wintersmith Family Papers, KHS.

13. Nothing would come of these plans either. TOH to Mrs. R. C. Wintersmith, Jan. 15, 1865, Wintersmith Family Papers, KHS.

14. Davis, *Breckinridge,* 479–82; TOH to AG, Feb. 7, 1865; TOH to S. Cooper, Feb. 21, 1865, AGO Correspondence, RG 109, NARS; Weinert, "Hard Fortune of Theodore O'Hara" 42.

15. "Memorandum for Information of Secretary of War," undated, TOH MSR.

16. TOH to J. C. Breckinridge, Feb. 20, 1865, TOH MSR, RG 109.

17. Kentucky and Alabama Representatives in the Confederate Congress to J. C. Breckinridge, Feb. 16, 1865, TOH MSR, RG 109.

18. O'Hara's alter ego John T. Pickett was there too and during the evacuation of the capitol somehow managed to secure the seal of the Confederacy, which he had copied in copper, silver, and gold. See R. A. Brock, "Seal of the Southern Historical Society and the Great Seal of the Confederate States of America," *SHSP,* 16:418. Also see William B. Smith, "Recovery of the Great Seal of the Confederacy," *SHSP,* 41:22–26, 29, 31–33.

19. Breckinridge was "accompanied by Major Wilson, Major O'Hara, Capt. James B. Clay, his sons Cabell and Clifton and a small escort commanded by Major John P. Austin [Ninth Kentucky Cavalry]." Unidentified clipping, June 10, 1901, in Theodore O'Hara Papers, UKL.

20. Davis, *Breckinridge,* 517–24; unidentified clipping, June 10, 1901, Theodore O'Hara Papers, UKL.

21. John T. Wood, "Escape of the Confederate Secretary of War," *Century Magazine* 47:111.

22. Kenny, *Catholic Culture in Alabama,* 119; Herbert, "Colonel Theodore O'Hara," 65–66; Richard C. Beatty, Floyd C. Watkins, Thomas D. Young, and Randall Stewart, *The Literature of the South* (New York, 1952), 188–89; Hollingsworth, "Theodore O'Hara," 420–21.

23. The date of this fire has not been determined. It is possible that it occurred even before the war ended. Gen. James Wilson's raid in April 1865 resulted in the destruction by fire of some three hundred thousand bales of cotton and a number of buildings in Columbus. This event could have been the catastrophe that ruined O'Hara.

24. Johnston, "Sketch of Theodore O'Hara," 70; Kenny, *Catholic Culture in Alabama,* 119; Herbert, "Colonel Theodore O'Hara," 65–66; Beatty et al., *Literature of the South,* 188–89; Hollingsworth, "Theodore O'Hara," 420–21; Julian A. C. Chandler et al., eds., *The South in the Building of the Nation,* 12 vols. (Richmond, 1909), 12:241; Hume, *O'Hara,* 51; O'Sullivan, "Theodore O'Hara," 494; Weinert, "Hard Fortune of Theodore O'Hara," 43.

25. Hawkins fell in love with an Alabama girl and married her, ultimately renouncing his Catholic faith to join her in the local Eufala Baptist congregation. Hollingsworth, "Theodore O'Hara," 420–21; *Memorial Record of Alabama,* 2 vols. (Madison, Wisc., 1893), 1:435, 468–69; Anne K. Walker, *Backtracking in Barbour County* (Richmond, Va., 1941), 295–97; Thompson, *History of the First Kentucky Brigade,* 394.

26. Marguerite T. Roseberry, "Theodore O'Hara Was Soldier-Poet," *United*

Daughters of the Confederacy Magazine 21 (July 1938):19; Hume, *O'Hara,* 51; Johnston, "Sketch of Theodore O'Hara," 70.

27. Hollingsworth, "Theodore O'Hara," 420–21; W. C. Woodall, "Poet O'Hara, Rose Hill Marriages," *Columbus (Ga.) Ledger Enquirer,* Aug. 10, 1969.

28. Theodore O'Hara's mother, Mrs. Helen O'Hara, died the following fall or winter, leaving what remained of her husband's property to her great grandson, Kean O'Hara Tremere. *Columbus Daily Sun,* June 9, 1867, quoted in *New York Times,* June 16, 1867; *Mobile Register,* June 26, 1867; Hollingsworth, "Theodore O'Hara," 420–21; O'Sullivan, "Theodore O'Hara," 494; Herbert, "Colonel Theodore O'Hara," 65–66; Weinert, "Hard Fortune of Theodore O'Hara," 43; Armstrong, *Biographical Encyclopaedia,* 445.

29. W. Preston to J. C. Breckinridge, Aug. 6, 1867, William Preston Papers, FC.

30. Hume, *O'Hara,* 53; Johnston, "Sketch of Theodore O'Hara," 70; *Louisville Evening Post,* Feb. 22, 1916.

31. *New York Times,* June 16, 1867.

32. Here is the complete text of Van de Graaf's poem, "Bring Back the Hero's Dust":

> Son of the "dark and bloody ground"
>   Thou must not slumber there;
> Tho' sister states thy praises sound
>   Along the southern air.
> Kentucky's soil should be thy grave—
>   Thy native soil thy tomb.
> The noble cause you fought to save,
>   With thee, is wrapt in gloom.
> The Celtic breast was fired to arms
>   Regardless of the cost;
> A tyrant's act awoke alarms—
>   The battle now is lost.
> Thou lent an ear to Honor's voice—
>   True instinct of the brave—
> And kindred hearts will now rejoice
>   To guard their hero's grave.
> The song you sung o'er warriors dead,
>   The fitter requiem be;
> For freely, too, thou wouldst have bled,
>   And smiled at Fate's decree.
> Thy gallant life has gone to God—
>   A soldier's sleep be thine.
> Tho' stiff thy form and cold the clod,
>   Thy soul was e'er divine.
> Then let thy sacred dust be laid
>   In Valor's proudest spot;
> And may the lyre, so sweetly played,
>   By friends be not forgot—
> But tuned by some great master hand

>   To strike one pensive lay,
>   And call thy spirit to the land
>   Made hallowed by thy clay.

Herbert, "Colonel Theodore O'Hara," 65–66

33. Johnston succeeded S. I. M. Major as editor of the *Yeoman* in 1868.
34. Hume, *O'Hara*, 53.
35. Commonwealth of Kentucky, *Journal of the House of Representatives, Commonwealth of Kentucky, 1874* (Frankfort, Ky., 1874), 624, 736; Commonwealth of Kentucky, *Journal of the Adjourned Session of the Senate of the Commonwealth of Kentucky, 1874* (Frankfort, Ky., 1874), 972–73.
36. *New York Times,* July 4, 1874; Collins, *History of Kentucky,* 1:411; Hume, *O'Hara,* 54.
37. Herbert, "Colonel Theodore O'Hara," 64–66; Morton, "Theodore O'Hara," 52–53.
38. Five years later, without fanfare, the faithful Thomas T. Hawkins would be buried next to O'Hara. Hollingsworth, "Theodore O'Hara," 421; Ranck, *Bivouac of the Dead,* 41–42; Morton, "Theodore O'Hara," 53; Johnson, *History of Franklin County,* 184–85.
39. Mrs. Price viewed Stanton as somewhat of a rival and much preferred O'Hara's admirer and future biographer, George W. Ranck of Louisville.
40. Hume, *O'Hara,* 50; Ranck, *Bivouac of the Dead,* 41–42; Morton, "Theodore O'Hara," 54.

12. The Public Poet, the Private Man

1. "Bivouac of the dead" became a buzz phrase in the second half of the nineteenth century. An example is its use as a heading, without explanation nor attribution, for a column in the *Las Vegas (N.M.) Daily Optic* in 1882. A correspondent had visited the grave of Billy the Kid near the ruins of old Fort Sumner. Inside the badly eroded adobe walls of the cemetery itself he found Billy resting close to rustlers he had killed or caused to be killed. Nearby lay a cluster of American soldiers killed in fights against the Indians soon after the Civil War.
   The correspondent commented pensively about these lonely graves, this silent city of the dead. These patriotic soldiers deserved better, he believed, than to rest beside criminals. These servants of our country, like the soldiers of which the "unknown poet" wrote, ought to have the dignity of a final bivouac, where "Glory guards, with solemn round," their "eternal camping-ground." *Las Vegas Daily Optic,* Jan. 16, 1882.
2. Statement of Maj. Gen. J. L. DeWitt, Quartermaster General, quoted in a letter of Jan. 9, 1934 from William N. Morell, Chrm., National Pilgrimage Committee of the American Legion to H. P. Caemmerer, Secretary and Administrative Officer of the Commission of Fine Arts, Washington, D.C. Letter in the files of the commission.
3. *Lexington Herald,* July 1, 1934.

4. 74th Cong., 1st sess.

5. *New York Times,* Feb. 13, 1934; *Lexington Herald-Post,* Feb. 15, 1934.

6. Charles H. Atherton, secretary, Commission of Fine Arts, to Thomas C. Ware, Aug. 13, 1992.

7. "'The Bivouac of the Dead' Will Receive Recognition," *Louisville Herald-Post,* Feb. 16, 1933.

8. Charles H. Atherton, secretary, Commission of Fine Arts, to Thomas C. Ware, Sept. 15, 1992.

9. Mynders, "O'Hara's Poem 'Bivouac of the Dead'; Restored in National Cemetery," *Chattanooga Times,* Oct. 24, 1962.

10. The current superintendent at the Chattanooga National Military Cemetery is now attempting to discover what happened to them.

11. This omission, however, appears to be an editorial mistake. See 7th ed., New York, 1982.

Bibliography

Manuscripts

Alderman Library, Univ. of Virginia, Charlottesville
    Theodore O'Hara Papers
Commission of Fine Arts, Washington, D.C.
    Correspondence of the Secretary, 1933–34
    Minute Book, 1934
Duke Univ. Library, Durham, North Carolina
    Campbell Family Papers
    Clement Claiborne Clay Papers
    Charles Edgeworth Jones Papers
    John Moore McCalla Papers
    Papers of Spanish Ministry of Foreign Affairs, Charleston Consulate
Filson Club, Louisville, Kentucky
    Orlando Brown Papers
    Marion Cartwright Taylor Diary
    Historical File (Library)
    Logan Hunton Letters
    J. Stoddard Johnston Papers
    Miscellaneous Collection
    J. J. Neely Papers
    Theodore O'Hara File
    Theodore O'Hara Papers
    William Preston Papers
    Henry T. Stanton Papers
    E. P. Thompson Papers
    Wintersmith Family Papers
Florida State Univ. Archives, Tallahassee

Hebel, Ianthe Bond. "Colonel H. T. Titus, Founder of Titusville, Florida, 1865."

Getz Museum, St. Joseph's Roman Catholic Church, Bardstown, Kentucky

In possession of Thomas R. Hay, Locust Valley, New York
    William H. Emory Letters

The Historical Society of Pennsylvania, Philadelphia
    George Cadwalader Collection
    Ferdinand J. Dreer Collection
    Simon Gratz Collection

Houghton Library, Harvard Univ., Cambridge, Massachusetts
    Frederick M. Dearborn Collection
    John A. Quitman Papers

Howard-Tilton Memorial Library, Tulane Univ., New Orleans, Louisiana
    Mrs. Mason Barret Collection of A. S. and W. P. Johnston Papers
    Callender Irvine Fayssoux Papers

Kentucky Historical Society, Frankfort
    Biographical Section
    Nat Ewing Letter
    Capt. G. W. Lee Letter
    Theodore O'Hara Collection
    Theodore O'Hara File
    James Taylor and Family Collection
    Robert Burns Wilson Collection

Library of Congress, Washington, D.C.
    John Forsyth Papers
    Narciso López, Miscellaneous Manuscripts Collection
    John T. Pickett Papers
    James K. Polk Papers
    Leonidas Polk Papers

Mississippi Dept. of Archives and History, Jackson
    John A. Quitman Papers

National Archives and Record Service, Washington, D.C.
    Adjutant General, Letters Received, 1822–1860, RG 94
    Compiled Service Record, Fifty-fourth Tennessee Volunteer Infantry, RG 109
    Correspondence of the Adjutant General, RG 94
    General Orders, Adjutant and Inspector General's Office, RG 109
    Josiah S. Johnston MSR, RG 109
    Letters Sent, Adjutant and Inspector General's Office, RG 109
    Letters Sent, Dept. of Texas, the District of Texas, and the 5th Military District, 1856–58 and 1865–70
    Miscellaneous Letters Received, Secretary of the Navy, RG 45
    Theodore O'Hara MSR, RG 109
    William Preston Diary, RG 109
    Quartermaster General Consolidated Correspondence File, RG 92
    Register of Letters Received, Adjutant and Inspector General's Office, RG 109
    Telegrams Received and Sent by Gen. Breckinridge's Command, December 1861–November 1863, RG 109 (chap. 2, vol. 311)
    Treasury Dept.
        Appointment Division Records

Settled Miscellaneous Treasury Accounts
War Dept. General Orders, 1838–61, RG 107
New York Historical Society, New York City
John C. Breckinridge Papers
St. Joseph's College, Bardstown, Kentucky
Academic Yearbook, 1838–39
Southern Historical Collection, Univ. of North Carolina, Chapel Hill
W. W. Mackall Papers
Theodore O'Hara Papers
Edmund Kirby Smith Papers
M. J. Wright Papers
Tennessee State Library and Archives, Nashville
Washington Curran Whitthorne Diary
Tufts Univ. Library, Medford, Massachusetts
Ryder Collection
U.S. Army Military History Institute, Carlisle, Pennsylvania
Theodore O'Hara File, Aztec Club Archives
Univ. of Kentucky Libraries, Lexington
Luther C. Jefferies Papers
Theodore O'Hara Papers
William Preston Mexican War Journal
In possession of Thomas C. Ware, Chattanooga, Tennessee
O'Hara Family Papers
Western Reserve Historical Society, Cleveland, Ohio
William P. Palmer Collection

Newspapers

Columbus (Ga.) Daily Sun
Daily American Star (Mexico City)
Danville (Ky.) Advocate-Messenger
Frankfort (Ky.) Argus of Western America
Frankfort (Ky.) Commonwealth
Frankfort (Ky.) Tocsin
Jacksonville (Fla.) Florida Republican
Kentucky Yeoman
Las Vegas Daily Optic
Lexington Herald-Post
Louisville Courier-Journal
Louisville Evening Post
Louisville Times
Mobile Daily Register
National Intelligencer
New Orleans Crescent
New Orleans Delta
New York Times
Richmond Examiner

Official Documents

Commonwealth of Kentucky
  Adjutant General's Office. *Report of the Adjutant General of the State of Kentucky: Mexican War Veterans.* Frankfort, Ky., 1889.
  Journal of the House of Representatives, Commonwealth of Kentucky, 1874. Frankfort, Ky., 1874.
  Journal of the Adjourned Session of the Senate of the Commonwealth of Kentucky, 1874. Frankfort, Ky., 1874.
Confederate States of America. *Journal of the Congress of the Confederate States of America, 1861–1865.* 58th Cong., 2d sess. Senate Document No. 234. Washington, D.C., 1904–5.
Franklin County, Kentucky, Circuit Court Order Book, 1852, Franklin County Courthouse, Frankfort, Ky.
Franklin County, Kentucky, Deed Books E, 4, 5, and 6, Franklin County Courthouse, Frankfort, Ky.
Franklin County, Kentucky, Tax Lists, 1801–34, Franklin County Courthouse, Frankfort, Ky.
Franklin County, Kentucky, Will Book 2, Franklin County Courthouse, Frankfort, Ky.
Henderson County, Kentucky, Tax Lists, 1810–16.
Jefferson County, Kentucky, Tax List, 1800.
Mercer County, Kentucky, Tax List, 1818.
Mobile, Alabama, *City Directory, 1859.*
U.S. House of Representatives. House Executive Doc. 83, 32d Cong., 1st sess.
———. *House Joint Resolution 20.* 74th Cong., 1st sess., Jan. 3, 1935.
U.S. Navy Dept. *Official Records of the Union and Confederate Navies in the War of the Rebellion.* 31 vols. Washington, D.C., 1894–1919.
U.S. War Dept. *Official List of Officers with the Army under Command of Major-General Winfield Scott.* Mexico City, 1848.
———. *The War of the Rebellion: A Compilation of the Official Records of the Union and Confederate Armies.* 70 vols. Washington, D.C., 1880–1901.
Woodford County, Kentucky, Tax Lists, 1800–1812, courthouse, Versailles, Ky.

Books

Abbott, Edith. *Immigration, Select Documents and Case Records.* New York, 1969.
Alderman, Edwin Anderson, Joel Chandler Harris, and Charles William Kent, eds. *Library of Southern Literature.* 17 vols. New Orleans, 1970.
Allardice, Bruce S. *More Generals in Gray.* Baton Rouge, La., 1995.
Amos, Harriet E. *Cotton City: Urban Development in Antebellum Mobile.* Tuscaloosa, Ala., 1985.
Andrews, J. Cutler. *The South Reports the Civil War.* Princeton, N.J., 1970.
Aries, Phillipe. *The Hour of Our Death.* Translated from the French by Helen Weaver. New York: Alfred A. Knopf, 1981.
Armstrong, J. M., ed. *Biographical Encyclopaedia of Kentucky of the Dead and Living Men of the Nineteenth Century.* Cincinnati, 1878.

Aytoun, William Edmondstone. *Lays of the Scottish Cavaliers*. Edinburgh: William Blackwood and Sons, 1872.

Barnard, J. G. *The Isthmus of Tehuantepec: Being the Results of a Survey for a Railroad to Connect the Atlantic and Pacific Oceans . . . with a Resume of the Geology, Climate, Local Geography, Productive Industry, Flora and Fauna, of that Region*. New York, 1852.

Bauer, K. Jack. *The Mexican War, 1846–1848*. New York, 1974.

———. *Zachary Taylor: Soldier, Planter, Statesman of the Old Southwest*. Baton Rouge, La., 1985.

Beatty, Richard C., Floyd C. Watkins, Thomas D. Young, and Randall Stewart. *The Literature of the South*. New York, 1952.

Bemis, Samuel Flagg. *A Diplomatic History of the United States*. New York, 1950.

Benjamin, Judah P. *Memoir Explanatory of the Transcimos and Tehuantepec Route between Europe and Asia*. Washington, D.C., 1851.

Bevins, Ann Bolton, and Rev. James R. O'Rourke. *"That Troublesome Parish": St. Francis/St. Pius Church of White Sulphur, Kentucky, Mother Church of the Diocese of Covington*. Georgetown, Ky., 1985.

Boyd, Minnie C. *Alabama in the Fifties*. New York, 1931.

Brooks, U. R. *Stories of the Confederacy*. Columbia, S.C., 1912.

Brown, Charles H. *Agents of Manifest Destiny: The Lives and Times of the Filibusters*. Chapel Hill, N.C., 1980.

Brown, J. H., ed. *Lamb's Biographical Dictionary of the United States*. Boston, 1903.

Bruce, Dickson D., Jr. *Violence and Culture in the Antebellum South*. Austin, 1979.

Caldwell, Robert G. *The López Expeditions to Cuba, 1848–1851*. Princeton, N.J., 1915.

Chaffin, Tom. *Fatal Glory: Narciso López and the First Clandestine U.S. War Against Cuba*. Charlottesville, 1996.

Chance, Joseph E. *Jefferson Davis's Mexican War Regiment*. Jackson, Miss., 1991.

Chandler, Julian A. C., Franklin L. Riley, James C. Ballagh, Joseph W. Walker, Walter A. Fleming, John B. Nenneman, Edwin Mims, Thomas E. Watson, and Samuel L. Mitchell, eds. *The South in the Building of the Nation*. 12 vols. Richmond, 1909.

Collins, Lewis. *History of Kentucky*. 2 vols. Louisville, 1874.

Connelly, Thomas Lawrence. *Army of the Heartland: The Army of Tennessee, 1861–1862*. Baton Rouge, La., 1967.

———. *Autumn of Glory*. Baton Rouge, La., 1971.

Costigan, Giovanni. *A History of Modern Ireland, with a Sketch of Earlier Times*. New York, 1969.

Coulter, Ellis Merton. *The Confederate States of America, 1861–1865*. Vol. 7, *A History of the South*. Edited by Wendell Holmes Stephenson and E. Merton Coulter. Baton Rouge, La., 1950.

Cozzens, Peter. *No Better Place to Die*. Chicago, 1990.

———. *Shipwreck of Their Hopes: The Battles for Chattanooga*. Urbana, Ill., 1994.

Craighead, Ervin. *From Mobile's Past: Sketches of Memorable People and Events*. Mobile, Ala., 1925.

Crist, Lynda Lasswell, and May Seaton Dix, eds. *The Papers of Jefferson Davis*. 9 vols. Baton Rouge, La., 1971–97.

Crute, Joseph H., Jr. *Units of the Confederate Army*. Midlothian, Va., 1987.
Darnell, Erma Jett. *Filling the Chinks*. Frankfort, Ky., 1966.
Davis, J. C. *History of the Late Expedition to Cuba*. New Orleans, 1850.
Davis, William C. *Battle at Bull Run*. Baton Rouge, La., 1977.
———. *Breckinridge: Statesman, Soldier, Symbol*. Baton Rouge, La., 1974.
———. *The Orphan Brigade: The Kentucky Confederates Who Couldn't Go Home*. Garden City, N.Y., 1980.
Dufour, Charles L. *Gentle Tiger: The Gallant Life of Roberdeau Wheat*. Baton Rouge, La., 1957.
Eggleston, George C. *American War Ballads and Lyrics*. 2 vols. in 1. New York, 1889.
Elliott, Lawrence. *The Long Hunter: A New Life of Daniel Boone*. New York, 1976.
Elliott, Marianne. *Partners in Revolution: The United Irishmen and France*. New Haven, Conn., 1990.
Ellis, John Tracy. *American Catholicism*. 2d ed., rev. Edited by Daniel Boorstin. The Chicago History of American Civilization. Chicago, 1969.
Ellison, Rhoda C. *History and Bibliography of Alabama Newspapers in the Nineteenth Century*. University, Ala., 1954.
Evans, Clement Anselm. *Confederate Military History*. Expanded ed. 12 vols. Atlanta, 1899.
Evans, Eli N. *Judah P. Benjamin, the Jewish Confederate*. New York, 1988.
Faragher, John Mack. *Daniel Boone: The Life and Legend of an American Pioneer*. New York, 1992.
Finding, John E. *Dictionary of American Diplomatic History*. Westport, Conn., 1989.
Foner, Philip S. *A History of Cuba and Its Relations with the United States*. 2 vols. New York, 1963.
Frazer, Robert W. *Forts of the West*. Norman, Okla., 1963.
Freeman, Douglas Southall. *R. E. Lee: A Biography*. 4 vols. New York, 1934–35.
Fremantle, Arthur J. L. *The Fremantle Diary*. 2d ed. Edited by Walter Lord. Boston, 1954.
Glenn, Nettie Henry. *Early Frankfort, Kentucky, 1786–1861*. Frankfort, Ky., 1986.
Hamilton, Holman. *Zachary Taylor*. 2 vols. Indianapolis, 1941–51.
Hamilton, Peter J. *Mobile of the Five Flags: The Story of the River Basin and Coast about Mobile from the Earliest Times to the Present*. Mobile, Ala., 1913.
Hamlin, Percy G. *Old Bald Head (General R. S. Ewell)*. Strasburg, Va., 1940.
Hardy, Richardson. *The History and Adventures of the Cuban Expeditions from the First Movements Down to the Dispersion of the Army at Key West, and the Arrest of General López*. Cincinnati, 1850.
Hart, Herbert M. *Old Forts of the Southwest*. Seattle, 1964.
Hartje, Robert G. *Van Dorn: The Life and Times of a Confederate General*. Nashville, 1967.
Heitman, Francis B. *Historical Register and Dictionary of the United States Army, 1789–1903*. 2 vols. Washington, D.C., 1903.
Hendrick, Burton J. *Statesmen of the Lost Cause: Jefferson Davis and His Cabinet*. New York, 1939.
Horn, Stanley F. *The Army of Tennessee*. Norman, Okla., 1941.
Hubbell, Jay. *The South in American Literature, 1607–1900*. Durham, N.C., 1954.

Hughes, Nathaniel C., Jr. *General William J. Hardee, Old Reliable*. Baton Rouge, La., 1965.

——. *The Life and Wars of Gideon J. Pillow*. Chapel Hill, N.C., 1993.

Hume, Edgar Erskine. *Colonel Theodore O'Hara, Author of The Bivouac of the Dead*. In *Southern Sketches* 6, edited by J. D. Eggleston. Charlottesville, Va., 1936.

Jillson, Willard Rouse. *Early Frankfort and Franklin County, Kentucky*. Louisville, 1936.

——. *The Newspapers and Periodicals of Frankfort, Kentucky, 1795–1945*. Frankfort, Ky., 1945.

Johannsen, Robert W. *Stephen A. Douglas*. New York, 1973.

Johnson, Allen, and Dumas Malone, eds. *Dictionary of American Biography*. 22 vols. New York, 1928–58.

Johnson, L. Frank. *History of Franklin County, Ky*. Frankfort, Ky., 1912.

——. History of the Franklin County Bar. Frankfort, Ky., 1932.

Johnson, Richard W. *A Soldier's Reminiscences in Peace and War*. Philadelphia, 1886.

Johnston, J. Stoddard. *Memorial History of Louisville from Its First Settlement to the Year 1896*. 2 vols. Chicago, 1896.

Johnston, William Preston. *The Life of Gen. Albert Sidney Johnston, Embracing His Service in the Armies of the United States, the Republic of Texas, and the Confederate States*. New York, 1878.

Kenny, Michael. *Catholic Culture in Alabama: Centenary Story of Spring Hill College, 1830–1930*. New York, 1931.

Kentucky Historical Society. *Genealogies of Kentucky Families*. 3 vols. Baltimore, 1981.

Klotter, James C. *The Breckinridges of Kentucky, 1760–1981*. Lexington, Ky., 1986.

Kunitz, Stanley J., and Howard Haycraft, eds. *American Authors, 1600–1900, a Biographical Dictionary of American Literature*. New York, 1938.

Levin, H., ed. *The Lawyers and Lawmakers of Kentucky*. Chicago, 1897.

Mackall, William W. *A Son's Recollections of His Father*. New York, 1930.

McDonough, James L. *Stone's River—Bloody Winter in Tennessee*. Knoxville, 1980.

McMurray, W. J. *History of the 20th Tennessee Regiment Volunteer Infantry, C.S.A.* Nashville, 1904.

McPherson, James M. *Battle Cry of Freedom: The Civil War Era*. New York, 1988.

May, Robert E. *John A. Quitman: Old South Crusader*. Baton Rouge, La., 1985.

——. *The Southern Dream of a Caribbean Empire, 1854–1861*. Baton Rouge, La., 1973.

Meade, Robert Douthat. *Judah P. Benjamin, Confederate Statesman*. New York, 1943.

Memorial Record of Alabama. 2 vols. Madison, Wisc., 1893.

Merk, Frederick. *Manifest Destiny and Mission in American History: A Reinterpretation*. New York, 1963.

Military Society of the Mexican War. History of the Aztec Club. 1909.

Miller, Emily Van Dorn. *A Soldier's Honor: With Reminiscences of Major-General Earl Van Dorn. By His Comrades*. New York, 1902.

Moore, Albert Burton. *History of Alabama*. Tuscaloosa, Ala., 1951.

Moses, Montrose Jonas. *The Literature of the South*. New York, 1910.

National Cyclopaedia of American Biography. 63 vols. New York, 1893–1919.

Nogues, Dewitt C. Desha Genealogy: A Survey. Austin, Tex., 1983.

O. D. D. O. [J. C. Davis]. The History of the Late Expedition to Cuba. New Orleans, 1850.

O'Donoghue, D. J. The Poets of Ireland. Dublin, 1912.

Opatrny, Josef. U.S. Expansionism and Cuban Annexationism in the 1850s. Lewiston, N.Y., 1993.

O'Rorke, Terence. History of Sligo; Town and County. 2 vols. Sligo, Ireland, 1889.

Owen, Thomas McA. History of Alabama and Dictionary of Alabama Biography. 4 vols. Chicago, 1921.

Painter, F. V. N. Poets of the South. New York, 1903.

Parrish, T. Michael. Richard Taylor: Soldier Prince of Dixie. Chapel Hill, N.C., 1992.

Portell Vilá, Herminio. Narciso López, y su Epoca 1848–1850. 3 vols. Havana, 1938–58.

Price, George F. Across the Continent with the Fifth Cavalry. New York, 1883.

Quisenberry, Anderson Chenault. López's Expeditions to Cuba, 1850–1851. Louisville, 1906.

Railey, William E. History of Woodford County, Kentucky. Versailles, Ky., 1968.

Ranck, George Washington. The Bivouac of the Dead and Its Author. New York, 1898. Reprint, New York, 1909.

———. O'Hara and His Elegies. Baltimore, 1875.

Rauch, Basil. American Interest in Cuba: 1848–1855. New York, 1948.

Ray, Bess A., ed. Biographical and Critical Materials Pertaining to Kentucky Authors. Louisville, 1941.

Reid, Samuel C., Jr., The Case of the Private Armed Brig of War Gen. Armstrong. New York, 1857.

Rister, Carl Coke. Robert E. Lee in Texas. Norman, Okla., 1946.

Roland, Charles. Albert Sidney Johnston, Soldier of Three Republics. Austin, 1964.

Rosengarten, Frederic. Freebooters Must Die. Wayne, Pa., 1976.

Russell, William H. My Diary North and South. 2 vols. London, 1863.

Rutherford, Mildred Lewis. The South in History and Literature, a Handbook of Southern Authors from the Settlement of Jamestown, 1607, to Living Writers. Athens, Ga., 1906.

[Scott, John A.]. Encarnación Prisoners. Comprising an Account of the March of the Kentucky Cavalry from Louisville to the Rio Grande, together with Authentic History of the Captivity of the American Prisoners. Including Incidents and Sketches of Men and Things on the Route and in Mexico. Edited by Theodore O'Hara. Louisville, 1848.

Scroggs, William Oscar. Filibusters and Financiers; the Story of William Walker and His Associates. New York, 1916.

Steffan, T. G., E. Steffan, and W. W. Pratt, eds. Lord Byron: Don Juan. New Haven, Conn., 1982.

Stout, Joseph Allen, Jr. The Liberators. Los Angles, 1973.

Sword, Wiley. Shiloh: Bloody April. Dayton, Ohio, 1983.

Symonds, Craig L. Joseph E. Johnston: A Civil War Biography. New York, 1992.

Thomas, Hugh. Cuba: The Pursuit of Freedom. New York, 1971.

Thompson, Ed Porter. History of the Orphan Brigade. Louisville, 1898.

Townsend, John Wilson. Kentucky in American Letters, 1784–1912. 2 vols. Cedar Rapids, Iowa, 1913.

Walker, Anne K. Backtracking in Barbour County. Richmond, Va., 1941.

Wallace, Edward S. *Destiny and Glory.* New York, 1957.

Webb, Benjamin J. *The Centenary of Catholicity in Kentucky.* Louisville, 1884.

Williams, Samuel. *Kentucky Memories of Uncle Sam Williams.* Edited by Nathaniel C. Hughes, Jr. Chattanooga, 1978.

Wilson, James Grant, and John Fiske, eds. *Appleton's Cyclopedia of American Biography.* 6 vols. New York, 1900.

Wittke, Carl B. *The Irish in America.* Baton Rouge, La., 1956.

Woodworth, Steven E. *Jefferson Davis and His Generals: The Failure of Confederate Command in the West.* Edited by Theodore A. Wilson. Modern War Studies. Lawrence, Kans., 1990.

Works Progress Administration. *The American Guide Series.* Washington, D.C., 1937.

Wyatt-Brown, Bertram. *Southern Honor: Ethics and Behavior in the Old South.* New York, 1982.

Articles and Parts of Books

"Alfred Beckley's Recollections of Kentucky." *Register of Kentucky History* 60:312–13.

Alexander, John. "Theodore O'Hara, Famous Poet, Was Born at Danville." *Lexington Herald Leader,* Sept. 27, 1957.

Aswell, James B., Jr. "Danville Personages—Letters and Surgery." *Danville Advocate-Messenger,* Aug. 22, 1924.

"'Bivouac of the Dead' Will Receive Recognition." *Lexington Herald-Post,* Feb. 16, 1933.

Brackett, Albert Gallatin. "Colonel Theodore O'Hara." *Louisville Courier Journal,* Aug. 1891. Reprinted in *Southern Historical Society Papers* 19:275–81.

———. "Colonel O'Hara's Career Made Famous By a Poem, 'The Bivouac of the Dead,' in Washington, D.C." *Vedette,* Dec. 1892, 3–4.

Broussard, Ray. "Governor John A. Quitman and the López Expeditions of 1851–1852." *Journal of Mississippi History* 28 (1966):103–20.

Buckner, John A. "Greatest Martial Eulogy." Undated clipping in possession of Thomas C. Ware.

Bullock, Barry. "Theodore O'Hara." *Register of the Kentucky State Historical Society* 11 (Sept. 1913):76–78.

Burnett, Henry. "López's Expeditions to Cuba, 1850–1851: Betrayal of the Cleopatra, 1851." Edited by L. M. Perez. *Publications of the Southern History Association* 10 (1906):345–62.

Clay, H. B. "On the Right at Murfreesboro." *Confederate Veteran* 21:588–89.

Crane, R. C. "Robert E. Lee's Expedition in the Upper Brazos and Colorado Country." *West Texas Historical Association Year Book* 13 (Oct. 1937):53–63.

Crimmins, M. L. "Camp Cooper and Fort Griffin, Texas." *West Texas Historical Association Year Book* 17:32–43.

———. "First Sergeant John W. Spangler, Company H, Second United States Cavalry." *West Texas Historical Association Year Book* 26:68–75.

———. "Major Van Dorn in Texas." *West Texas Historical Association Year Book* 16:121–29.

———. "Robert E. Lee in Texas: Letters and Diary." *West Texas Historical Association Year Book* 8:3–24.

Curti, Merle E. "George Nicholas Sanders." *Dictionary of American Biography* 8:334.

De Bow, James Dunwoody Brownson. "The Late Cuba Expedition." *DeBow's Review* 9:164–77.

De la Cova, Antonio Rafael. "Cuban Filibustering in Jacksonville in 1851." *Northeast Florida History* 3 (1996):17–34.

———. "Filibusters and Freemasons: The Sworn Obligation." *Journal of the Early Republic* 17 (Spring 1997):95–120.

Dienst, Alex. "Contemporary Poetry of the Texas Revolution." *Southwestern Historical Quarterly* 21:156–84.

Dixon, Susan B. "Bivouac of the Dead." *New York Times,* Aug. 11, 1900.

———. "The Bivouac of the Dead." *Southern Bivouac,* n.s., 11, no. 10 (Mar. 1887):641–43.

———. "Mutilation of a Great Poem." ——— *Dispatch,* Aug. 1900. Unidentified clipping in possession of Thomas C. Ware.

DuPuy, William Atherton. "Kentucky Confederate Official Poem of the Martial Dead." *Louisville Courier Journal,* May 25, 1913.

Eckdahl, Andrew. "'Bivouac of the Dead' Eulogizing Kentuckians Who Fell at Buena Vista." *Lexington Herald Leader,* Mar. 1, 1959.

Farley, Paul. "Uncle Sam's Official Poet." *Columbia,* New Haven, Conn., Apr. 1930.

Fitcher, Joseph H., and George L. Maddox. "Religion in the South, Old and New." In *The South in Continuity and Change,* edited by John C. McKinney and Edgar T. Thompson. Durham, N.C., 1965.

"General López, the Cuban Patriot." *United States Magazine and Democratic Review* 25 (Feb. 1850):97–112.

Genzmer, George H. "Theodore O'Hara." *Dictionary of American Biography* 14:4–5.

Gonzales, Ambrosio José. "The Cuban Crusade: A Full History of Georgian and López Expeditions." *New Orleans Times Democrat,* Mar. 30, 1884.

Henry, Ruby Addison. "Captain Theodore O'Hara, Soldier-Poet." In *These Things Are Our Kentucky.* Louisville, 1955.

Herbert, Sidney. "Colonel Theodore O'Hara, Author of 'Bivouac of the Dead.'" *Kentucky State Historical Society Register* 15:62–66. Reprinted in 39:230–36; *Atlanta Journal,* May 29, 1897.

Hollingsworth, Annie Mae. "Theodore O'Hara, Immortal Poet of One Song." *Alabama Historical Review* 7:416–24.

Holman, C. Hugh. "A Cycle of Change in Southern Literature." In *The South in Continuity and Change,* edited by John C. McKinney and Edgar T. Thompson. Durham, N.C., 1965.

Hume, Edgar Erskine. "Colonel Theodore O'Hara and Cuban Independence." *Bulletin of the Pan American Union* 71 (May 1937): 363–67.

Idol, John L., Jr. "Theodore O'Hara." In *Southern Writers, a Biographical Dictionary,* by Robert Bain, Joseph M. Flora, and Louis D. Rubin, Jr., 333–34. Baton Rouge, La., 1979.

"Inscription for Theodore O'Hara's Tomb." *Register of the Kentucky Historical Society* 11:43.

Johnston, Josiah Stoddard. "Kentucky's Greatest Poem, Cut Down to Half Its Original Length." *The Illustrated Kentuckian,* Louisville, n.d. In Theodore O'Hara Papers. Univ. of Kentucky Libraries.

———. "Sketch of Theodore O'Hara." *Register of the Kentucky Historical Society* 11, no. 33 (Sept. 1913):67–72.

"The Life of Theodore O'Hara, the Famous Poet Who Was Born in Danville and Composed the Immortal 'Bivouac of the Dead.'" *Danville Advocate-Messenger,* Mar. 3, 1921.

McFarland, Baxter. "A Forgotten Expedition to Pensacola in January, 1861." *Publications of the Mississippi Historical Society* 9:15–23.

McIntyre, W. O. "Endorse O'Hara Monument in McDowell Park." *Danville Advocate-Messenger,* Mar. 3, 1921.

Mallalieu, W. C. "William Owsley." *Dictionary of American Biography* 7:122–23.

Mansfield, J. K. F. "Colonel J. K. F. Mansfield's Report of the Inspection of the Department of Texas in 1856." *Southwestern Historical Quarterly* 41:122–48.

Morton, Jennie Chinn. "Biographical Sketch of the Life and Writing of Theodore O'Hara, Author of 'The Bivouac of the Dead.'" *Register of the Kentucky Historical Society* 1:49–62.

———. "Kentucky's Bard." *Register of the Kentucky Historical Society* 12:5–11.

Mynders, Alfred. "O'Hara's Poem, 'Bivouac of the Dead'; Restored in National Cemetery." *Chattanooga Times,* Oct. 24, 1962.

Neff, Robert O. "The Best and the Bravest." *Confederate Chronicles of Tennessee* 2 (1987):81–142.

O'Conner, Clem J. "On Many a Tombstone." *Louisville Courier Journal,* n.d. In Theodore O'Hara Papers. Univ. of Kentucky Libraries.

O'Sullivan, Daniel E. "Theodore O'Hara." *Southern Bivouac,* n.s., 11 (Jan. 1897):489–94.

Ottey, Passie Fenton. "Theodore O'Hara's Martial Elegy." Undated clipping in possession of Thomas C. Ware.

Park, Robert E. "The Twelfth Alabama Infantry, Confederate States Army." *Southern Historical Society Papers* 33:193–296.

Patton, James W. "John Louis O'Sullivan." *Dictionary of American Biography* 7:89.

Perez, L. M. "The López Expeditions to Cuba, 1850–1851: Betrayal of the Cleopatra, 1851." *Publications of the Southern Historical Association* 10:345–62.

Pickett, William D. "A Reminiscence of Murfreesboro." *Nashville American,* Nov. 10, 1907.

Quisenberry, Anderson Chenault. "Col. M. C. Taylor's Diary in López's Cárdenas Expedition, 1850." *Register of the Kentucky Historical Society* 19 (Sept. 1921):79–89.

Ranck, George Washington. "The Poet O'Hara." *Southern Journal of Education,* n.d., 24–28. In Theodore O'Hara File, Biographical Section, Kentucky Historical Society Library, Frankfort.

Rawlings, Robert. "Kentucky History: The Death of the Yeoman Recalls Many Interesting Events." *Cincinnati Enquirer,* May 7, 1866.

"Review of the Work of the Kentucky State Historical Society and the O'Hara Memorial." *Register of the Kentucky State Historical Society* 2:93–103.

Roseberry, Marguerite T. "Theodore O'Hara Was Soldier-Poet." *United Daughters of the Confederacy Magazine* 21 (July 1938):18–19.

Schlesinger, Louis. "Personal Narrative of Louis Schlesinger, of Adventures in Cuba and Centra." *United States Magazine and Democratic Review* 31 (Sept.–Dec. 1852):200–224, 352–66, 553–70.

Schmidt, Martin E. "The Early Printers of Louisville, 1800–1860." *Filson Club History Quarterly* 40:307–34.

Schoonover, Thomas. "John T. Pickett." In *Encyclopedia of the Confederacy,* edited by Richard N. Current, Paul D. Escott, Lawrence N. Powell, James I. Robertson, and Emory Thomas. 4 vols. New York, 1993.

Scroggs, William O. "William Walker." *Dictionary of American Biography* 10:364.

"Slighting Southern Literature." *Literary Heritage* 46:1224–26.

Steward, Luther N., Jr. "John Forsyth." *Alabama Review* 14:98–123.

Sweeny, William M. "Theodore O'Hara, Author of Bivouac of the Dead." *Journal of the American Irish Historical Society* 25 (1926):202–6.

"Theodore O'Hara." *Confederate Veteran* 7 (May 1899):202.

"Theodore O'Hara." Unidentified clipping in Theodore O'Hara Papers, June 10, 1901. Univ. of Kentucky Libraries.

Thomas, John B., Jr. "Best of Breed: Col. H. Milburn McCarty as a Country Editor." *Filson Club History Quarterly* 63:24–41.

Thompson, Alan S. "Southern Rights and Nativism as Issues in Mobile Politics, 1850–1861." *Alabama Review* 35:127–41.

Townsend, John Wilson. "Kean O'Hara and His Son Theodore: A Proposed Adventure." Unidentified clipping in Theodore O'Hara Papers. Univ. of Kentucky Libraries.

Urban, Chester Stanley. "The Abortive Quitman Filibustering Expedition to Cuba, 1853–1855." *Journal of Mississippi History* 18 (1956):175–96.

———. "New Orleans and the Cuban Question during the López Expeditions of 1849–1851." *Louisiana Historical Quarterly* 22 (Oct. 1939):1104–18.

Wakelyn, Jon L., Walter J. Fraser, Jr., and R. Frank Saunders, Jr. "Antebellum College Life and the Relations Between Fathers and Sons." In *The Web of Southern Social Relations: Women, Family, & Education.* Athens, Ga., 1985.

Ware, Thomas C. "'Where Valor Proudly Sleeps': Theodore O'Hara and 'The Bivouac of the Dead,' the Odyssey of an Irish-American Soldier-Poet." *Markers: Journal of the Association for Gravestone Studies* 11 (1994):82–111.

Weinert, Richard P. "'The Hard Fortune of Theodore O'Hara.'" *Alabama Historical Quarterly* 28:33–43.

Westcott, Allan. "Samuel Chester Reid." *Dictionary of American Biography* 8:480–81.

Wheat, Leo. "Memoir of Gen. C. R. Wheat, Commander of the Louisiana Tiger Battalion." *Southern Historical Society Papers* 17:47–60.

Wilson, Robert Burns. "Theodore O'Hara." *Century Magazine* 18:106–10.

———. "Theodore O'Hara." *Library of Southern Literature* 9:3831–34.

Wood, John T. "Escape of the Confederate Secretary of War." *Century Magazine* 47:110–23.

Woodall, W. C. "Poet O'Hara, Rose Hill Marriages." *Columbus (Ga.) Ledger Enquirer*, Aug. 10, 1969.

Poems and Speeches

Bullock, Barry. "'Theodore O'Hara,' Address Delivered at the Banquet of the Press at Enid, Oklahoma." *Register of the Kentucky Historical Society* 11:76–78.

O'Hara, Theodore. *Obituary Addresses Delivered upon the Occasion of the Reinterment of the Remains of Gen. Charles Scott, Major Wm. T. Barry, and*

Capt. Bland Ballard and Wife, in the Cemetery at Frankfort, Nov. 8, 1854. Frankfort, Ky., 1855.

Unpublished Studies

Chestnut, David. "John Forsyth, the Southern Partisan." Master's thesis, Auburn Univ., 1967.

Cockrell, Monroe Fulkerson. "'The Bivouac of the Dead' and 'The Old Pioneer,' by Theodore O'Hara: A Venture into the Shadows of Yesterday." Library of Kentucky Historical Society, Frankfort.

De la Cova, Antonio R. "Ambrosio José Gonzales: A Cuban Confederate Colonel." Ph.D. diss., West Virginia Univ., 1994.

Cusick, Dennis Charles. "Gentleman of the Press: The Life and Times of Walter Newman Haldeman." Master's thesis, Univ. of Louisville, 1987.

Ellwanger, Ella Hutchison. "A Soldier of Fortune Who Won Fame Through a Single Poem." Unpublished study in Kentucky Historical Society, Frankfort.

Hughes, Nathaniel C., Jr. "William Joseph Hardee, U.S.A., 1815–1861." Master's thesis, Univ. of North Carolina, 1956.

Luetze, James. "Judah P. Benjamin and the Tehuantepec Canal." Master's thesis, Univ. of North Carolina, 1961.

Mauck, Jeffrey Gordon. "The Gadsden Treaty: The Diplomacy of Transcontinental Transportation (Mexico)." Ph.D. diss., Indiana Univ., 1991.

Meier, Matthias S. "History of the Tehuantepec Railroad." Ph.D. diss., Univ. of California, Berkeley, 1954.

Middagh, Severyn H., comp. "The History of the Fifth U.S. Cavalry from March 3, 1855 to December 31, 1905." In Oversize Document Collection, RG 94, Adjutant General's Office, National Archives and Record Service, Washington, D.C.

Poore, Ralph. "History of the *Mobile Press Register*." In possession of Ralph Poore, Mobile, Ala.

Townsend, John Wilson. Script for a radio talk on WHAS. Louisville, Kentucky, June 1, 1932, 1. In possession of Thomas C. Ware.

Interviews

Ralph Poore. Conversations with author. *Mobile Register* 10 (Apr. 14, 1992).

Colonel Frederick P. Todd, Curator, United States Military Academy Museum. Interview by author. West Point, N.Y., Mar. 29, 1956.

Index

Theodore O'Hara: Poet-Soldier of the Old South was designed and typeset on a Macintosh computer system using PageMaker software. The text is set in Sabon, and the chapter openings are set in Caslon Antique. This book was designed by Kay Jursik, composed by Kimberly Scarbrough, and printed and bound by Thomson-Shore, Inc. The recycled paper used in this book is designed for an effective life of at least three hundred years.